ELEANOR MARX

ELEANOR MARX

Volume One

by YVONNE KAPP

Pantheon Books, New York

Copyright © 1972 by Yvonne Kapp

All rights reserved under International and Pan-American Copyright Conventions. Published in the United States by Pantheon Books, a division of Random House, Inc., New York, and simultaneously in Canada by Random House of Canada Limited, Toronto. Originally published in Great Britain as *Eleanor Marx, Volume I: Family Life, 1855-1883* by Lawrence and Wishart, London.

Kapp, Yvonne Mayer, 1903–
 Eleanor Marx.

 Bibliography: v. 1, pp. 308–313.
 Includes indexes.
 1. Aveling, Eleanor Marx, 1855–1898. 2. Labor and laboring classes—Great Britain—Biography.
 3. Socialists—Great Britain—Biography.
 HD8383.7.A93K36 1977   335.4′092′4 [B]   77-77538
 ISBN 0-394-42143-4 (v. 1)
 ISBN 0-394-73456-4 pbk. (v. 1)

Manufactured in the United States of America

First American Edition

Dedicated to

Bianca Margaret Mynatt

CONTENTS

ILLUSTRATIONS

AUTHOR'S NOTE

This book covers the first 28 years of Eleanor Marx's life, up to and throughout the year of her father's death in 1883. It has a section devoted to her common law husband, Edward Aveling, whom she had met before the end of this period.

The research done and material gathered since 1966 cover also Eleanor Marx's last 15 years, when, emerging from her internationalist background, here described, she entered the British working class movement in which she played a significant part, to be dealt with in the second volume. Thus my acknowledgments refer to more matter than appears in the present book.

This applies also to a number of memoirs and autobiographies mainly if not entirely concerned with later events. It may be said in passing that, by and large, such secondary sources have not proved of paramount value. Though written by contemporaries with personal knowledge of the people and affairs involved, they were more often than not set down in old age when faulty memory and hindsight can play strange tricks. Many of these beguiling reminiscences are contradicted on matters of fact by the testimony of private letters and public prints of the day, by official records, trade union archives, school and university registers and verifiable information from surviving kin, as also by pilgrimages to the houses, streets and neighbourhoods where Eleanor Marx lived. So if any reader feels disappointed that some of the more familiar legends about the Marx family are not included here, it means merely that no reliable evidence could be found to bear them out.

My staple source material has been the German edition of the works of Marx and Engels (*Marx Engels Werke*. Dietz Verlag, Berlin 1956–1968), in particular the correspondence which appears as Volumes 27–39. At the risk of distressing the academic historian no separate references to this pervasive source are given, save where the first appearance of a publication, or where the writer, recipient or date of a letter is enlightening. When the holograph was written in a language other than German—for the photostat of which I am indebted

to the Moscow Institute of Marxism-Leninism and the Berlin
Institute of Marxism-Leninism—acknowledgment is made.

For the translation of quotations from the *Marx Engels Werke*,
as of those from other foreign sources, I am responsible unless
otherwise stated. Here a slight difficulty arises. Marx and
Engels frequently interspersed letters written in another lan-
guage with English expressions, phrases and whole passages.
Where these are used, naturally they are left unchanged.
Thus there are instances where my rendering of a mainly
German—or French—text is combined with its original
English interpolations: always clear and forceful but sometimes
rather odd. The erratic punctuation in extracts from Eleanor
Marx's and her sisters' original letters, where not an obstacle
to sense, has been retained.

Other material to which attribution is not always made,
since much has been traced and is acknowledged to its primary
source, comes from the collected pieces by divers hands known
in English as *Reminiscences of Marx and Engels* (Foreign Languages Publishing House, Moscow, n.d. probably 1956) and,
in German, with slight variations of text, as *Mohr und General*
(Dietz Verlag, Berlin, 1964).

All certificates of births, marriages, deaths and all copies of
Wills registered in England were obtained from Somerset
House. A few foreign birth and death certificates were traced
to the appropriate Registries abroad. Census returns were
examined at the Public Record Office, contemporary local
Directories at the Guildhall Library. Information on weather
conditions was supplied by the Meteorological Office or
found in *The Times* newspaper of that date. Changes of street
names and house numbers since the 19th century were obtained
from the Greater London Council. Ratebooks, by permission
of the Borough Treasurer, were investigated under conditions
of extreme cold, dirt, peril and difficulty in the basements of
St. Pancras Town Hall.*

All other source material is numbered and the references
will be found at the end of each section. (For page numbers
where these Notes appear see Contents.) This has the dis-

---

* Now Camden Town Hall. I understand that the Ratebooks—dusted, repaired
and accessibly ranged according to date and Ward—have been removed to another
place since January 1967.

advantage of spangling the text with numerals of no possible interest to the general reader who may, however, like to feel assured that the book is properly documented.* Abbreviations for the most frequently used sources are given at the head of each series of Notes.

These references are not furnished with the full scholarly apparatus of page numbers in published works or piece numbers of unpublished documents. The reason is not that it would have been too much trouble to put them in: indeed, having served their purpose for work in progress, they have been deliberately omitted because I have often felt depressed by such elaborate annotations to otherwise unpretentious books: mountainous appendages to mouselike products. This is not a doctoral thesis, inadvertently published, nor yet a textbook. Further, I believe that the reader who may be unfamiliar with some of the magnificent published sources will find it more rewarding if his attention is directed, not to a page—or to learn whether an extract has been faithfully quoted—but to those works as a whole.

To avoid deadening each page with references, footnotes are reserved for additional matter thought pertinent but not essential to the text (except in the few Appendices where references are given in footnotes).

While the Reference Notes provide a fairly representative sample of the chief works consulted, a Select Bibliography is given on pp. 308–313 in conformity with custom and good practice.

But the acknowledgments are another matter altogether.

No writer venturing into a fresh and specialised field can have met with more cordial goodwill at every step from scholars and historians, from archivists, librarians and from friends both old and new in many countries. Nor could any writer feel more sensible of this generosity.

Among the names appended below, in alphabetical order, my sole fear is that, by oversight, some may have been omitted, so widespread has been the help extended. The shortcomings of the book are all mine.

First and foremost my thanks are owed to the Director and

---

* I have allowed myself to use one qualifying word—"battered"—for which there is no documentary evidence whatsoever.

Staff of the Institute of Marxism-Leninism in Moscow, but for whose interest and encouragement the long period of research could not have been sustained. To my regret I was unable to avail myself of invitations to examine the archives in Moscow but, to compensate, the Institute sent me photostats of much important material from those archives, including letters, documents and answers to questions relevant to my subject.

Equally great is my indebtedness to the Institute of Marxism-Leninism in Berlin, where I spent much profitable time studying documents, newspaper articles and conference reports. The Berlin Institute also gave me photographs from their valuable collection and, by courtesy of the Moscow IML, photostats of original material.* I wish to place on record the friendly co-operation of all the members of the Berlin IML staff in whose sections I worked and, above all, the extreme kindness of Professor Dr. Heinrich Gemkow and Mrs. Rosie Rudich of the Marx-Engels Department.

Dr. Emile Bottigelli of the University of Paris (Nanterre), the fruits of whose ripe erudition have been offered me again and again, not only allowed me access to those Marx family letters—formerly the property of the Longuet heirs—of which he is the custodian, but provided every facility, including the privilege of working in a room set aside for me in his own house. My warmest thanks are extended for this and other hospitality from Dr. and Madame Bottigelli at a time when they were under the considerable pressure attendant upon the Happenings of Paris May Week 1968.

With all efficiency the International Institute of Social History in Amsterdam produced from the wealth of their archives all the material I asked to see and, by an exceptional act of courtesy, gave me permission to reproduce certain items in this biography.

Some other names are not included in the appended list because they represent such rare experiences that it will not be thought invidious, I hope, if, like those already mentioned, they are singled out.

I wish to pay a special tribute of appreciation and respect to Mrs. Gwendoline Redhead and her younger sister Mrs. Aileen Reynish, nieces of Edward Aveling and the daughters of the

* Where these are used, the Moscow Institute is acknowledged as the source.

Rev. Frederick Wilkins Aveling (1851–1937), the brother closest in age to Edward with whom he shared his schooldays and remained in touch until the end. These ladies, who received me on separate occasions in the summer of 1967, subsequently keeping up an informative correspondence, gave me not only some enjoyable hours of their company, answering my questions with the greatest patience and civility, but also the use of unique family documents, photographs and anecdotes for the purposes of this book.

With similar friendliness Mrs. Muriel Radford, the daughter-in-law of Caroline ("Dollie") Maitland and Ernest Radford who, both before and after their marriage, were among Eleanor Marx's closest friends, allowed me to visit her and to draw upon family papers, photographs and her own recollections.

To Miss Blanche Ward, the niece and close companion in the last days of Edith ("Biddy") Lanchester (1870–1966), I owe the pleasure of a memorable occasion in February 1967 when she submitted with grace to a recorded interview, again both preceded and followed by correspondence and material compiled from her aunt's reminiscences.

Throughout the writing of this book I have enjoyed the constructive criticism of Mrs. Noreen Branson of the Labour Research Department and the privilege of drawing freely, not to say importunately, upon the immense scholarship of Mr. Andrew Rothstein of the Marx Memorial Library and the wisdom of Mr. Bob Stewart.

It is common form to acknowledge research assistance, but in Mrs. Elisabeth Whitman I have had a matchless collaborator, without whose aid in Paris and Amsterdam and, since 1969, continuous team-work and independent research, the book could not have been written.

I am also greatly obliged to Mrs. Ann Kirkman and Mrs. Janet Rubidge for their conscientious typing of the final manuscript.

I now express my liveliest sense of gratitude to these outstanding benefactors, to all those whose help is acknowledged in the body of the book and to: Mr. Bert Andréas of the Graduate Institute of International Studies in Geneva; Mr. Robin Page Arnot; Professor Shlomo Avineri of the Hebrew

University of Jerusalem; Dr. Theodore Barker, M.A., Ph.D., of Keynes College, Kent University; Miss P. H. Bodington, former Headmistress of South Hampstead High School for Girls; Dr. J. P. Bodmer of the Manuscript Department of the Zentralbibliothek, Zurich; Mr. Michael Brook, Reference Librarian of the Minnesota Historical Society; Mrs. Peggy Burkel; Miss Betty England of the Labour Research Department; Professor Philip Foner of Lincoln University, Pennsylvania; Mr. Edmund Frow; Mr. Henry Grant for his new and the brilliant reproduction of old photographs used in this book; Mr. H.-P. Harstick and Miss Marie Hunink of the International Institute of Social History, Amsterdam; Mr. Malcolm Holmes and Mr. E. Jeffcott, former Librarians of the Chester Road Library, Highgate which, until 1969, had the custody of the most valuable St. Pancras archives, including the local newspapers of the 19th century; Mr. Walter Holmes for the use of the late Dona Torr's unpublished papers; Mr. Bernard Honess, Manager and Librarian, and his assistant, Mr. Derek Leask, of the Memorial Hall; Mr. G. Allen Hutt; Mr. Frank Jackson, formerly Librarian of the Communist Party of Great Britain; Mr. Alfred Jenkin; Mr. Mick Jenkins; Mr. James Klugmann for his sage advice; the London County Council—now Greater London Council—research staff at County Hall and, in particular, Mr. V. R. Belcher and Mr. J. F. C. Phillips, the former and present curators of the Map and Prints Collection, Miss J. Coburn and Mr. M. Pearce of the Record Room, Miss Anne Riches of the Historic Buildings Department and Dr. J. O. Springhall, Historical Research Assistant; Professor Henry Mayer of the University of Sydney; M. Paul Meier of the University of Paris (Nanterre); Mr. B. Y. Michaly, Manager of the Archive and Museum of the Jewish Labour Movement, Tel-Aviv; Mr. A. L. Morton; Mr. Alastair Pettigrew, Administrative Assistant to the Registry of King's College, London; Mr. G. Radice, Research Officer of the General & Municipal Workers' Union; Mr. Boris Rudyak, Mrs. Irma Sinelnikova and Mrs. Olga Vorobyova of the Institute of Marxism-Leninism, Moscow; Miss Pauline Seear of the History Research Library, Lewisham; Professor Dr. Johannes Siebert of Dresden; the late Mrs. Dorothy Thornycroft, the daughter of Eleanor Marx's friend, Edward

Rose; the late Sir Stanley Unwin for permission to read the letterbooks of Swan Sonnenschein & Co.; Mrs. Hertha Walcher, formerly secretary to Clara Zetkin; Mr. H. E. Wells-Furby, M.A., Headmaster of Christ's College, Blackheath; Mr. Edward Weber, Curator of the Labadie Collection at the Library of the University of Michigan; Miss Bernadette Wilson (now Mrs. Harris), formerly of the Long Room in the Public Record Office; and the Public Relations Officers of the British Museum, the Ministry of Agriculture and Messrs. Philips Electrical Ltd.

Y.K.

London, June 1971.

PART I

THREE SISTERS

Jenny Julia Eleanor—all Karl Marx's female children were named Jenny after their mother—was born at 28 Dean Street, Soho, in the borough of Westminster, between six and seven o'clock on the cold grey snowy morning of Tuesday, 16 January 1855. Her father was nearly 37, her mother 41, and she was the sixth child—the fourth daughter—of their twelve years of marriage; the only one to be born, to grow up, to live, to work, to cast her lot with an Englishman and to die in England.

A few days before her birth Marx wrote of his wife "approaching the catastrophe with firm steps". He announced to Frederick Engels* the arrival of "a *bona fide* traveller"— meaning one who, by law, cannot be refused sustenance and lodging—"unfortunately of the *sexe par excellence*", adding "had it been a male the matter would be more acceptable". It does not sound a particularly warm welcome.

But circumstances were hardly such as to occasion great rejoicing. Already one boy, Henry Edward Guy, known as Guido or Föxchen, after Guy Fawkes,† and one girl, Jenny Eveline Frances, known as Franziska,‡ had died in London, while the surviving son Henry Edgar, the beloved Mouche,§ had for a year past shown grave and progressive symptoms of the mesenteric disease, possibly of tubercular origin, from which he died, aged eight, three months after Eleanor's birth.

Wilhelm Liebknecht has left an account of the infant Eleanor as "a merry little thing, round as a ball, all cream and roses". Less obligingly, her nephew Edgar Longuet—writing from

---

* On 15 November 1850 Engels had re-entered his father's Manchester textile business, Ermen & Engels. At the time of Eleanor's birth he was contributing to the Chartist journals *Notes to the People* and the *People's Paper* and also writing articles for the *New York Daily Tribune*.

† b. 5 November 1849 at 4 Anderson Street, Chelsea; d. of meningitis 19 November 1850 at 64 Dean Street, Soho.

‡ b. 28 March 1851 at 28 Dean Street; d. of broncho-pneumonia 14 April 1852 at the same address.

§ b. in December 1846 at 42 rue d'Orléans, Brussels. d. 6 April (Good Friday) 1855 at 28 Dean Street.

distant hearsay, since he was not born until his aunt was 24—described her as "so puny that she was daily expected to die". The only certain facts, since they were recorded at the time and with some vexation, were that she screamed a great deal, "grew every day worse", disturbed the whole household and had to have a change of wet-nurse. So much, then, is clear: whether a sicklier or merely a hungrier and lustier than normal baby, she was breast-fed, but not by her mother, and managed to get on everybody's nerves.

However, once the "hospital atmosphere" created by a sick wife, a dying child and a yelling baby was dispelled, Eleanor grew more popular. She earned herself a pet-name, Tussy,* the forerunner of many but the one that was to stick. A sympathetic account of her at nine months was recorded by her sister Jenny, aged eleven, who wrote in her far from perfect English† to tell her father on a visit to Manchester that "Tusschen" was very lively, jumping and crawling. "She is quite in raptures when the little crucked (sic) greengrocer calls. I think this little man is her first amour."[3] She was, indeed, much cossetted by the whole family who transferred to her the protective concern inspired by the loss of Edgar and the great love they had borne him.

Conditions in the Dean Street lodgings to which the Marxes had moved five years earlier (2 December 1850, barely a fortnight after Guido's death) were so cramped that the other infant born there, Franziska, had been put out to nurse since it was found impossible to cope with her and three other small children.‡ The census returns of 30 March 1851 show that at

---

* Virginia Bateman (Mrs. Edward Compton, 1853–1940) recalled in 1935 meeting Tussy half a century before and that the parents pronounced their daughter's name to rhyme with pussy and not fussy.[1] Unreliable in other respects—she believed she had called upon the Marxes in St. John's Wood where they never lived—her memory is here corroborated by others, such as Mrs. Muriel Radford, the daughter-in-law of Eleanor's two close friends Dollie Maitland and Ernest Radford, who often spoke of "Toossy" in her hearing.[2] There was a great fondness for nicknames in the Marx family and everyone had several. Marx himself, however, was generally known as Mohr—the Moor—and her children called Mrs. Marx Möhme or Möhmchen: a Teutonised form of Mummy.

† Jenny's first language was French. In the last years of her life, married and back in France, her English became rather peculiar again. She complained of a servant railing at her "like a fishmonger".[4]

‡ The circumstances of the family before Eleanor was born are movingly described in her introduction to the series of articles she edited in 1896 under the title *Revolution and Counter-Revolution*, believing them to have been written by Marx in the years 1851–1852. As is now known, they were in fact mainly the work of

MRS. MARX SHORTLY AFTER HER MARRIAGE IN 1843

CENSUS RETURN FOR 28 DEAN STREET, 1851

the time there were eight people—four adults including a
midwife and four children—living in the Marxes' two furnished
rooms, while at no stage in the years that followed were they
ever fewer than six.

The Marxes rented these rooms for £22 a year as sub-tenants
of Morgan Kavanagh,[5] an Irishman who penned a number of
controvertible works on the origins of myth and language,
while his daughter Julia gained unlasting fame as a novelist.*
But it is to his landlady that Marx refers in his letters, and with
no more cordial feeling than is usual in that relationship,
writing to Engels in September 1852 to say that the thing most
to be desired was that she should throw him out, which would
at least save the rent, but she was unlikely to prove so obliging.

In that one Dean Street house†—still standing and now, since
August 1967, bearing a commemorative plaque to Marx's
residence—there were in all 13 people. That this was not
conspicuous overcrowding for that time and place is made clear
by the Report on the 1851 census which shows that the 1,354
inhabited buildings in the Soho parish of St. Anne housed a
population of 17,335: an average of 14 persons to each house
and 327 to the acre.‡

This was the period, and even briefly the scene, of Edwin
Chadwick's labours to establish elementary sanitary conditions
and domestic drainage for London's 300,000 houses, since the
Metropolitan Commission of Sewers in Greek Street, Soho,

Engels. Eleanor drew upon her mother's unfinished autobiographical notes,
set down in the mid-'60s but not published for nearly a century, when an incom-
plete version appeared (in Russian, English and the original German): *Kurze
Umrisse eines bewegten Lebens (Short Sketches of an Eventful Life)*.
* A quotation from one of her mawkish works[6] has a certain relevance: " 'What
has the world done for me that I should love it? . . . Why did I see my children die
from hunger, when others had more wealth than they could spend? I once said
. . . that it seemed to my poor judgment the world would be better arranged if
all human creatures shared in its wealth alike . . .' 'Well, but what is to be done?'
'I know not . . . how should I? But there are wise men in the land paid to find
out everything. Let them find out that . . .' " The authoress might have learnt
from the lodger more about this subject, including the fact that such men were not
exactly paid and that their own children also hungered and died. She is said by the
Dictionary of National Biography to have devoted herself to the care of an "aged and
infirm" mother who, however, outlived her by many years. Neither of these ladies
was at 28 Dean Street on the night of the 1851 census. They lived much abroad.
† Built *c.* 1735 under a 65-year lease granted by the Portland family to John Nolloth,
carpenter.
‡ Compared with 42·1 to the acre in the Soho Ward covered by the 1961 Census,
a figure which does not greatly differ from the average for the London Administrative County as a whole.

was for a few years his base of operations. This obstinate, arrogant but dedicated little public servant—Dickens' "indefatigable Mr. Chadwick"—who was honoured by neither friend nor foe, fought tirelessly against opposition, ignorance and apathy to introduce a primitive Public Health Act* in the belief that "the sullen resentment of the neglected workers might organise itself behind the Trade Union leaders and the Six Points men" and that "if a Chartist millennium were to be averted, the governing classes must free the governed from the sharp spur of their misery by improving the physical conditions of their lives".[7]

In the year of Eleanor's birth England's population was almost 18 million† and of the 425,703 deaths registered in that year, 97,503, or almost 24 per cent, were infants under one year of age.‡

In that year, too, Louis Pasteur, then a young professor of chemistry and Dean of the Faculty of Sciences at Lille University, examined microscopically fermentation processes which led him to the germ theory and laid the foundations of modern biochemistry and bacteriology, revolutionising medical practice.

It was a time when an engineering fitter in London—among the highest paid of skilled workers—earned 34s for a 58-hour week. It was also a moment of great technological inventions, of which the Bessemer steel process was possibly the most important. But in fact Eleanor's life of little over 40 years witnessed the expansion of the railways by the opening to traffic of over 12,000 track miles,§ saw the introduction of the telegraph as a world-wide means of communication, the mechanisation of manufacture in a score of industries, the introduction of the modern sewing-machine, the typewriter, the telephone, the bicycle, the gramophone, electric generators and lighting, the turbo, the gas, the Diesel and the petrol engine, though she barely lived to know the motor car, since it was not a commercial proposition in Britain until after the repeal of the Red Flag Act of 1897. However, a power-driven plane

---

* Passed in 1848.
† Roughly 20 million in England and Wales. The population of London had just passed the 2 million mark.
‡ Compared with 3·2% for England and Wales exactly a century later.
§ 13½ thousand track miles—rather more than were opened between 1855 and 1897—were closed between 1963 and 1969.

took off and landed safely in 1857, while the first two street letterboxes appeared in London, the Colt revolver and the Gatling machine-gun and the system of competitive examination for entrance to the Civil Service came into the world almost at the same time as she did, when the Crimean War was in full swing and Lord Aberdeen's Tory and Peelite government was about to fall on a vote of censure concerning "the condition of the army before Sebastopol", making way for Palmerston's Liberal administration. In that same year too, and in the street where she was born, St. Anne's churchyard, where some tens of thousands of bodies had been interred in its three-quarters of an acre, was finally closed, and the new burial ground, the London Necropolis, where Eleanor herself was cremated, was bought at Woking.

In this world Eleanor grew up as one of three sisters, though Jenny* and Laura† were so much her seniors that she enjoyed to some extent the status of an only child while sharing precociously in the interests of her elders. But there was one circumstance of the utmost importance to her early development.

In April 1845 Mrs. Marx, then pregnant with Laura, received from her mother, the widowed Baroness von Westphalen, "the best present she could send her: dear faithful Lenchen". This feudal gift consisted of Helene Demuth, a young person then in her 25th year, who had been born at St. Wendel in the Palatinate where her father, of peasant stock, was a baker. At the age of eight or nine the child left home for Trier, some 30 miles away, to go into domestic service, bettering herself three years later, after some harsh experiences, by entering the Westphalen household. Jenny von Westphalen, her mother's only surviving daughter, was then 21 and already secretly betrothed to the 17-year-old Karl Marx, though the engagement was not formally—or easily—recognised for another two years nor the marriage celebrated until 1843, by which time her father, Baron Ludwig von Westphalen, had been dead for

* Jenny Caroline. b. 1 May 1844 at 28 rue Vaneau, Paris. d. 11 January 1883 at 11 boulevard Thiers, Argenteuil, Val d'Oise. Her death certificate states that she was born 4 May; but since Eleanor told Liebknecht that Jenny was born in 1845 and Eleanor's own birth date is incorrectly carved upon the present Marx monument in Highgate Cemetery, too much attention should not be paid to these little slips of the pen and chisel.

† Jenny Laura. b. 26 September 1845 at 5 rue de l'Alliance, Brussels. d. 26 November 1911 at Draveil, Seine-et-Oise.

a year and Jenny was 29. Thus, when bundled off to Brussels to rejoin her young mistress, Lenchen had been but briefly separated from her.

This abrupt transfer from her homeland and from the placid round of waiting upon the petty nobility in a sleepy provincial town to the hugger-mugger family life of a revolutionary, hounded from one European capital to another, certainly tested Lenchen's stoicism but failed to daunt her. She shared the experience of cheap hotels and squalid lodgings, of expulsions and evictions, flitting from country to country with the hard-pressed Marxes, whose children were born and whose children died, while Lenchen's wages were seldom paid and her clothes more often than not in pawn. If she had time off it was as porter of the laden picnic basket on family outings, or else she played chess with Marx when not running his errands and beating off his creditors. Yet in that heyday of overworked and underpaid slaveys who were also despised, Helene Demuth was never looked upon by any of the Marxes as less than a most valued friend.

It was not, however, until 1856, after twelve restless years, that she came into her own. There was still no money, but in the haven of a small suburban house with a settled family whose numbers were not again to vary—save for the advent of a last-born child who lived but a few hours—Lenchen ordered and sustained the whole establishment where bread was baked, clothes were made and patched, boots were mended, linen was washed and beer was brewed. Her own son, born in 1851, had early been put out to foster-parents* and on Eleanor she lavished all her motherliness.

It was during the years of Eleanor's childhood that some of Marx's most significant work was done. She was six weeks old when the inaugural meeting of an international committee, foreshadowing great things, was held under the chairmanship of Ernest Jones, with Marx in attendance, at St. Martin's Hall, Long Acre. In 1855 and early 1856 Marx wrote his famous articles on the conduct of the Crimean War and the fall of Kars,[8] in 1857 those on the Indian Mutiny.[9] In June 1859 his *Critique of Political Economy* appeared; in December 1860, *Herr Vogt*; in September 1864 the International Working Men's

* See Appendix I, p. 289.

Association, the First International, was founded, Marx's *Inaugural Address* and *Provisional Rules* being published that November. In June 1865 he gave the address to the General Council of the IWMA known to later generations as *Value, Price and Profit*, while September 1867 saw the first edition of Volume I of *Capital* on which Marx had worked for ten years, plagued throughout by ill-health and debt.

Mrs. Marx, who was also often unwell, spent a good deal of her time running to the pawnbroker to pledge the linen and plate, her own and her family's personal belongings and attire and all such household objects as were not immovable. Occasionally, when impending guests made the denuded home an embarrassment positively more acute than the need for ready cash, she ran to redeem a few of these articles. When not so engaged she was copying out by hand the successive drafts of Marx's manuscripts. Doting mother though she was, dwelling on her daughters' beauty, brains, prizes and attainments in letters to her friends, she had scarcely more time than Marx himself—an extremely loving father—to devote to the small Eleanor. Nor is there evidence that, apart from the true affection that bound all members of the family, her big sisters, who were either at school or busy mastering the ladylike accomplishments so unsuited to their actual—and future—circumstances, paid overmuch attention to the child.

So she was Helene Demuth's baby, nurtured by that warm and sturdy peasant soul. Something of its down-to-earth simplicity, its *Demut*,* its kindliness and unselfish devotion were reflected in Eleanor all her days.

Unlike the other members of the family Eleanor cannot be regarded as a Soho character. She spent her first seven months there, during some part of which her parents were in Manchester and her mother, when in London, was frequently laid up. She was then taken to Camberwell—a suburb so pastoral compared to the environs of Leicester Square that the Marxes referred to it quite simply as "the country"—to live in a cottage lent by Peter Imandt, a German exile. There she spent the summer, returning to Dean Street, a few days after the fall of Sebastopol, to remain until the following May when she went with her mother and sisters to Trier until September to stay for

* The word means modesty, humility.

the first and last time with her maternal grandmother who died during the visit in July, shortly after her 81st birthday.

For this expedition and on the strength of a little over £100 which came to her on the death of a 90-year-old uncle,* Mrs. Marx paid off some of the most pressing debts, redeemed certain items from the pawnbroker and made the journey to her old home with her children "newly attired".

Now, on her return, she could look to another legacy, enough to make the break from Dean Street and, indeed, within a month she was househunting. It turned out, however, that her half-brother, as is usual in such circumstances, was holding up her inheritance, that endless debts, large and small, had again accumulated and that everything was back in pawn.

The househunting went on blithely nonetheless and, with Engels' help, the family moved into No. 9 Grafton Terrace, Kentish Town, in the borough of St. Pancras,† on 29 September 1856. Eleanor was nearly 21 months old.

---

* Heinrich Georg von Westphalen. Six years later Mrs. Marx wrote to Mrs. Bertha Markheim, a lady who had made the acquaintance of the Marx family in 1854, stating that she had inherited £150 to £200 in 1856 from a Scottish relative, using the occasion to mention her Campbell and "Argyle" (*sic*) connections.[10] Later still, in her reminiscences, she referred to this as "a small English inheritance". There is no reference in the correspondence of the time to any legacy from such a source and no means of tracing the Will, since the testator, whether Scottish or English, is never named.
† Now, since 1965, Camden.

THE YOUNG HELENE DEMUTH

NO. 9 GRAFTON TERRACE

Grafton Terrace, where Eleanor lived until she was nine, was in what we should now call a development area. It had been built in the late forties on a parcel of land sold as two Lots of just under half an acre each at the auction in August 1840 of a portion of freehold ground rents on Lord Southampton's Haverstock Hill and Kentish Town estate.* The presumed building value of the combined plots at the time of the sale was £140 a year.

This short terrace of 14 paired and three singlefronted brick cottages—or "third-class houses" as they were designated by the District Surveyors of the short-lived Metropolitan Building Office (1844–1855)[11]—was built in a slightly whimsical style, with balconies and stone coping, quoins, balustrade and window surrounds. It was as yet an island in a morass of churned London clay and building operations, the street unlit and unpaved. It represented a fairly typical example of small builder's enterprise, spurred by the exodus of Londoners from the centre to the outskirts which, thanks to the railways, was one of the distinguishing features of London life in the second half of the 19th century.† The speed of the suburban spread to the northwest may be judged from the fact that in 1843 a duel was fought at Chalk Farm as one of the "least frequented parts". By the end of that decade it had become a favourite out-of-town Sunday resort for costermongers because it had "plenty of life",[12] yet within two years of the Marxes' move, that is, by 1858, all the fields surrounding Grafton Terrace had been completely built over, prefiguring the neighbourhood where Eleanor was to spend the best part of the next 27 years.

* The St. Pancras almshouses begun in 1850 on a site facing the length of Grafton Terrace, and the public house opposite—The Lord Southampton, frequented by Marx—which forms the corner of Grafton Terrace and what is left of Southampton Road, are still extant.
† The population of St. Pancras increased by an average of 3,723 and the number of houses by 397 in each year of the decade 1841–1851. Over the 20 years 1841 to 1861 the population rose from 48 to 74 persons to the acre.

To Mrs. Marx this mean little house in Kentish Town,* covering an area of 16 ft. (frontage) by 20 ft. with its eight small rooms on four floors, including a basement, seemed in truth "a princely abode compared with our former holes".[13] She had inherited something like £120 from her mother. She now proceeded to take her household goods out of pawn again, to pay off some of the Soho tradesmen† and to spend £40 on furniture, mostly "second-hand rubbish" as she described it.[13] This, supplemented by some rickety chairs and a tea-table cast off by Peter Imandt when he left Camberwell to settle in Dundee, more than met her needs: she pronounced the living room (15 ft. by 12) positively magnificent, sold a few old dresses and shoes to buy ornaments, and the money was gone; in fact they were short of £15 for the move. It then struck Marx that if he did not pay at least his first quarter's rent punctually he would be "utterly discredited".

Marx considered the place a bargain at £36 a year, attributing the low price to its "unfinished surroundings". In fact, its rateable value at the time and for most of the years he remained there was £24 a year and the gross estimated rental—which in those days bore an intelligible relation to rateable value—was £27, with rates of £2 5s. 10d., some part of which covered the lighting and paving which were not there. The truth is that throughout his seven-and-a-half years' tenancy of No. 9‡ Grafton Terrace, Marx was never able to pay for the upkeep of this princely abode. "We were permanently hard up," Mrs. Marx recalled, "our debts mounted from day to day," and when Engels undertook in January 1857 to provide £5 a month— which was rapidly stepped up as one crisis followed upon another—it was in response to Marx's dismayed recognition that the hand-to-mouth existence of Dean Street was no longer feasible for a householder and ratepayer with three daughters to bring up.

There were other disadvantages for the parents. Though

---

* The house is still standing. Its rateable value is £134 p.a. and it is occupied by several families.
† Though not all: three years later the Dean Street milkman and baker were still owed the substantial sum of £9.
‡ Now, and since October 1888, No. 46. For some years, from 1872, with the extension of the street, the renaming of adjacent terraces and the renumbering of the first houses, it became No. 36.[14]

exile was nothing new to the Marxes who had known little else since their repeated expulsions from France, Prussia and Belgium, this was a new form of it.

The England where they had landed seven years before had been no more than their last country of immigration,* the London to which they came was but another foreign city that turned out to be home for the rest of their lives. Apart from the first few months in Chelsea, their stamping ground had been Soho—the German Hotel at No. 1 Leicester Square, then 64 Dean Street for half a year and 28 Dean Street for close on six years: a Soho flooded with the 1848 refugees from Poland, Hungary, Russia, Italy, France and Germany—a tide that was not to recede for nearly a decade—and the Marxes had been among the "incongruous elements" described by Herzen as "caught up from the Continent and deposited . . . by those ebbs and flows of revolution . . . in the alleys . . . of Leicester Square and the adjoining back streets . . . a wretched population wearing hats such as no one wears, and hair where none should be, a miserable, poverty-stricken, harassed population . . ."[15] whose "dissolute habits" shocked the easygoing Engels.[16] But the Marxes' Dean Street lodgings had been a homing point for new arrivals and the natural meeting place for socialist friends already in London, few of whom had any means of support and most of whom fell a prey to the internecine strife, mutual recrimination and spy-mania endemic to political émigré circles.

Now many of the old friends had departed, while to those still left Kentish Town seemed wildly inaccessible. The Marxes missed the social life of the Clubs and pubs they had used to frequent in the West End. Nor did they relish going out at night to encounter the hazards of darkness, refuse, mud and rubble of this "barbarous region",† preferring the comfort of their own hearth. In any case, Marx felt, his time was too valuable to spend on the futile plottings and petty squabbles of refugee politics, and he retreated more and more into his study, or

---

* Following Marx's refusal to accept banishment by the authorities from Paris to Vannes: at that time a swamp in Morbihan (Brittany).

†The rubbish from building, railway cutting and sewer works was tipped into the fields behind Haverstock Hill abutting Grafton Terrace at the rate of some 37,000 loads a year (1 load = 1 cubic yard) in the period when Hampstead, added to the metropolis in 1846, was being developed.

repaired to the British Museum where now, in 1857, the rotunda Reading Room was opened.

For the children it was an unqualified change for the better. Jenny and Laura had been to a little school in Soho, but now their education made strides. They were coached for a brief period by Wilhelm ("Fridolin") Pieper who had formerly been Marx's secretary. Marx did not think much of him as a tutor and he was extremely tiresome into the bargain. So the girls were sent to the rather high-sounding South Hampstead College for Ladies at Clarence House, 18 Haverstock Hill, run by the Misses Boynell and Rentsch. Here they constantly won prizes, came out top in everything though the youngest in the form, and cost their father a good deal of money, for the fees were £8 a term, to which were added extra lessons in languages and drawing. "And now I have to engage a music fellow", Marx wrote ruefully to Engels in April 1857, which step was followed by the hire of an inferior piano.

Eleanor, not to be outdone by so much brilliance and something of a wag, announced that she had two brains—one for each of her years presumably—and exercised them both to good purpose with incessant chatter. She later recalled that when she had whooping cough, which lasted the best part of the year 1858, she "took advantage of the fact to insist upon open house being kept for every street child in the neighbourhood". As there were no fewer than 50 young children living on their side of Grafton Terrace alone*—and it may be remarked that some of the little maids-of-all-work were barely in their 'teens—social life at No. 9 must have lacked a certain restraint. It was perhaps fortunate that for some part of that time Marx himself was stopping with Engels in Manchester. But then, as Eleanor wrote, she had made "bond slaves" of the family and "as is usual in slavery, there was general demoralisation".[17] Three years later she went down with jaundice. Adept at turning her afflictions to good account and perceiving that she was yellow, she decided that she had become Chinese and that her rather frizzy hair should be made into a little pigtail. Her renown as a hostess, by no means

---

* There was, for example, the family of John Withers, master-baker, who lived at No. 1 at the end of the street with three small daughters. The Marxes' neighbour, at No. 10, was Samuel Sawyer, a builder, also with three daughters and a son under seven. In later years both these families played some part in Marx's affairs.

dependent upon her indispositions, was so widespread that the Marx family was known in the neighbourhood to children and grown-ups alike as "the Tussies"; and such was her conviviality that, as Lenchen recalled in after-years, Tussy could not be induced to come to table in summertime but sat on the doorstep with a mug of milk and then, snatching a slice of bread, was off to join her companions at their street games. She was something of a romp and what was called a tomboy; fearless in play with the bigger, wild urchins.[18]

All Eleanor's recollections are of an unclouded childhood. One of the earliest is of careering over fields and round the long narrow garden of Grafton Terrace on her father's shoulders at the age of three with convolvulus flowers in her hair. She remembered the unending tale which Marx spun for her, month after month, concerning one Hans Röckle, a magician who kept a toyshop but was "never able to meet his obligations either to the devil or the butcher and was therefore, much against the grain, constantly obliged to sell his toys . . .". She listened entranced to the fairy stories of the Brothers Grimm until she not only had them by heart but had picked up fluent German in this way.*

Then Marx began to read aloud, as to her sisters before her, "the whole of Homer, the whole *Niebelungenlied, Gudrun, Don Quixote*, the *Arabian Nights*" and Shakespeare, who was "the bible of our house, seldom out of our hands or mouths". By the time she was four she knew long passages by heart and, at six, "recited whole scenes", one of her favourites being that between Hamlet and his mother. As Mrs. Marx occasionally played the Queen, Eleanor "fancied that the line: 'Mother, you have my father much offended' must have been the attraction".[19]

She did not learn her letters at some prodigiously early age. Indeed, her mother claimed that she could not read to herself with ease until she was eight.[20] Eleanor's own recollections blur or belie this, for she relates that on her sixth birthday she was given *Peter Simple* and then went on to the rest of Marryat and to Fenimore Cooper, Marx also reading these books so that he could discuss each one in detail with her. When, fired by Marryat's tales, she "declared she would become a 'Post-

* She never learnt to write German correctly.

B

Captain' (whatever that may be)* and consulted her father as to whether it would not be possible for her to 'dress up as a boy' and 'run away to join a man-of-war', he assured her he thought it might very well be done, only they must say nothing about it to anyone until all plans were well matured".[21] It was at this period too that Eleanor, convinced that Abraham Lincoln could not do without her advice on the conduct of the American Civil War, wrote—or possibly dictated—long letters to the President for Marx to read and post. These letters so amused him that he preserved them, though they have not come down to us, and many years later showed them to her.

"Children should educate their parents", said Marx, and lived up to the dictum by keeping in step with the reading, entering the fantasy life, encouraging the confidences and adjusting his views to meet the religious scruples of his engaging Tussy. He told her the story of the Passion—"the carpenter whom the rich men killed"—adding that much could be forgiven Christianity because it had taught the adoration of the child.

Mrs. Marx, who admitted that her sporadic efforts to teach her elder daughters German were vain, for they "had no mind to obey", while her authority, like their respect for her, "left much to be desired",[13] was also quite good at learning. She derived instruction from Tussy's facility in making up stories, in which she rivalled her father, and her more than facile gymnastic ability. To the child herself it seemed in after-years that there had never been a more "merry pair" than these two whom she helped to educate.

It is hard to realise that the laughing, loving parents of Eleanor's childhood memories were racked by the most sordid misery and distress; that her father was brought to the point of desperation and her mother to the verge of a mental breakdown in those same years. It is a tribute of a kind rarely paid to Karl Marx that what Eleanor knew—unlike Maisie—was untainted.

Almost from the time they moved to Grafton Terrace, Mrs. Marx, who immediately became pregnant with her seventh child which did not survive, was ailing and also exceedingly

* It is curious that Eleanor, writing as an adult, should have been puzzled by what she had known as a child, for "Post Captains" do not occur only in Marryat but also in Jane Austen. They were naval officers with the substantive rank of Captain, having "taken post".

ill-humoured, "for which at heart I can't really blame her under present auspices", Marx wrote, "though it annoys me".

This was the year (1857) of world economic crisis, starting in November in America, with the result that the *New York Daily Tribune* reduced Marx's contributions, thus halving this source of income.* It was now that he began his first draft of *Capital*, but before the year was out he was threatened with the broker's men for failure to pay his rent while hordes of "hungry wolves", the angry shopkeepers, also suffering hard times, were at the door.

A cold snap in January 1858 found the family without coal or money in the house and, feeling that the position was fast becoming insupportable, unable to work, Marx spent his time trying to raise loans and borrowing from one tradesman to fend off another. These shifts were not calculated to produce a lasting solution to any of the problems and, but for Engels' help, the family could barely have survived. By the summer Dr. Allen of Soho Square with a surgery in Dean Street, who still attended them†—and was himself owed £10 in fees—insisted that Mrs. Marx must have a change of air, which was the last straw. Marx sent Engels a detailed account of his present debts, amounting to £113, of which £30 was owed to the pawnbroker and over £32 to the local butcher, baker, grocer, milkman, greengrocer and newsagent, the last not having been paid for a twelvemonth. "Even if I were to reduce my expenses to the utmost", Marx wrote, "by, for example, removing the children from school, going to live in a strictly working-class dwelling, dismissing the servants and living on potatoes", the sale of the furniture would not realise enough to satisfy his creditors, while such drastic steps could have dangerous consequences for his wife in her nervous state and were hardly suitable for his growing girls.

Although at this point Engels, having poked some gentleman in the eye with his umbrella for insulting the "bloody foreigner", was being sued for £200 damages,‡ he still came to the rescue

---

* He had at first received £1 an article, then £2 for each one published. Later the editor (Dana) agreed to pay for every article sent, whether printed or not.
† Doing so until 1868 when he suffered a paralytic stroke and was unable to make his rounds.
‡ In the event he got off with £30 damages and £20 costs, though Marx had thought the only course open was for Engels to flee the country.

of the Marxes, as he did again and again, not only with cash but also with crates of wine—regarded on all sides as the sovereign remedy for every bodily ill—yet when winter came round the household was "more dreary and desolate than ever", an atmosphere of gloom prevailed and Mrs. Marx, unable to provide any Christmas cheer for the children, tore herself free of the rabid creditors to celebrate the festive season by paying yet another visit to the pawnbroker and copying out the MS. of the *Critique of Political Economy*. "Never, I think, was money written about under such a shortage of it", said Marx.

The year 1859 saw no change in this state of affairs; rather was it aggravated by Marx's recurrent liver complaint and toothaches. Indeed, this whole wretched string of years, with all its incongruities, could be summed up in the scene presented by the family that Christmas when, with a County Court summons pending, the instalments to the tallyman for Marx's very trousers sorely in arrears, most of the others' clothing at the pawnshop and everyone ailing in one way or another, they gathered round the imaginary *Weihnachtsbaum* to drink the champagne Engels had sent.

It is among other inconsistent features of this poverty-stricken household that letters in which Marx recounts the most seamy efforts to raise money, while being sued for debt and about to have the water and the gas supply cut off, were written to the accompaniment of Laura and Jenny singing delightful duets at the piano, having made good progress with their music lessons.

These girls, now aged 15 and 16, left school in 1860 but they continued to take the "single class in any subject" offered by the South Hampstead College to learn French, Italian, drawing and singing, while there were now two servants to wait upon the family, Helene Demuth having been joined by Marianne Kreuz as housemaid.

For three months of that year Marx was continuously ill, while money troubles gathered ever more ominously about him, but in the late summer he managed to send the family to Hastings for a fortnight, where it rained all the time. In November, though twice vaccinated, Mrs. Marx contracted smallpox. The nature of her illness had to be kept a great secret for some reason, though not, it must be thought, an anti-social one, for

immediate steps were taken to isolate the invalid and the
children were sent to stay with the Liebknechts nearby. Marx
remained in the house and, with Lenchen's help, tended his
wife who was fed on sips of claret. Though not allowed to come
near the members of the contagious household—and, indeed,
Jenny had to post a letter from just round the corner "as
the thoroughfare to 9 Grafton Terrace is closed"[22]—Eleanor,
viewing her father in the street from Liebknecht's windows,
cried in true hunting style "Halloo, old boy!". There was some
scheme for sending the girls temporarily to a little boarding
school, which they scotched by objecting to the "religious
rites" they would have to perform. In any case Mrs. Marx was
sufficiently recovered for them all to return home by Christmas,
to everyone's relief, for Marx had been obliged to pay for the
upkeep of two séparate establishments in their absence, Liebknecht being in no position to provide for three additional
hungry young persons.

The homecoming was festive, but almost at once in the New
Year Marx, worn out by nursing his wife who was still far from
well, inclined to be crotchety and extremely demanding, went
down with an attack of his chronic liver trouble which now
became acute. For fear of incurring fresh medical expenses he
doctored himself for some weeks with such lamentable results
that, suffering a severe relapse, he had to call in Dr. Allen,
who came every three days and prescribed horse riding and a
change of air. "I'm as plagued as Job, if less godfearing",
wrote Marx to Engels as, sardonically reporting the doctor's
advice, he remarked that he was being sued for rates and school
fees while grocer and butcher were refusing both further credit
and supplies. But Dr. Allen must not be told the truth or "where
the shoe pinches". Once more Marx set about exploring the
possibilities of a Loan Society, but his guarantees were not
sound enough.

With the usual timely £10 from Engels he settled the gas
bill and the rates, beat off the bailiffs once again and prepared
to go to Holland. He was there from March till May 1861.
Eleven years earlier, desperate at the prospect of the fifth child
then on the way, Mrs. Marx had gone to Holland to beg her
husband's uncle Lion Philips for help, which was refused. Marx
had little taste for courting a similar rebuff and had set his face

against an expedient long urged by Engels. But there was no alternative. His income from the *New York Daily Tribune* had dwindled to nothing and was about to cease; that from the *New American Cyclopaedia*, to which he had contributed since July 1857, had completely dried up in the autumn of 1860.

Lion Philips, a successful businessman in Zaltbommel, near Nijmegen, married to Marx's aunt Sophie, managed the affairs of his sister-in-law, Marx's mother, herself of Dutch origin.* Marx hoped to borrow an advance on his expectations from the old lady, widowed for the past twenty-three years and now aged 74. Apart from occasional loans against IOUs, grandmother Marx had not been generous, usually answering her son's appeals with prolonged silence and holding the view that he would be better employed accumulating capital than writing about it. His mission was moderately successful. He established excellent relations with his Dutch cousins and eventually came back to London with £160; but not before he had used the opportunity to go, without papers, into Prussia† where he tried but failed to reclaim citizenship and to travel widely in Germany and the Low Countries, while laying the groundwork for contributing regular articles to the Vienna *Presse*. He also involved himself in highly complicated man-oeuvres to arrange a long-term loan on the Continent. Though he claimed to have been bored to death in Berlin, where he was lionised, this brief interlude was something of a respite for him.

During his absence it was Lenchen's turn to fall ill and she was out of commission for several weeks. Mrs. Marx was obliged to turn to Engels for money, at which juncture her husband was trying to raise his return fare.‡

---

* "My grandmother", wrote Eleanor,[23] ". . . belonged by descent to an old Hungarian Jewish family driven by persecution to Holland . . . [they] became known by the name of Presburg (*sic*), really the town from which they came. These Presburgs, of course, intermarried, and my grandmother's family name was afterwards Phillips (*sic*) . . . To the day of her death . . . I believe . . . [she] spoke very bad German." Pressburg is now Bratislava. The Philips family founded the firm of Philips Lamps Ltd. in Eindhoven in 1891.

† While there he obtained a passport valid until May 1862. An amnesty for political refugees had been granted on the accession of Wilhelm I in January 1861. It did not, however, apply to Marx who—like most other Prussian revolutionaries —had lived abroad for over ten years and thus became a "foreigner".

‡ From Carl Siebel (28 March 1861), in order to travel back *via* Elberfeld, Cologne, Trier, Aachen, Zaltbommel again, Amsterdam and Rotterdam.

He arrived home to be confronted by the familiar mountain of debt, swallowing up every penny he had brought back—and small wonder, since £40 went on school and doctor's fees alone—so that by June he was again unable to meet an inexorable rate demand.

§3

With an inflammation of the eyes that prevented him from reading or writing, a variety of summonses and a law-suit hanging over his head—not for the first time—but without the means to employ a solicitor, Marx had now to take stock of the fact that his wife could no longer withstand the stresses of their situation. Her loyalty to his interests, which she shared, was unfaltering, her determination that he should "pursue his purpose through thick and thin, not allowing bourgeois society to turn him into a money-making machine"[24] was as steadfast as his own—she always looked back on the days spent in his tiny study "copying out his scrawled articles" as the happiest of her life—but the struggle had been too nasty, brutish and long.

Mrs. Marx was not an hysteric but nor was she cast in the heroic mould. The truth is that, while she met uncommonly trying circumstances with more than common fortitude, her origins were against her. Though much has been made of her high birth, she came of no ancient or exalted aristocracy.

Her paternal grandfather, Christian Heinrich Philip West-phalen (1724–1792) had been an able administrator who rose to become the Duke of Brunswick's general factotum and acting Chief of Staff, or Quartermaster General, in the Seven Years' War. Having refused military honours both from Brunswick and the British Government, he accepted the German title of Baron on his alliance with Jean Wishart (1746–1811), a kinswoman of the third Duke of Argyll, herself the daughter of an Edinburgh minister. On her mother's side, Mrs. Marx was descended from a minor Prussian functionary called Heubel. She was born in Salzwedel in the Mark.

There was more in her make-up of the good provincial *bourgeoise*—except in the matter of thrift—than of the great lady who gives not a snap of the fingers for anyone. Her indignities and deprivations were so much the harder to bear. She cared very much what others thought, was intensely house-proud and entertained meek worldly ambitions for her daughters. Her courage is thus the more to be admired as she stood perpetually on the brink of the relentless tide of debt that rose to disaster level every few weeks, threatening to engulf the whole family. It never quite swamped her but it damped her spirits. Nevertheless, there was an unquenchable optimism in her nature and more than a touch of Mrs. Bennet.

Something of her attitude to the upbringing of children can be discerned from letters written many years later, and is wholly sympathetic. Describing a meal at the house of a widower she wrote: ". . . the children are constantly watched and called to order: they must eat correctly, they must speak correctly; the only thing that is not done according to rule is drinking; to my great astonishment there was neither beer nor wine on the table. . . . The children have never yet tasted spirits . . .".[25] ". . . The little boy, a friendly though ugly child, was in a fearful state over an unmanageable duck's leg. He very much wanted to get the little bit of meat off it, but as he did not dare lay a finger on the bone (the governess's eye never leaves the children) the piece of leg slid off the plate. You should have seen the poor boy and, indeed, the whole to-do at the table, the tittering of his sisters, the threatening glare of the governess, the flurry of domestic servants and, on top of it all, G.'s grave sermonising on good table manners. . . ."[26]*

Since Mrs. Marx found this behaviour so absurd it is clear that her own children were never drilled and corrected in a like manner; but as the years advanced she grew more querulous, showing signs of nervous depression until there were times when Marx thought she was taking leave of her senses. Looking back at the age of 58 over her troubled life she wrote to Wilhelm Liebknecht: "In all these struggles, the harder because the pettier part falls to us women. While the men are invigorated

---

* Mrs. Marx also expressed horror at the cruelties inflicted upon children in the name of medical science. "Poor little H. is in an advanced stage of dropsy. He has a dreadful abdomen and is otherwise like a skeleton . . . The cure is appalling. Just imagine, the child is given nothing whatever to drink, not a drop of water, no tea, no coffee, but on the other hand every four days a few glasses of wine. Neither is he allowed a morsel to eat except quite stale bread, dry rusks and nothing else, nothing. At night he is wrapped in wet towels and swaddled in long bandages of linen, flannel, etc., and so put to bed; then dry bread again, without water. And this is supposed to cure dropsy! It is frightful to see . . .".[27]

by the fight in the world outside, strengthened by coming face
to face with the enemy, be its number legion, we sit at home
and darn stockings. It does not banish care and the little day-
to-day worries slowly but surely sap one's vitality. . . . I can
truly say that I did not easily allow my spirits to flag. Now
I am too old to hope for much any more . . .".[28] But now, in
1861, she still hoped, and reacted, with passion, so that the
mere mention of the interminable negotiations for a loan—at
high interest—which figured so largely in Marx's correspondence, provoked outbursts of a most disquieting nature.

Whether undermined by the combination of her husband's
absence abroad, the lack of friendships with women of her own
kind, Lenchen's indisposition, Tussy's jaundice, her aversion
from the scheme to resume Prussian nationality and the after-
effects of smallpox, which had prematurely ravaged her looks,
or whether by her time of life—she was 47—Mrs. Marx's
fortitude collapsed.

Even Dr. Allen was alarmed by her condition whose etiology
he guessed—diagnosing before his time a psychosomatic illness
—but had the delicacy not to name. "This dog's life isn't
worth living", wrote Marx: now that Jenny was old enough to
realise the situation, its vileness and horror were telling on her
health; daily Mrs. Marx bemoaned the fact that she and her
children were not in the grave. All this was going on, and felt,
and said. Yet it was impossible to admit to the family doctor or
allow him to mention their hopeless straits.

This keeping up of appearances is not to be mocked. To be
sure, a century later it strikes one as grotesque that a man of
such powerful intellect, a woman of such proper spirit as Karl
Marx and his wife should have deigned to hide their circumstances; should have persisted in employing two domestic
servants and encouraged their almost full-grown daughters to
draw and sing and thump upon the piano with indifferent talent
while the household fell about their ears.

What has to be seen is that, at the time, the gulf between
the respectability of the professional class to which the Marxes
belonged and its alternative, a proletarian way of life, was vast
and unbridgeable.* It was not a question of doing without cer-

* It is of interest to note that in the Debates on the abortive Reform Bill in 1859
it was recognised that no working man could afford to pay £10 a year for a

tain fribbles or cutting down on luxuries, as they would now be regarded; the Marxes did without and cut down on sheer necessities. There was often neither food nor fuel in the house. Rather it was a matter of social and historical realities pressing no less on Marx than on his contemporaries. The interesting thing about him is not that he was subject to these pressures, but that it was he who evolved an entirely new concept of both society and history. "Men's social being determines their consciousness" he wrote and nowhere claimed exemption from the rule.

In 1861 nearly a quarter of the male and over one-third of the female population of England and Wales were illiterate, while the professional classes represented under 3 per cent: considerably less than the proportion of paupers. In every trade, nine-tenths of the workers were unskilled with an earning capacity that rarely reached 20s. a week; the Scottish miner (with a family of above the average of six children to support) earned 24s, the Manchester carpenter 28s. and the craftsman in the London building trade 32s. Their living conditions were atrocious and had not greatly changed since Engels wrote his *Condition of the Working Class in England in 1844.* Indeed, he was able to say in the new preface he wrote to the English edition of that work in 1892: ". . . the most crying abuses described . . . have either disappeared or have been made less conspicuous. . . . But what of that? Whole districts which in 1844 I could describe as almost idyllic, have now, with the growth of the towns, fallen into the same state of dilapidation, discomfort and misery. Only the pigs and the heaps of refuse are no longer tolerated. The bourgeoisie have made further progress in the art of hiding the distress of the working class. . . . Police regulations have been as plentiful as blackberries; but they can only hedge in the distress of the workers, they cannot remove it."

By the 1860s the arts of hiding and hedging were not yet widely cultivated. As late as 1875 "the average age at death of the Manchester upper middle class was 38 years, while the average age of the labouring class was 17; while at Liverpool those figures were represented as 35 against 15. It thus appeared that the well-to-do classes had a lease of life which was more

house. When the 1867 Bill finally went through the franchise included householders paying £7 p.a. at which date Marx's rent was some ten times that amount.

than double the value of that which fell to the lot of the less-favoured citizens."[29]

Keeping up appearances meant most to Marx where his daughters were concerned. He might rail against his wife's mild pretensions as false and pernicious, as "roasting him over a slow fire", yet he shared her aspirations for the girls and took offence at any suggestion that they should attempt to earn their living, for which, in however restricted a field, their polite studies might be thought to have equipped them.

He lamented that they could not join in the amusements of their young friends, whose visits to the house they dreaded; he pitied them because they were not presentable enough to attend either their classes or the 1862 International Industrial Exhibition,* for which he himself obtained a permanent press ticket in August as correspondent of the Vienna *Presse*, though it is not known that he ever took his daughters with him. But that they might become self-supporting he looked upon as a mortification outweighing any to which they were daily and hourly exposed. Marx treated as an impertinence Lassalle's well-intentioned proposal that they should go to Berlin as companions to the Countess Hatzfeldt; and when he expounded to Engels his plan to declare himself bankrupt, let the landlord sell his furniture, find another situation for Lenchen and move with Mrs. Marx and Tussy into a Model Lodging-House at 3s a week, quite the cruellest aspect of the whole design was that Laura and Jenny—then 18 and 19—should take posts as governesses.

Even training for a profession was unthinkable. When Jenny approached Mrs. Charles Young† with a view to studying for the stage, she did so without her parents' knowledge and naturally nothing came of this reprehensible step, even though

---

* Open from 1 May until 1 November 1862 in South Kensington (hence Exhibition Road). Its success was slightly marred by the death from typhoid of the Prince Consort on 14 December 1861. The domes and other distinctive features of the buildings (known as the "Brompton Boilers"), designed by Captain Francis Fowke, R.E.—who was also partly responsible for designing the Albert Hall—were used in the construction of Alexandra Palace, completed in 1873, where, two years later, to commemorate the 21st anniversary of the charge of the Light Brigade, a banquet was given for the 195 survivors.

† Jane Elizabeth Thomson (1827–1902), an American actress who made her first appearance in England in 1857. Previously the wife of an American actor, Charles Young, whose name she used at this period, she married Hermann Vezin (1829–1910) in 1863 and became well-known under her second husband's name.

her mother told Mrs. Bertha Markheim in January 1863 that, were Jenny's health not so delicate, they would do nothing to discourage her from such a career.

Mrs. Marx might be driven to try to sell her husband's books when all else had been sacrificed; she might suffer another paroxysm at the renewed threat of the broker's men and make scenes that caused Marx to go more frequently to the British Museum than he required for his reading; but it never struck her that her girls might with greater dignity pursue an independent life.

With his children's and his servants' footwear in pawn, so that none of them could leave the house on which a whole year's rent was owing, the plight of Marx's family appears as great as that of the most miserably paid worker. In some ways it was worse, for preoccupation with these base problems effectively stopped Marx working for weeks on end, contributing to and aggravating his ill-health to complete the vicious circle. But, however their situation compares with that of the proletariat in the England of the 1860s, one matter is beyond dispute: a middle-aged, middle-class, Middle-European Doctor of Philosophy simply could not have been assimilated into it. He had either to struggle on against all odds—as a few of his kind, but not many, did—to emigrate again or to go into commerce. In August 1862, conceding that it was a little late in the day to entertain the thought, he wrote to Engels: "If I but knew how to start a business"; and, a month later, in a throwaway postcript, he announced that he might be going to work in the office of an English railway company in the New Year. Luckily or unluckily, he was not sure which, his application was turned down on the grounds of his bad handwriting,* and nothing more was heard of these fantasies.

The fact was that at this period Marx was not only writing articles on the American Civil War[31] but, despite the strain of trying to make ends meet, his "brainbox", rather to his surprise,

---

* It was indeed appalling and special training was needed to decipher it. Such training Engels gave to Eduard Bernstein and Karl Kautsky in the late '80s when his eyesight troubled him, so that others might be able, if he failed, to complete the work of preparing for publication the "hieroglyphic script" of Marx's literary remains. It was a not inconsiderable factor in the confusions that arose over the Marx-Engels *Nachlässe*. It proved almost impossible to assign correctly the authorship of individual manuscripts: Engels had frequently written out *en clair* his friend's work.[30]

was positively working better than for years past and he produced the whole first draft of Volume I of *Capital*.

For three weeks in the late summer of 1862 Mrs. Marx took
the children to Ramsgate. (No distinction was ever made
between the two grown girls and their little sister: they were
always "*die Kinder*".) Tussy was still slightly "Chinese" and
Jenny, who had been asthmatic since childhood, now had a
persistent cough and was rapidly losing weight, a source of
uneasiness—and doctor's bills—for many months. During their
absence, his negotiations for a loan having proved fruitless,
Marx again visited his uncle in Zaltbommel and his mother in
Trier. Reunited in September, the family found that progress
had been made: everyone was in a better state of health and
Marx had set in train new and even more hopeful and elaborate
transactions to raise a loan. Nevertheless,the butcher was owed
£6, the tide of debt was rising irresistibly again and there was
no money in the house. Engels' rescue operations temporarily
stemmed the inundation, while Mrs. Bertha Markheim now
sent Mrs. Marx three separate money orders from Germany in
as many months at the end of 1862 and the beginning of 1863,
one at least of which was known to be for £6.[32]

That winter, when Tussy was nearing her eighth birthday,
her parents' misfortunes reached their high-water mark. As
though all the malign forces, from the merely mischievous to the
near-tragic, had awaited this moment to conspire, the Marxes
were buffeted by wave upon cruel wave.

For a year past the second servant, Marianne Kreuz, had
been on the list of Dr. Allen's patients. She suffered from a heart
complaint that caused him serious misgivings in mid-December
1862, at which juncture Mrs. Marx had just left for France.

Prone to minor accidents, Mrs. Marx had but to step out on a
frosty morning to fall and sprain her hand* or to bite upon
something hard to lose two of her front teeth, whereas should
she go to the dentist in frightful pain, an unoffending tooth
that had not caused a single pang was bound to be drawn; but
what befell her on this excursion defies the laws of probability.

She intended to see Monsieur Arbabanel, a banker who had

---

* In extenuation it should be noted that, where they existed, the pavements in
Kentish Town until late in the 19th century were of slate, notoriously treacherous
in wet or icy weather.

befriended her and Marx in their Paris days. Her purpose goes
without saying. On crossing to Boulogne the Channel packet
ran into a high storm and while it did not positively founder,
as did a sister-vessel, it tossed about horridly so that the
passengers were much alarmed. Monsieur Arbabanel lived
outside Paris. To reach his house Mrs. Marx took a train whose
locomotive broke down, necessitating a halt of two hours for
repairs, during which interval M. Arbabanel had a stroke, lying
paralysed and at death's door when she arrived.* On her return
to the city after this hapless errand, she boarded an omnibus
which was at once involved in a collision. Shaken but uninjured
she made her way back to London where, not feeling at her best,
she allowed herself the luxury of a fly whose wheels became
somehow interlocked with those of another. In consequence
she had to get out and walk, two small boys carrying her
trunks. She arrived at Grafton Terrace to be met by the news
of Marianne's death which had occurred during the hour when
she was plodding her homeward way. It was 23 December and
the funeral had to be postponed until Christmas was over.
Marianne was buried on 27 December.†

Still the storm did not abate. At the culminating crisis of
Marx's money troubles and in the oppressive atmosphere of a
house in mourning, with the bailiffs at the door, came the news
that on the night of 6 to 7 January Mary Burns, with whom
Engels had lived for twenty years, had died very suddenly at
the age of 40 "of natural causes", as the coroner's inquest
established.

Marx's first response to this event, a dismissive phrase of
condolence followed by a lengthy and precise account of his

---

* He did not in fact die for another month.
† Mrs. Marx in her reminiscences said that Marianne had been with the family
for five years before her death. This would have meant that she had come to them
in 1858 and certainly in the summer of that year Marx referred to his domestic
servants in the plural. Eleanor, on the other hand, in the passage she wrote for
incorporation in Liebknecht's memories of Marx, speaks of Marianne joining the
household "after your time", that is, August 1862 when Liebknecht went back
to Germany. Here Eleanor is mistaken, for Marianne appears in the 7 April 1861
census returns at 9 Grafton Terrace, aged 25. It is curious nonetheless that in his
intimate picture of the Marx household as he knew it Liebknecht never mentioned
her existence. Although she is entered in the census returns under the surname
Kreuz, as her death certificate confirms, she was in fact Lenchen's half-sister,
having been of unknown paternity to her widowed mother, whose maiden name
she used.

own troubles, came near to wrecking a friendship of the utmost importance to both men.

Owing largely to his exceptional qualities, and also a little to Marx's isolated life, Engels was at this stage of history the only person in the world who recognised Marx's towering genius and the true importance of his work. Without Engels' support, intellectual and moral no less than financial, *Capital* could not have been written. Whether Marx's letters dealt with the most far-reaching and profound questions of economic, political and philosophical theory or with his own practical and domestic difficulties, Engels responded unstintingly with advice, encouragement, the fruits of his own knowledge and with money. Now, for the first and only time, it was he who had a need— the need for sympathy—and Marx failed him.

This stark insensibility, which Engels chose to interpret as great fortitude of mind, cut him to the quick. There were delays in writing and then there were gaps in what had been a continuous, at times a daily—even twice daily—correspondence.*

Engels' reply, a modified version of his first draft, expressed his bitterness, but briefly and with all restraint, and he turned immediately to Marx's concerns, promising £25 and suggesting the name of a life insurance society for a loan. With his innate charity of mind he snatched wholeheartedly at Marx's half-hearted apology; for it was this moment that Marx chose to unfold his desperate scheme to declare himself bankrupt with all it entailed, thus compounding while professing to repent of his initial lack of grace. Upon this Engels sent £100, borrowed at some risk to himself, to stave off the extreme measures threatened. Thanking for this "great and unexpected help", Marx threw the blame for the rift on Mrs. Marx's shoulders— with musings upon the irrational nature of women—and so it was healed. For a short moment the calamity of losing this friendship loomed darker for both men than any part of their separate anguish. They averted it, but narrowly. Perhaps Engels never quite forgot the injury, for when his sister, Marie

* There were twelve postal deliveries on weekdays in Kentish Town at this time and one on Sundays. The gaps in the correspondence of this period cannot be attributed to the known destruction of letters by Engels after Marx's death and by Laura and Eleanor after Engels'. Those that have survived are not only clearly in sequence but there are references to the absence of communication.

Blank, died of scarlet fever in 1869, he wrote to her husband:
"No condolences can help in such cases . . . and I do not write
to condole but simply because I know it does one good to be
shown the sympathy of those from whom one can allow oneself
to expect it."

For the next many weeks Engels felt his loneliness unbearably.
He tried to learn Slavonic which proved small consolation and
turned to less exacting diversions. He also took to sending
Tussy stamps for her collection. She could not be dissuaded
from acknowledging these in person and there must have been
a brisk exchange of letters for, in May 1863, not having heard
from Marx for some time, Engels wrote to ask whether he
was ill, deep in economics or had he perhaps appointed Tussy
as his secretary to deal with his correspondence. Though Marx
had done nothing quite so reckless, he had now enlisted Laura
as an assistant and she accompanied him to the British Museum,
for which she held a Reader's ticket.³³ *

Marx was in fact still anxious about Jenny's continued loss of
weight and exasperated by Mrs. Marx's latest symptom, which
took the form of partial deafness, so it was with relief that, on the
strength of a further remittance from Mrs. Markheim, he
packed off the family to Hastings attended by Mr. Henry
Banner, the girls' music teacher, from 14 August to 1 September.
That autumn of 1863, by which time his long established habit
of working far into and sometimes throughout the night had
taken its toll, Marx underwent the first operation for the abscesses and carbuncles that were to plague him from now on.†
This condition was not at the time always dealt with by surgery
and the recommended treatment was more usually large doses
of opium. Marx, however, was prescribed four times his usual
intake of food, four glasses of port and half a bottle of claret
daily. This regimen failed to cure him and he could not sleep,
so one-and-a-half quarts of the strongest London stout were

---

* The lower age limit for the Reading Room was raised from 18 (in 1842) to 21
in 1863. Laura's ticket, issued on 18 May 1863, was granted on the recommendation
of Mr. A. Deutsch who was employed at the Museum. Regrettably, for she was
not 18 until the following September, Laura signed a declaration that she was over
21.
† Marx's liver complaint and his carbuncles could well have been connected, both
conditions arising from a generalised staphylococcal infection, which could not
have been diagnosed as such until the late 1880s. Both ailments were liable to be
aggravated by alcohol.³⁴

added to his diet. Still he did not recover; and he was in considerable pain when, at 4 p.m. on 30 November—the hour and the date of her marriage fifty years before—his mother died. A week later, borrowing the fare from Engels, he set out for Trier, then travelled to Frankfurt to see his aunts, Esther Kosel and Babette Blum, and finally to Zaltbommel to settle the formalities of his mother's Will with Lion Philips, her executor. The strain told on him: fresh boils and carbuncles broke out and he was obliged to stay in Holland for nearly two months, by which time he received his inheritance of some £750.[35] Part if not all of the money he received in 1,000 Dutch gulden notes which he changed on his return journey *via* Rotterdam in February 1864.[36]

It looked as though the direful years were over. Eleanor was nine and can safely be left to speak for herself.

JENNY (STANDING) AND LAURA

MARX, ENGELS AND THE THREE SISTERS, 1864

§4

Not that she had been exactly silent, for Eleanor was a great talker, a passionate partisan of the North in the American Civil War, with a sneer at *The Times* leader which expressed admiration for Lee's strategy—"It considers this very canny, I daresay"—and, in general, pronouncing her views upon international affairs in and out of season. That she was well informed on worldly matters and never excluded from their discussion in the family is illustrated by her comment upon Ferdinand Lassalle who, at the end of August 1864, was killed when he was 39 in a senseless duel fought over Helene von Dönneges, whom he had wished to marry. According to Laura, Lassalle had always made clear to each lady in her turn that he was constitutionally unable to love her for more than six weeks. Tussy, on the *nil nisi bonum* principle, remarked kindly that at least he could be relied upon—she used the grand word "warranted" —for that length of time.

She also emerges in another sense, for now one can see what she looked like. Perhaps the best-known photograph of her— it has so often been reproduced—is also the earliest to have survived. There she is, the centre of a group composed of her father, Engels and her two large sisters who, with their hats like ornamented pancakes and voluminous skirts sweeping the ground, look about 45 though they were not yet 20. Smug and neat in her little sporting topper, Eleanor, apparently perched on her sisters' crinolines, her thin legs and elastic-sided boots dangling, looks away from the camera with dark, amused eyes. She is not so much a pretty as an attractive child, anxious to please, one feels, and confident of succeeding; a little girl who would have had some difficulty in keeping still and even more in keeping quiet for the photograph to be taken. But the wide, firm, good-humoured mouth and resolute chin are unmistakably those of Abraham Lincoln's adviser.

During these years, as may be imagined, her schooling

had been irregular and her treats rare. These, when they occurred, were sedate and free of charge. At five or six she was taken to a Roman Catholic Church—arousing qualms in so confirmed an atheist—to listen to the music; at eight she went twice to hear a secular preacher make Voltairean quips at the Bible. She never resented this lack of lighter entertainment, though in after years she did complain that little had been spent on her education. At the time it troubled her not at all. She was far too busy with her letter-writing, her chess, her stamp collection, her political interests and the dressing of dolls. Thanks to Engels she was also a wine connoisseur from the tenderest age.

She kept up a correspondence on and off all her life with Wilhelm Liebknecht, about whom a word must be said, if for no other reason than that Eleanor sent almost her last, as she wrote her very first letter to him. This is not the place to record his career as a revolutionary socialist, a member of the Reichstag and a most frequent inmate of German gaols. Born in Giessen, Hesse, on the east bank of the Lahn near Marburg in 1826, he took part in the Paris street fighting of 1848 and the Baden insurrection of 1848–49 after which he was "forcibly transported through France from gaol" to Switzerland. In 1850 or 51—the date is somewhat uncertain—he came to London where he stayed for a time in a Model Lodging-House in Old Compton Street and then, for some years, at 14 Church Street,* Soho. He was a daily visitor to the Marxes in Dean Street. Shortly after they moved to Kentish Town he followed them, living at 3 Roxburgh Terrace until he went back to Germany in August 1862. He maintained a continuous correspondence with both Marx and Engels and many of their letters to him—as to each other about him—are peppered with irate not to say furious criticism: he was slapdash, a donkey, a dunderhead, almost invariably did the wrong thing at the wrong time, a wretched, even catastrophic, tactician, he muffed his chances and his inefficiency was unspeakable. He so exasperated them that the letters would scarcely lead one to believe that they held him in deep affection. Yet such was the case and during his many terms of imprisonment Engels never

---

* Renamed Romilly Street in 1937. The French socialist émigrés of 1848 founded their London club in this street in 1850.

failed to send words of comfort and material help to his wife. It is the only case in his published letters in which Engels did not mince his words—Marx was never a mincer—and is to be explained by the fact that he expected more and better things of one he loved and in whom he unreservedly placed trust.*

Liebknecht's importance to the biographer of Eleanor—as also to other biographers—lies not only in the correspondence but also in the publication of his reminiscences of Marx[37] incorporating a long passage he had asked Eleanor to write.† Liebknecht came to England in the early summer of 1896 to stop with Eleanor and together they made a pilgrimage to the old haunts he had known: to Dean Street and to Grafton Terrace, noting the familiar landmarks that remained and the bewildering changes that had taken place.

Her earliest letter to him—written at the age of six when he was 35 years old—is a note of small consequence, as one would expect between close neighbours. It is in a less rounded hand, more in the German style, than her efforts of a year or two later —as though it had been taken down by someone else at her dictation and painstakingly copied—addressed to "Dear Library", as the family called him,‡ and signed, mysteriously, "*Niemand*".§[38] Later, when the Liebknechts had left London, she also kept up a correspondence with Alice Liebknecht, two years her junior, to whom she was always inclined to show off, boasting first of her stamp collection and then of her "measels", while affectionately regretting that her little friend, now in Berlin, was no longer there to play with the cats and go for long walks on Hampstead Heath.

While her father was staying with the Philips family in the

---

* Engels later described him as "an optimist by nature who sees everything through rose-coloured glasses. This keeps him cheerful and is one of the main reasons for his popularity, but it also has its drawbacks". (May 1883.)
† While of the greatest interest, his sympathetic account is not a completely trustworthy guide. Wrong dates are given for the births and deaths of the Marx children, some of the misinformation being supplied by Eleanor who seems to have been rather hazy on these points, while a letter she wrote to Liebknecht correcting her first version of Helene Demuth's early life was never used in this little volume of 1896 which, perpetuating the errors of fact, has remained a source-book for students ever since.
‡ Although Liebknecht himself never understood how he derived this nickname, it seems fairly obvious that in England the natives found his name altogether too difficult and pronounced it in a garbled manner that suggested to the Marx children the first syllable of the familiar word "library".
§ "Nobody".

winter of 1863 Eleanor started a genial correspondence with her
great-uncle Lion.

"My dear Uncle", she wrote, "Although I have never seen
you I have heard so much about you that I almost fancy I
know you, and as there is no chance of my seeing you I just
write these lines to ask you how you are. Are you enjoying
yourself? I am, and always do at Christmas time which I think
is the jolliest in the year. I wish you a very happy new year,
and dare say you are as glad to get rid of the old one as I am.
I hear from papa that you are a great politician so we are
sure to agree. How do you think the Poles are getting on? I
always hold up a finger for the Poles those brave little fellows.*
Do you like A.B.?† He is a good friend of mine.

But I must say goodbye now, but dare say you will hear from
me again.

Give my love to cousin Nettchen‡ and to Dada.

Goodbye, dear Uncle.

I am

your affectionate

Eleanor Marx."[40]

It speaks volumes that Christmas, a season which had heralded with awful regularity the climax of her parents' tribulations, was for Tussy the "jolliest in the year". Here is Mrs. Marx
on the same subject: "Our last two Christmases"—she is
speaking of 1862 and 1863—"were inexpressibly sad. Two
years ago we were all lamenting our poor little Marianne who
had just relinquished her sweet young life. . . . Last year my

---

* From early in 1863 there had been a general insurrection in Poland, put down by
the Russians with great violence, including the execution of prisoners. At the time
of Eleanor's letter the final defeat of the uprising was not yet assured. On 12 November 1863, at the Bell Inn, Old Bailey, George Odger, secretary of the London
Trades Council, read out the text of an appeal to the governments of England and
France calling for a united effort in support of Poland's freedom, "to prevent
. . . the devil's tragedy" being "played over again . . . making that fair land once
more a huge slaughterhouse to the everlasting shame and disgrace of the civilised
world". The Inaugural Address of the IWMA, written by Marx in October 1864,
included the words: "The shameless approval, mock sympathy, or idiotic indifference, with which the upper classes of Europe have witnessed heroic Poland being
assassinated by Russia . . ." Marx's own writings of this period on the subject
were found amongst his unfinished MSS. after his death and not published until
nearly a century later.[39]

† (Louis) Auguste Blanqui.   ‡ Annette Philips.

My dear uncle

Although I
have never seen you I
have heard so much about
you that I almost fancy
I know you; and as there
is no chance of my seeing
you, I just write these

may; but then say you will
hear from me again.
Give my love to my cousin
Clothilde and to Dada.
Goodbye, dear uncle
I am
Your affectionate
Eleanor Marx.

LETTER TO A GREAT-UNCLE, 1863. *pp. 1 and 4*

... lines to ask you how you
are. Are you enjoying
yourself? I am, and always
do at Christmas time what
I think is the jolliest in
the year. I wish you every,
happy new year, and dear
say you are as glad to
get rid of the old one as
I am. I hear from Papa

that you are a great Politician so we are sure to
agree. How do you think
Poland is getting on? I
always hold up a finger for-
the Poles those brave little
fellows. Do you like
A. B..? He is a great
friend of mine.
But I must say goodbye

LETTER TO A GREAT-UNCLE, 1863. *pp. 2 and 3*

husband was recuperating from a dangerous and painful illness. . . ."[41]

To Eleanor's great satisfaction Philips sent her a doll, for which she thanked him in a letter with an enclosure purporting to be written in Chinese characters. Her Chinese leanings* were, indeed, so marked at this period that her father called her the "Chinese Successor"; but that may have been because occasionally Jenny was known as the Emperor, and sometimes the Empress, of China and had evidently abdicated.

A bitterly cold wet March confined Tussy to bed with a cough, interrupting the correspondence with her great-uncle to whom she continued to send greetings and communicate her opinions on the political scene. "In regards to the Danish question", her father wrote to Philips on 29 March, "she begs me to tell you that 'she don't care for such stuff' and that 'she considers one of the parties to the quarrel as bad as the other and perhaps worse'."†

To cement the bonds with her relations in Holland she learnt to read Dutch and to get by heart some Dutch children's songs. The next letter to her great-uncle, written in June that year, provides a thumbnail self-portrait of Tussy at nine.

"My dear Uncle,
It was very kind of you to send me your Carte de Visite. I am getting on very well with my chess. I nearly always win and when I do Papa is *so* cross.
What do you think of affairs in America? I think the Federals are safe, and though the Confederates drive them back every now and then, I am sure they will win in the end. Were you not delighted about the Alabama?‡ Of course you know all about

---

* In case these should be thought a trifle bizarre, it may be recalled that between 1853 and 1860 Marx wrote a series of articles on China for the *New York Daily Tribune*.[42] China and the "Opium Wars" of 1856 and 1859, the capture of Pekin and destruction of the Summer Palace in 1860, and Gordon's campaigns in 1863 and 1864 must have been matters of common table-talk in Grafton Terrace.

† This refers to the dispute between the Danes and the Prussians over Schleswig and Holstein. Lord Palmerston cannot have known about Tussy when he said that only three people had ever understood the Schleswig-Holstein question: the Prince Consort, who was dead, a German professor who was mad, and Palmerston himself, who had forgotten all about it.

‡ *Alabama*, a steam vessel built by Laird's at Birkenhead for the Confederate service, was launched on 15 May 1862 under the name *Eurica* and ostensibly on trials. Once in the open sea, she made for Holyhead, dropped the name—and the passengers who had acted as neutral cover for her warlike purpose—and picked up her armament at the Azores. After doing considerable damage to Federal

it; at all events a Politician like you ought to. As for poor Poland I am afraid there is no help for it. But I have had enough of Politics.

I hope to see you soon in Holland and till then goodbye. Don't forget to give my love to Nettchen.

I am, dear Uncle,

Your affectionate friend,

Eleanor Marx.

They tell me this is the longest day but to me it seems as short as any other—perhaps shorter. Can you make that out?"[43]

Meanwhile, of course, she kept up with Engels who was the main source of supply both for her stamp collection and her dolls' wardrobe. He sent her pieces of cotton whose quality, she asked Marx to convey to him that summer, had "somewhat improved". She also wrote frequently to "lupus", Wilhelm Wolff, who enjoyed her letters during his last illness in the spring of 1864. He was thought—though there was some disagreement among the doctors—to have meningitis but, whatever the cause, he died on 9 May at the age of 55. Marx was the main beneficiary under his Will.*

Legacies, like misfortunes, seem never to have come singly to the Marxes. Now the double inheritances from Wolff and Marx's mother—assessed in all at some £1,500—as those from Mrs. Marx's relatives eight years before, floated them to a new house. Without an instant's delay, Marx having got back from Holland only on 19 February, they moved before the end of

mercantile shipping as a privateer, she was destroyed on 19 June 1864 off Cherbourg by the Federal ironclad *Kearsage*. The government litigation and claim for damages dragged on for years. When, in 1872 an international court settled that the British government should pay over £3 million in compensation, it was a moment of such prosperity and large revenues that the nation was said to "have drunk itself out of the *Alabama* difficulty". Extra concessions, wrung from the British in the course of the lengthy negotiations, were attributed by Marx to the anti-British pressure of the Irish in America.

* Born on 21 June 1809 in Tarnau, the son of a Silesian farmer, Johann Frederick Wilhelm Wolff was imprisoned in Prussia for four years in the 1830s for his part in the revolutionary students' movement. He emigrated to Brussels where he first met and worked with Marx in 1845, from which time they remained on the closest terms. After a stay in Switzerland, Wolff came to England in 1851, lived for a short time in London and then moved to Blackburn where in 1856 he earned £60 a year as a teacher of languages. He died at 29 Carter Street, Chorlton upon Medlock. His Will provided that if Marx predeceased him, the inheritance should be divided among the Marx girls at the age of 21 or on marriage. Marx dedicated Volume I of *Capital* to Wilhelm Wolff: "My unforgettable friend; intrepid, faithful, noble protagonist of the proletariat."

March 1864 into No. 1 Modena Villas* where they were to stay for the next eleven years.

This house, one of two dwellings of the better sort built near to Haverstock Congregational Chapel, was in Maitland Park, "a pleasing and elevated locality on which new buildings of a neat and commodious character have within a few years been erected", according to the first (1862) St. Pancras Directory.†
It was barely a stone's throw from Grafton Terrace but in every way more elevated and commodious than anything the family had known, Marx working in a large airy study on the first floor overlooking the park, not yet then entirely built over, while each girl had a room of her own.

Marx took a three-year lease from the landlord, Mr. Sawyer,‡ at £65 a year, with rates of £4 8s. 0d., an increase of over 80 per cent on the expenses at Grafton Terrace.§ Naturally before they left the old home the debts and duns had to be paid off. Mrs. Marx then spent £500 on the move and, subscribing to the view that "it is a sad thing to pass through the quagmire of parsimony to the gulf of ruin", let herself go with rollicking improvidence. Early in July Marx recorded that she was attending auction sales. Later that month she wrote to the first

* Also spelt 'Medina' on contemporary maps and in Directories, justifying Engels' pretty pun that Marx's home was "the Medina of the emigration". It is now demolished, so that the size and character of the house can be deduced only from descriptions and the Ratebooks. But when Engels planned to live in London he stipulated his need for two living rooms, a study and four or five bedrooms, adding: "it does not have to be as big as your house and smaller rooms would do for me".
† In 1842 Ebenezer Maitland bought 13 acres of a property known as "Morgan's land", adjoining the former Southampton Estates, where he financed the building of new premises for an Orphan Working School of which he was the president. This non-sectarian institution, for children of both sexes between the ages of seven and eleven, had been founded in Hoxton in 1758, moved to the City Road in 1773 and to Maitland Park in 1847. It was incorporated by Act of Parliament in 1848. In 1860 the orphanage was enlarged to house some 400 children, at which time the whole of Maitland Park was developed as a residential area. Damaged by bombing in the Second World War, the old houses were pulled down to make way for the site of the present Maitland Park Estate of Council flats the first block of which was opened in 1948.
‡ This was Samuel Sawyer, a builder, who had occupied the next-door house in Grafton Terrace. He appears in the 1861 census as "Sanger", but that need not worry anyone, for his neighbour is entered as "Karl Mara" under which surname even Helene (Demuth) appears. The 1862 Directory, more reliable in its spelling, gives the occupant of No. 10 as Sawyer.
§ The rateable value of No. 1 Modena Villas when Marx first occupied it was £64 and the gross estimated rent £75, so this time, unlike the last, Marx was getting a bargain. There was also a "House Duty", imposed instead of window tax in 1851, for all dwellings rented at over £20 a year for domestic as distinct from farm or trade purposes.

Mrs. Liebknecht (Ernestine), referred to the inheritance from her mother-in-law and went on to say that, after redeeming their belongings from pawn: "the first thing we did with the rest of the money . . . was to move to our present new house. You have no idea how hateful to me the old house had become since the death of our little Marianne and how happy we all feel in the cheerful new rooms. . . . If only I could show you into our drawing-room or, better still, into the charming conservatory, decked out with flowers and climbing plants which flourish under Jennychen's excellent care. But before I take you into the holy of holies, let me acquaint you with the setting of the palace. Do you remember the small chapel at the entrance to the Park? Close by two pretty, elegant houses have been built. The first of these—not next to the church but the first as you enter the Park—is our present domicile. Elegant wide steps lead through a small flower garden into the house whose spacious pleasing entrance-hall strikes everyone. We bought the so-called fixtures from the previous tenant* and instead of being obliged to furnish as before in the most sparing fashion, this time we set aside something more for the furniture and decorations, so that we can receive anyone without embarrassment. I thought it better to put the money to this use rather than to fritter it away piecemeal on trifles. Both girls have arranged their charming bedrooms for themselves and Jennychen's is a sort of Shakespeare museum. . . . But the best thing about the house is its open healthy situation, standing, so to speak, entirely on its own, without neighbours or anyone opposite and at the same time with a large well laid-out garden. . . . Tussy has shot up and engages in a host of unprofitable pursuits. She is a first-rate chess-player and Mr. Wilhelm Pieper came off so badly against his young opponent that he lost his temper.

"I cannot tell you how deeply pained we were by the death of our dear good lupus . . .".[44]

Flown with pleasure in her new house, Mrs. Marx quite forgot to mention the legacy from dear good lupus. Probate had now been granted and Marx had received some £230 in

---

* A Mr. Henry John Watkins in whose day, curiously enough, and up to the year before the Marxes occupied the house, the rateable value and gross estimated rent were considerably higher.

early June, using part of it to speculate in American funds, on which he made a killing of £400: "squeezing a bit out of the enemy", as he called it. A further £350 from the Wolff estate came in early July, a week or so before Mrs. Marx penned her euphoric letter.

The year 1864 certainly went with a swing. After the excitements of the move the glorious spending spree was kept up. In the summer Jenny accompanied her father to Ramsgate for three weeks' convalescence. There they were joined by Laura and Tussy and, for a few days a little later, by Lenchen. Upon their return Mrs. Marx took a fortnight's holiday by herself as a "parlour boarder" with a family in Brighton. There was also a plan for Marx to take the girls to Zaltbommel in September, frustrated at the last moment by an outbreak of smallpox in the Philips household, though not before "the children" had been finely rigged out for the visit.

Tussy now went punctually to school. Another innovation was that the family dined at 5 p.m.—it is uncertain when and if they had dined in former days—while the girls embarked on a course of calisthenics to strengthen their physique.

It was indeed a year of beginnings, great and small, for on 28 September the First International was inaugurated at a meeting in St. Martin's Hall, Long Acre,* and now Tussy gave her first real party, though admittedly a makeshift.

"It has become possible to provide the girls with a pleasant and respectable setting, so appointed that now and again they can receive their English friends without fear or shame", wrote Mrs. Marx to Ernestine Liebknecht. "We had placed them in a false position and the young are still thin-skinned and sensitive."[45] They had been asked out so often and unable to return hospitality that they had reached the point of declining all invitations. Now they themselves could entertain. Accordingly on 12 October they gave a ball for 50 young people who kept

---

* Where on 27 February 1855 the inaugural meeting of an International Committee had been held (see p. 26). The Hall was built by subscription in 1847 and presented to John Pyke Hullah, a Worcester-born composer who enjoyed great renown in his day. It was inaugurated in 1850 as a concert hall and burnt down ten years later. It was in the rebuilt hall, dating from 1861, that the foundation meeting of the IWMA took place. This was demolished in 1867. In the years 1865–1866 the headquarters of the General Council was at 18 Greek Street. (In 1961, at the same address, a night club known as The Establishment was opened and flourished briefly as a satirical cabaret.) From January 1866 to June 1867 the General Council met at 18 Bouverie Street.

up the revelry until four in the morning. It was a lavish affair
with so many good things left over that on the next day an
impromptu children's party was arranged for Tussy.

This whirl of pleasure, with no thought of the morrow, continued into the next year. The Marxes began to behave like
people who enjoy a tolerably good and perfectly assured
income. In February 1865 Tussy wrote to "My dear Frederick,"
(Engels) to say that she and her sisters were organising a little
party "in honour of Mama's birthday"* and "should be very
much indeed obliged if you would send us a few bottles of
hock and claret". As they were giving the party without the
help of their elders they wanted it "to go off very grandly".
This gift was to be in the nature of a Valentine, but "to be
sent as early as you can, please".[46] Engels was prompt and
efficient as always and received a warm acknowledgment
from his "affectionate friend Eleanor Marx".[47]

House guests were entertained too. In March Marx's brother-
in-law Jan Juta, a Dutch merchant, bookseller and publisher
who had settled in the Cape, came to stay for a week bringing
with him Caroline Schmalhausen, the daughter of Marx's
elder sister, Sophie, from Maastricht.

At this point Eleanor, now ten, wrote her "Confession", a
popular pastime of the day.[48]

Your favourite virtue	Truth
„ „ „ in man	Courage
„ „ „ in woman	(left blank)
„ chief characteristic	Curiosity
„ idea of happiness	Champagne
„ „ „ misery	Toothache
The vice you excuse most	Playing the Truant
„ „ „ detest „	Eves Examiner†
Your aversion	Cold mutton
Your favourite occupation	Gymnastics
„ „ poet	Shakespeare
„ „ prose writer	Captain Marryat
„ „ hero	Garibaldi

* On 12 February.
† The detestable vice referred to was *The School Examiner* by Charles Eves, a volume
published in 1852 containing some 4,000 exercises on Sacred History, Geography,
English Grammar, Arithmetic and the like.

Your favourite	heroine	Lady Jane Grey
,,	,, flower	All flowers
,,	,, colour	White
,,	,, names	Percy, Henry, Charles, Edward
,,	,, maxim and motto	"Go a head"

Eleanor's favourite hero, Garibaldi, had visited London the year before, when the largest procession of workers that London had ever seen, trade union banners flying, took six hours to escort him from Nine Elms Station to Stafford House* in Stable Yard, St. James's Palace.

This little document was filled in on 20 March 1865, the day after Marx had left for Holland, where he stayed for three weeks with the Philipses.

Although it was only now that the Wolff estate was finally wound up† the money had vanished into thin air. It was not a year since he had received his handsome legacies, yet Marx could not find the fare to escort his niece Caroline back to Maastricht. During his absence Mrs. Marx had to appeal to Engels for £3 in order to be able to carry on. The tide of debts flowed back. Back came the familiar round of borrowing, pawning and raising loans. The old pattern of life was re-established.

Engrossed in *Capital*, which had been going well, and his work for the International Working Men's Association‡ Marx

* This sumptuous mansion was originally built on borrowed money at the instigation of the Duchess of Rutland by Benjamin Dean Wyatt in 1825–26 for George IV's brother, the Duke of York, thus finally ruining his unsound finances. He died before it was completed and it was taken over by the then Marquess of Stafford who became the first Duke of Sutherland. The Crown lease was sold to the second duke in 1841 when the building was completed by Charles Barry and Robert Smirke. It was here that the third duke accorded Garibaldi the scant hospitality of one room. Herzen commented: "One could easily without inconveniencing the owners have lodged in [Stafford House] all the peasant families turned homeless into the world by the duke's father."[15] Renamed Lancaster House in 1912, when it was bought by Sir William Lever, a Lancashire man better known as Lord Leverhulme, who presented it to the nation, it housed the London Museum from 1914 until after the Second World War. A relief bust of Garibaldi remained to commemorate the brief visit of 1864.

† Probate was granted on an estate of £1,348 17s. od. on 1 June 1864 but the final winding up of the accounts did not reach Marx until 11 March 1865. Bequests, lawyer's fees, funeral expenses, death duties and a small outstanding debt left a residue of £842 14s. 9d. and some £50 worth of books and other personal effects for Marx.

‡ Including his answer to propositions on wages put to the General Council on 2 April by John Weston, an old Owenite, and defended by him in *The Bee-Hive*.[49] The answer, given as an Address to the General Council on 20 and 27 June, was

was not earning a penny. Now the well-appointed house—on the furnishing of which he had tried to keep an account, for he was truly amazed that the money had melted away—and the way of life it had inaugurated became a gross and unbearable burden. But how to retrench?

The facts had to be faced: it was not as if he and his wife were on their own; they had three girls of whom two had reached marriageable age—it would have been a different matter had they been boys—and there were still three more chapters of the theoretical section of *Capital* to be written. A new standard of living had been set, the girls were no longer placed in a "false position" but in one of apparent ease and refinement, occupying an altogether more desirable station in life and one likely to improve their prospects. Already there was a young French medical student, Paul Lafargue, who had first met Marx in February 1865, made a good impression and, on his return to London in the autumn, was brought to the house where it became clear that his admiration was not confined to the father. On the occasion of Jenny's 21st birthday on 1 May 1865, celebrated in a subdued manner, most of the principal guests being leading members of the IWMA* and of her father's generation, Laura received a proposal of marriage from a younger man, Charles Manning, for whom she "didn't care a pin". But it was evident that suitors would appear, whether acceptable or not and, in the interests of the Misses Marx, it was imperative to maintain at least an air of solvency.

It is worth enquiring at this point how much it really cost the Marxes to live. The Board of Trade did not officially record retail prices of consumer goods until 1893; but, taking the first (1904) Cost of Living Index "weights", which assigned between one-sixth and one-seventh of total minimum family income to rent (including rates and water charges), it appears that life in Modena Villas could not have been sustained on less than £430 a year.[51] In 1868 Marx himself wrote to Dr. Ludwig Kugelmann, a gynaecologist in Hanover, that it cost him between £400 and £500. This of course would not include balls and

found among Marx's papers after his death and, edited by Eleanor, was published in 1898 after her own death under the title *Value, Price and Profit*.[50]
* Ernest Jones, George Odger, William Cremer, Hermann Jung and Peter Fox.

parties or, indeed, any form of entertaining and now, towards the end of May, Edgar von Westphalen came to stay for six months.

This broken man, aged 46, was Mrs. Marx's only brother, after whom she had named her first-born son. She had not seen him for 16 years. In early life he had briefly played a small part in politics and then, when he was 26, he had emigrated to America, where he hoped to make his fortune in Texas, leaving behind a fiancée, Lina Schoeler, whom, in the event, he never married and who came to England in the year of Eleanor's birth to seek employment as a teacher, a position she took up in the autumn of 1856. Defeated and ill, Edgar returned to Europe in 1849, only to go back to Texas two years later. Still he did not prosper and, from 1862 onwards, he fought for the South in the Civil War, losing all he had, including his health. As Marx put it: "It is a most remarkable irony of fate that this Edgar, who never exploited anyone except himself and was a workman in the strictest sense of the word, should have fought for the slaveholders in a war of and with starvation."

Mrs. Marx loved him dearly and although his arrival was neither anticipated nor timely, for Marx was suffering from abscesses, toothache and debts, she gave a warm welcome to her "poor, sick, helpless brother".

Marx, while not antagonistic to Edgar, whom he pronounced a "rum customer", "as egotistic as a cat or a benevolent dog", had scant sympathy with this idle, vain, greedy, sexless, self-centred valetudinarian described on a rising note of exasperation in letters to Engels. Edgar's major crime, as the months passed, was that he showed no signs of leaving. Admittedly Marx was not the ideal host. He had been driven almost insane by Lassalle who, on his visit to London three years before, had assumed that, since Marx had no job and was engaged on purely theoretical work, he had nothing better to do than to devote his time to the coxcomb.*

Edgar had lived so long as a recluse that he was hardly fit for human intercourse, in Marx's view. His cold in the nose, his

---

* In his rage Marx repeatedly referred to Lassalle as the "Jewish nigger", the "parvenu", the "tuft-hunter" and so forth; but at his death Marx paid him a sober tribute: "after all, he was one of the old guard, and his enemies were our enemies", regretting that their relations had been clouded in the last years.

vegetable existence and pitiable preoccupation with clothes and food—"even his interest in sex has been transferred to his belly"—not to mention the expenses of his keep, became a sore trial.

There was a serious outbreak of cattle-plague that summer.* "Food prices went up so much", Mrs. Marx wrote to Ernestine Liebknecht,[52] "that an extra person with a particularly healthy appetite was noticeable in the exorbitantly higher bills from the . . . greengrocer, etc. Meat rose to 1/4 or 1/6 and milk is still today 5d. a quart with proportionate increases for everything else."

The girls took a gentler view of their uncle, Laura with mild irony calling him "an exceedingly bright fellah", while Jenny allowed that he and his deserted fiancée might congratulate themselves on having "safely got rid of each other". Tussy frankly liked him "because he's *so funny*".

There was no question of a seaside holiday and a letter from Marx to Eleanor in that summer was written on the inter. com. system. His address is given in an execrable pun as "Maidena Towers"—over which she probably split her sides—and the date is 3 July 1865:

"Dear Miss Lilliput,

You must excuse the 'belated' character of my answer. I belong to that sort of people who always look twice at things before they decide one way or the other. Thus I was rather startled at receiving an invitation on the part of a female minx quite unknown to me. However, having ascertained your respectability, and the high tone of your transactions with your tradespeople, I shall feel happy to seize this rather strange opportunity of getting at your eatables and drinkables. But, pray, don't neglect the latter, as spinsters usually have the bad taste of doing. Suffering somewhat under an attack of rheumatism, I hope you keep your reception room clear of

---

* The rinderpest, or steppe murrain, originating among the cattle herds of the Russian steppes, spread to Europe and was brought to London in 1865. Several weeks elapsed before the disease was recognised by which time it had been carried to all parts of the country by animals bought at Smithfield. It was calculated to have caused a loss of between £5 million and £8 million. On 21 February 1866 an Act of Parliament authorised the slaughter of the infected animals and provided for compensation. The next serious outbreak occurred in 1872. Unlike foot-and-mouth disease, it was eradicated in Britain in 1877.

anything like drafts. As to the ventilation required, I shall provide for it myself. Being somewhat deaf on the right ear, please put a dull fellow, of whom, I dare say, your company will not be in want of, at my right side. For the left I hope you will reserve your female beauty. I mean the best looking female amongst your guests.

I am somewhat given to tobacco chewing; so have the stuff ready. Having from former intercourse with Yankees taken to the habitude of spitting, I hope spittoons will not be missing. Being rather easy in my manners, and disgusted at this hot and close English atmosphere, you must prepare for seeing me in a dress rather Adamitic. I hope your female guests are somewhat in the same line.

Adio, my dear unknown little minx.

Yours for ever

Dr. Cranky.

No *British* wines, I hope!"[53]

It is evident that the Yankee did not curtail the family's social life nor yet Marx's political activities; for it was during his stay that *The Workman's Advocate*, the official journal of the IWMA,* was launched with an authorised capital of £1,000. Marx took five £1 shares: the only subscriber to do so. The others were Friedrich Lessner, tailor; William Cremer, joiner; Edwin Coulson, bricklayer; Robert Applegarth, joiner; George Eccarius, tailor; William Morgan, shoemaker; Hermann Jung, watchmaker; Thomas Grant Facey, painter; William Stainsby, tailor; and John Weston, handrail manufacturer, accounting in all for £23.[54]

When "with a heavy heart" poor Edgar† at last took his leave in November, matters hardly improved at all. Mrs. Marx felt desolate and her husband dared not tell her that the landlord was threatening to withdraw the lease on the house, so badly was the rent in arrears. However, she could not be

* This weekly journal under the editorship of Eccarius lasted barely six months in its original form. In February 1866 it was reorganised to appear as *The Commonwealth*.

† He was not altogether hypochondriac. On his return to Germany he was medically examined and found to have heart disease. Mrs. Marx believed this to be merely a convenient diagnosis for any condition the doctors did not understand and personally thought that his lungs and brain were affected. However, he lived to the age of 72.

spared from knowing that Laura was unwell and losing weight, that Tussy had a severe bout of measles, that Jenny had diphtheria and that there was no coal. Engels sent £15, port, sherry and claret. There seemed to be a ray of light when one of Marx's Frankfurt aunts, Esther Kosel, died intestate. (She had refused to draw up a will for fear that it might cause her death.) Her estate in the event was divided between 20 of the next-of-kin with equal claims upon it and Marx's share turned out to be £13. He decided that, once his book was finished, he would go abroad, possibly to Switzerland, to live more cheaply. He was ill with worry and by no means cheered when Lina Schoeler, who had tactfully kept clear of the house during Edgar's visit, but was owed money she had lent to her hosts during a previous stay, came for the month of December.

The New Year was ushered in for Marx, as usual, with blazing carbuncles and mounting debts. There were also serious difficulties with the French branch of the IWMA, founded in London during the previous autumn. The disagreements were over the Polish question and both Charles Longuet, the editor of the anti-Bonapartist paper *La Rive Gauche*, and Paul Lafargue, one of its contributors, were involved.

For Tussy, also as usual, the season brought good cheer. Using Laura's writing paper and desk, she left a letter there addressed on the outside in elaborate script "To Miss L. Marx from E. Marx", with many smudges and illegibilities within, to thank for "a darling dolly", "a regular angel", whose christening was her most pressing problem. She already had a Laura, a Beatrice, a Rose Blanch (*sic*), a Jenny, an Athalie, an Edith and an Alice. The stock of female names appeared to have run out, until she recalled her Dutch cousin Annette.[55] The cares of so large a family on her eleventh birthday did not prevent her from assisting at the first of the "Sunday Evenings for the People", held at St. Martin's Hall on 28 January in defiance of the Lord's Day Observance Acts, to hear music by Handel, Mozart, Beethoven, Mendelssohn and Gounod. The event proved so popular that over 2,000 people had to be turned away from the hall. As Mrs. Marx wrote: "Until then they had not been allowed to do anything but bawl 'Jesus, Jesus, meek and mild' "—Mrs. Marx was a little weak on her Charles Wesley—"or frequent gin palaces."

the several persons whose Names and Addresses are subscribed, are desirous of being formed into a Company, in pursuance of this Memorandum of Association, and we respectively agree to take the number of Shares in the Capital of the Company set opposite our respective names.

Names, Addresses, and Descriptions of Subscribers.	No. of Shares taken by each Subscriber.
Friedrich Lessner 4 Francis St, Tottenham Ct Road Middlesex. Tailor.	Two
William Randall, Engraver 31 Gt Titchfield St Fitzroy Square Middlesex. Joiner	One
Edwin Coulson 25 Hatfield Street, Newington City of N Surrey, J. = Bricklayer	Two
Robert Applegarth Joiner 11 Clergyer St Kennington Cross London Surrey	Two.
J. George Eccarius 1 Portland Place Westmorland Road Walworth Surrey. Tailor	One.
William John Morgan 27 upper Ogle St Marylebone W Middlesex poly St W shoemaker	Two
Karl Marx, 1 Modena Villas Maitland Park, Haverstock Hill, Middlesex Dr. Phil.	Five.
Hermann F. Jung 4 Charles Street Northampton Square City of London E.C. watchmaker	Four
W Pfant Facey 2 Carteret St Westminster SW London Middlesex	One
William Steinsby 13 Little Titchfield St Marylebone Middlesex Tailor W	Two
John Weston 60 White Cross St City Handrailman Middlesex London	One

SIGNATURES OF SHAREHOLDERS IN *The Workman's Advocate*, SEPTEMBER 1865

MARX IN THE YEAR OF THE PUBLICATION OF VOLUME I OF *Capital*

Marx's health reached a critical pass that winter and spring of 1866. He suffered abominably and wrote that "it would be all the same to me if I went to the knacker's yard, that is to say, kicked the bucket today or tomorrow", if only there were enough money for the family—"something above minus zero" —and his work were finished. In fact it was, but the "damned book" had been completed in December 1865 only by dint of reading all day at the British Museum and writing all night. However, it was not quite true that he would as soon have died, for he was distinctly enjoying himself. He had begun copying out his manuscript and revising the style. "Naturally", he wrote, "it gives me pleasure to lick the child clean after so many birth pangs."

He had now embarked on a course of arsenic, taking one grain daily as prescribed at long range and second hand *via* Engels by Dr. Gumpert.* Marx did not relish this treatment but Engels assured him that in any case it could do no harm even if it did no good to his carbuncles. On these, without anybody's advice at all, he performed a surgical operation, using one of the old razors inherited with Wilhelm Wolff's other effects. What he needed, Gumpert now advised, was sea air. He was willing to go away, but postponed his departure from day to day: first there was a meeting held at his house with the foreign "Corresponding Secretaries" of the International, including Paul Lafargue (for Spain) and Charles Longuet (for Belgium). Then, following a crisis in February, the shareholders of *The Workman's Advocate*, now re-issued as *The Commonwealth*, had to meet; and finally he attended and

---

* Edward Gumpert, M.D., Wurzburg 1855, established at 102 Bloomsbury, Manchester. He was a friend of Engels'. Marx—who said he was the only doctor he trusted—frequently sought his advice, both for himself and his family, either when Dr. Allen's bills were too long unpaid or because the forms of treatment Allen prescribed entailed rest and other interruptions of work to which Marx would not submit.

spoke at the General Council of the IWMA. Thus it was not until mid-March that he went to Margate where he spent the first night at the King's Arms, disliked it and looked for lodgings the next morning. These he found at 5 Lansell's Place: a large sitting-room and a bedroom facing the sea for which he paid 10s. a week to Mrs. Grach the landlady, who was as deaf as a post but considerate.

Undeterred by his weakened condition, he at once took a warm sea-bath and went for a five-hour walk. A couple of days later, a Sunday, after promenading the piers for two health-giving hours, he walked the 17 miles to Canterbury— "an old, ugly, medieval sort of town"—in under four hours, but was "happily" too tired and too late to visit the Cathedral. He came back by train to spend a sleepless night as a result of these exertions.

"Ellie", as she temporarily called herself, wrote to her "dear dada" at this point to recall him to his paternal duties. Although he was to have stayed away for an unbroken month the girls were having a party on 22 March which he had promised to attend. "Now, Dr. Karl Marx of bad philosophy", wrote Eleanor, "I hope you will keep your promise and come on Thursday",[56] as of course he did.

This spring festivity was in place of the Christmas party they had planned to give on receiving £5 from uncle Lion Philips. The gift had been instantly expropriated for "general purposes" and was only now restored. The least Marx could do was to be present at the tardy event. As soon as it was over he went back to Margate where he was shortly joined by Jenny and Tussy for ten days, Mrs. Grach letting them have a room without extra charge. Though no letters from Tussy at this period have been traced, she never forgot her Margate holiday, referring to it more than 30 years later, three weeks before her death, when she found herself again in Margate in very different circumstances.[57]

While the family was away Mrs. Marx wrote at some length to Ernestine expressing her views on the evil consequences of an atheistic upbringing. There were all manner of things she could tell Mrs. Liebknecht about her girls' little doings and acquaintances, but such relationships were often of so delicate a nature that she did not care to commit an account of them to paper. Laura and Jenny were of very different character, but for both of them "the peculiar bent of their education is bound to bring them into painful conflict with their friends. They have been brought up with notions and views that form a complete barrier to the society in which they move, and at the same time they are not materially independent." They could not expect their views, running so sharply counter to accepted opinion, to prevail. Had they been young persons of means, they might have managed without "baptism, church and religion"; as things were, they would both have to face bitter struggles. "I often think", wrote Mrs. Marx, "that if one cannot offer one's children riches nor complete independence of others, it is hardly the right thing to bring them up in harsh disagreement with society. They will always find themselves in a false position and these matters weigh heavily upon me." She then confessed that she often seemed cross-grained and peevish to her daughters; this was merely a reflection of her awareness that they would never be able to claim from life the degree of happiness to which their outer and inward endowments entitled them. Both of them, she felt she could truthfully say without the besotted delusions of a mother, were of radiant beauty "but perhaps for this very reason, all the more *out of place* and *out of time*". Naturally, this was strictly in confidence: "girls brought up in England and who have always lived under English conditions, do not much care for outpourings of this kind . . .".[58]

The "outpouring" appears to have been tapped by the news that Alice Liebknecht, at nine years of age, might have to be baptised, for which, in Mrs. Marx's view, her mother should be thankful, such rituals doing less harm than did their omission. Tussy had been proposed as Alice's godmother and was vastly amused by the notion. While on the subject of Tussy, her mother reported her equally irreverent attitude to her father's toothache. Since this affliction, according to her Confession, was her "idea of misery" it might have been expected to excite her sympathy but merely elicited the jeer that her father was frightened of the dentist's forceps. This had the desired effect and Marx went off bravely to have two teeth drawn (in keeping with his own Confession that his "favourite virtue in man" was Strength).

There is an undoubted connection between Mrs. Marx's pessimistic reflections in April and the fact that, at long last in the May of 1866, Jenny and Laura ceased their lessons, the younger giving up her music altogether, the elder, now 22, confining herself to one session a week. There could be no point in their pursuit of culture if they were foredoomed by their heathen upbringing to social ostracism. This precipitated a fresh crisis, for it is impossible to take final leave of a school without paying the bill and three full terms, amounting to £25, were owing. Engels, who had sent £50 in February and various minor sums throughout the spring, now promised another£50 in July and sent £10 in the meantime.

Toothache and bills were not Marx's only discomforts: the arsenic cure, though he was temporarily free of carbuncles, now appeared to be affecting his liver adversely; he was unable to work and turned again to Dr. Allen, but did not follow his prescriptions. The vexatious problems of *The Commonwealth* also came to a head. Always in difficulties and never fulfilling the early hopes that, as a London workers' organ, it would win enough support to become independent, the paper had accepted subsidies to keep it afloat from a Bradford manufacturer named Kell. Marx found this situation ludicrous: he recognised that with such backing and control the character of the journal must inevitably be lost and, thoroughly sick of the whole affair, he proposed selling out the bankrupt enterprise to Kell and his friends.

As soon as he was well enough, he attended the IWMA meetings where, in June, he heard Paul Lafargue address the General Council, though unfortunately in French, of which language nine-tenths of his audience did not understand a word.

This young man, despite political differences with Marx— for he was an adherent of Proudhon* and held the view, accord-

---

* Pierre Joseph Proudhon (1803–1865) had propagated and left a legacy of petty bourgeois socialism, attractive both to students and to workers employed in the more sophisticated trades of the metropolis, but without much appeal to the peasants or industrial workers of France as a whole. Marx's *Poverty of Philosophy*, an answer to Proudhon's *Philosophy of Poverty*, had ended their friendship as far back as 1847. Proudhonism, however, persisted as an active principle in French politics because, as Marx had put it long before: "Proudhon has the merit of being the scientific interpreter of the French petty bourgeoisie—a genuine merit, because the petty bourgeoisie form an integral part of all impending social revolutions. . . . Indeed, he does what all good bourgeois do. They all tell you that in principle. . .

ing to Marx that, "all Europe must and will sit quietly on its backside until the gentlemen in France abolish 'poverty and ignorance' "—was playing an increasing part in the Marxes' family life. The only son of a successful planter, born on 16 June 1842 in Santiago de Cuba, Paul Lafargue, the last of his line, was of extremely mixed descent. His paternal grandfather, a Frenchman who had emigrated to the Antilles, married a mulatto from St. Domingo, herself a refugee in Cuba from the French Revolution, and it was in St. Domingo that her husband was killed in a revolutionary uprising. Paul's mother's maiden name was Armagnac and she was the daughter of a Frenchman, assumed to be Jewish because he was called Abraham, who had married a Caribbean Indian. In 1851 Paul's parents left Cuba for Bordeaux where M. Lafargue went into the wine trade and Paul to school, later attending the *lycée* at Toulouse until he entered the Medical Faculty ot the University of Paris. There he contributed to *La Rive gauche*, edited by Charles Longuet, a fellow-student three years his senior. In 1865, when he was 23, Lafargue was sent to London to report on the French working class movement to the General Council of the IWMA, where naturally he met Marx. Later in the same year he helped to organise the first Students' International Congress, held in Liège, with the result that he and other delegates, including Longuet, were excluded from the university, a decision that provoked violent student riots. Paul hoped to take his finals in Strasbourg but, in the meantime, he returned to London where, without much urgency, he continued to study higher mathematics, physics and chemistry under Dr. Carrère, himself a refugee, at Bart's.

As if to confound Mrs. Marx's gloomy forebodings and undaunted by Laura's profanity, Paul now proposed to marry her and by the beginning of August they were "half-engaged". Engels, informed of this curious arrangement, was at a loss whether to offer his half, his whole or no congratulations. He did, however, send a further £50, for since 1864 he had been a partner in the firm of Ermen & Engels and he now

---

competition, monopoly, etc., are the only basis of life, but that in practice they leave much to be desired. They all want competition without its tragic effects. They all want the impossible, namely, the conditions of bourgeois existence without the necessary consequences of those conditions."[59]

guaranteed Marx £200 a year, with apologies that it could not be more.

Apart from young Lafargue's Proudhonism, there were other things about him not entirely to Marx's liking. He applied for references from Lafargue's former professor in Paris, Dr. Jules-Antoine Moilin;* he withheld a direct reply to a civil communication from Lafargue *père* asking him to accept Paul as a son-in-law, and finally he sat down and wrote a letter to the *demi-fiancé*, prompted by regard for Laura's welfare, bidding the young man mend his torrid manners if he wished to consort with her, but couched in such needlessly stern language as to exhibit the Victorian father at his least endearing.†

At the same time he was not only revising his completed draft of Volume 1 of *Capital* but he had just received and was incorporating the findings of the latest (5th) *Report of the Children's Employment Commission* and the (8th) *Board of Health Report*, an enquiry into the housing of the poor. On the Commission's report he commented: "Bourgeois complacency since 1850 could receive no more fearful blow than these five Blue Books."

He was also following with close interest the agitation over Gladstone's Reform Bill, now taken up by the London Trades Council‡ through the newly formed London Working Men's Association whose leadership was inspired by the IWMA. When the Bill was rejected, in terms so insulting that the class nature of the opposition was brought home in the sharpest way, there was an outcry. Demonstrations took place all over the country and vast meetings were held in Trafalgar Square, where, on 2 July, Benjamin Lucraft, a member both of the Executive Committee of the Reform League and of the General Council of the International, was the main speaker. "The workers' demonstrations in London, which are marvellous compared with anything we have seen in England since 1849", wrote Marx, "are purely the work of the International. . . . This shows the difference between *working* behind the scenes while not appearing in public and the Democrats' way§ of being self-important in public while doing nothing."

---

* 1832–1871. In 1870 Dr. Moilin was condemned to five years' imprisonment but was liberated on the Proclamation of the Republic, only to be shot in the Luxembourg Gardens by the Versaillais for his part in the Commune.
† See Appendix 2, p. 298.   ‡ Formed in 1860.
§ Under Bright, Cobden having died in 1865.

On 23 July a huge protest demonstration was called in Hyde Park, to forestall which Sir Richard Mayne, the Commissioner of Police, declared the meeting illegal and the Cabinet ordered the park gates to be closed.* The angry demonstrators in their thousands stormed the park in the Bayswater Road. Despite the massive presence of police and troops they tore up a hundred yards of the iron railings near to Marble Arch, and then, under the provocation of police brutality, proceeded to tear up the rest as far as Hyde Park Corner. "It was touch and go", wrote Marx. "If the railings had been used offensively and defensively against the police and some 20 of them had been struck dead, the military would have had to 'intervene' instead of merely parading. And then there would have been some fun. . . ."

While this great movement was shaking the British working class into furious activity, the first Congress of the International was held in Geneva at the start of September. Sixty delegates —English, French, German and Swiss—attended, and Paul Lafargue worked manfully, though not well, at translating the "Instructions to Delegates". With disarming honesty Marx admitted that he could not help liking the young man nor feeling a slight jealousy of him.

Still Laura's fate hung in the balance and, at the end of August, she took Tussy to Hastings where they boarded at a school run by a Miss Davies. One of the drawbacks to this arrangement, Laura wrote to her mother[60] was "the regular recurrence of meals . . . like the march of destiny . . . they haunt me like ghouls—the four monsters—breakfast, dinner, tea and supper; they cast shadows before them and behind. . . ." Not foreseeing the four monsters Laura, who feared that Tussy might starve, had laid in a stock of biscuits. It rained a great deal and they were often obliged to stay indoors, where the windows were hermetically sealed and a piano was played from morning till night. But, conceded Laura, it was not the fault of Hastings, "a divine place", that Miss Davies' school should contain compulsive pianists, unaired rooms, a white dog and an elderly maiden-lady called Miss Case. Firmly Laura announced that Tussy and she would neither go to church

* The demonstration was called in part to assert the right of assembly, challenged when the police had put down the mass meeting held on Primrose Hill in 1864 by the Working Men's Garibaldi Committee to protest against the abrupt curtailment, on political grounds, of their hero's too popular visit to England.

on Sunday nor undertake to be home before nine in the evening. Having asserted their spiritual and temporal independence the sisters enjoyed themselves to the top of their bent, using up the £5 Marx had sent them on bathing tickets and cab-rides and then asking him for a further £3. Jenny now joined them, while Mrs. Marx took a week's holiday by herself at the Rose and Crown in Dover and a further week at another resort.

Whatever doubts and reservations Marx still harboured, Laura's engagement was formally announced on 26 September 1866, her 21st birthday. She had insisted on having Engels' consent as well, which was readily given since he was a great believer in personal happiness. Mrs. Marx was jubilant. In glowing terms she described her son-in-law to Ernestine Liebknecht. Even his "dark olive complexion and extra-ordinary eyes", which proclaimed him a Creole on sight, did not detract from her enthusiasm. His parents, she wrote, who owned considerable estates in Cuba, had established a prosper-ous wine-merchant's business in Bordeaux. Paul had acquitted himself brilliantly at the university, taking his BM degree with honours after four years' study. "Fortunately", Mrs. Marx exulted, "he will not be dependent on his practice, always so precarious at the start. His parents are very well-off, owning plantations and house-property in Santiago and Bordeaux and, as Paul is their only child, naturally all this will pass on to him. They have behaved capitally towards Laura, welcoming her as their daughter with open arms and have promised the young couple a gift of 100,000 frs. on their wedding-day.* So you see, Frau Liebknecht, in respect of externals, there is nothing left to be desired; but what is even more important is the young man's fine character, his kindheartedness, his gener-osity and his devotion to Laura. What I consider a quite remarkable piece of luck is that he has the same principles, in particular where religion is concerned; thus Laura will be spared the inevitable conflicts and sufferings to which any girl with her opinions is exposed in society. For how rare it is nowadays to find a man who shares such views and at the same time has culture and a social position. . . . I always thought Laura would be a lucky girl! . . ."[61]

Poor Mrs. Marx, who had not thought so at all barely six

* Roughly £4,000.

months before. And poor Mr. Marx. For Paul Lafargue "in respect of externals" did not come up to scratch nor do what his father-in-law preached but rather what he practised, and for most of his married life, without a vestige of justification—since he was no genius and had no children to feed—Lafargue sponged shamelessly on Engels whose ears and purse were never closed to any of Marx's kin.

Tussy jubilated too and wrote to tell Alice of the engagement "at which you will be as surprised as we were"[62]—her powers of observation and her celebrated curiosity must have failed her here—and that Paul had given her "a *delicious* swing" on which, according to her mother, she performed marvels of daring the livelong day and forgot to go to school.

As though these excitements were not enough, the daughter of an "eminent and aristocratic family of their acquaintance", the Cunninghams, did Jenny and Laura the honour of inviting them to be the sole bridesmaids at her wedding. Mrs. Marx was so overcome by this mark of distinction that it was all she could do to collect her wits and what little money could be scraped together to buy the girls "bonnets, cloaks and heaven knows what else" for the occasion.

This incidental extravagance, though unwarranted, was as nothing to the expenses now incurred. Although Mrs. Marx did not approve of long engagements there could be no question of an immediate marriage and, for the time being, life would have gone on much as before, but for the rub that "the real state of things" must be scrupulously hidden from the prospective son-in-law who, until he took himself off to see his parents in Bordeaux early in November, was always about the place. The rent was unpaid; Marx borrowed from Withers the baker to pay Sawyer the landlord who held a promissory note from Marx for the wrong amount; and he wrote to his pen-friend the gynaecologist Dr. Kugelmann begging him to try to arrange for a private two-year loan of 1,000 thaler* at 5 or 6 per cent, revealing that he had been paying 20 and even 50 per cent to small lenders. This move miscarried too, for, unable to do what was asked of him, Kugelmann proposed appealing to Engels on Marx's behalf, for which innocent but officious design Marx coldly snubbed him.

* Roughly £175.

As he approached his annual nadir Marx declared that things were as bad as in his worst refugee days: he owed money everywhere; so many articles of clothing were in pawn that, given the season, his wife could hardly venture out of doors; he could not afford the new books he needed—not yet available in the British Museum nor at "Mudy"*—he was working at night and, though on arsenic again, horrifying carbuncles had appeared. To crown all, before 1866 was out, news came of the death not only of his old friend Joseph Weydemeyer in America, but also of his uncle Lion Philips, the last of his relatives to whom he could turn and a man he had grown to trust and admire.

There were just three flickers of light as the year went out: Engels sent another £50, port and a case of wine; James Stephens, the leader of the Fenians in Ireland, recently escaped from Dublin's Richmond jail, joined the IWMA; and the first batch of Marx's manuscript had at last gone off to Otto Meissner, the Hamburg publisher.

* Mudie's Lending Library was founded in 1842 and failed in 1937.

§6

It was of course the publication of his book that wholly absorbed Marx in the year 1867, though not without many distractions.

In January the tiresome Sawyer sold No. 1 Modena Villas to a Mr. Burton of Torquay where he did not choose quietly to remain but came only too often to London and made devilish trouble over the rent.* He established from the start the character of their future relations by holding a pistol to Marx's head: he must make up his mind here and now whether, when the lease fell in on quarter-day, he wished to take a longer lease, a yearly tenancy, or clear out; the rent was disgracefully in arrears and more satisfactory tenants were not hard to find. It gave Marx insomnia. Engels settled the arrears of rent and, since no more was heard of this problem—though plenty more was heard of Mr. Burton—and the family stayed on for another seven years, it may be assumed that the lease was renewed.

Until the end of March Marx worked intensively on his book, not even pausing to write to Engels. Though his carbuncles, as in the past three winters, were excruciatingly painful, he dropped the arsenic because it made him feel "too stupid" and so long as he was capable of writing his head must be clear. Then the work was done and he planned to take the rest of the manuscript to Meissner in person. He emerged from his concentrated labours to take note that the family was penniless—in which state he could not leave them while he went abroad—and that he would require his watch and some clothes,

* This gentleman had been hard hit by the failure of Overend & Gurney in 1866, a bankruptcy which not only dealt a blow at joint stock discount houses, from which they were said never to have recovered, but became a national scandal and a *cause célèbre* when the directors were prosecuted in 1869, though acquitted. Mr. Burton, following the crash, prudently decided to put what capital remained to him in house property whereby he hoped to live comfortably on rent for the rest of his days. His misfortune in acquiring Marx as a sitting tenant so soon after the earlier experience might well have shaken his faith in the whole system of rent, interest and profit, but did not do so.

presently at the pawnbroker, for his journey to Hamburg. Laura was languishing for no very clear reason but one that demanded a small bottle of champagne (costing £2), a course in gymnastics, to be paid in advance, and, as she regained her strength, claret of a quality better than her father could afford. Engels sent £35, but his mind, too, was on other things and: "Hurrah!" he wrote. "This exclamation was irrepressible as I read at last in black and white that Volume I is finished and that you are going straight off to Hamburg with it." He also sent a chit to Meissner instructing him to pay Marx money owing on his own work.[63]

Marx left London on 10 April and was away for nearly six weeks. He took a liking to Meissner, remained at hand to correct the proofs of his book, which was to be printed in four or five weeks by Hugo Wigand in Leipzig, and stayed with Dr. Kugelmann in Hanover, where he was overwhelmed and more than a little bored by the fanatical enthusiasm of the whole family for Engels and himself. Indeed, it came to him as a great surprise to find in what high esteem he was held among educated Germans.

During his stay he received a tragic letter from Liebknecht, whose wife Ernestine, Mrs. Marx's friend and *confidante*, was desperately ill. Her health had been undermined by the years of poverty in exile while the shock of her husband's expulsion from Prussia in the summer of 1865, followed by his arrest and three months' prison sentence in October 1866, at which time she was pregnant, had dealt a mortal blow. "It is frightful for me to watch her slowly dying", wrote Liebknecht.*

Marx reported this and other news in long and loving letters to his daughters who kept up a regular correspondence with him, including at least one letter from Tussy, written on 26 April:

"My dear Dada, Just as your letter came I was deciding that you never could stay away a whole fortnight without writing,

---

* A month later, on 29 May 1867, Ernestine Liebknecht died in great agony, leaving two little daughters: Eleanor's friend Alice, now ten, and the infant Gertrud. The one married Bruno Geiser the other Wilhelm Swienty. In 1868 Liebknecht took a second wife, Natalie. She presented him with three sons, of whom the younger, Karl, born on 13 August 1871, became the leader of the German *Spartakus* movement and was murdered, together with Rosa Luxemburg, on 15 January 1919.

and I never would forgive you but my rage began to evaporate amazingly quickly as soon as your letter was read and now I'm actually writing to you. . . . Paul has been keeping me in books, he got me Cooper's *Deerslayer, Homeward Bound, The Effinghams,* and I am going to read the *Watermate* and *Two Admirals.* You see I'm quite 'going the hog'. . . . On Good Friday I eat sixteen hot cross buns, Laura and Jenny eat eight. Louisa and Percy Freiligrath came here the other day. Percy jumped out of the window on the first landing, because I said he could not, and he wrote me he would jump out again if I ordered him to. . . . Paul and Laura have had three riding lessons. . . . The days after the lessons however both were rather stiff and I had to make Paul a cushion to rest his bruised behind upon. I was much surprised to receive a letter from Franziska.* Now dear Dady goodbye. Believe me, Your UNdutiful daughter Eleanor."[64]

There were also letters from Engels, who was providing for the family in Modena Villas, not forgetting Jenny's birthday, and who now, on 27 April, wrote to tell Marx that in all probability he and his partner, Godfrey Ermen, who did not hit it off, would separate at the end of their present contract in two years' time, if not earlier. In that case he would abandon altogether the filthy world of commerce, with its utterly demoralising waste of time. At all events, he wrote, his life as a businessman would cease in a few years. Of course this meant that the flow of income would be reduced to a trickle and, a matter always on his mind, what would he be able to do for Marx? But if things went as they now promised, that too could be arranged, even if the Revolution took place to put a stop to all financial schemes. Rejoicing at the prospects opening for Marx with the imminent publication of his book, Engels summed up the past unhappy years in a memorable passage: "It always seemed to me that this accursed book which you gestated for so long was at the root of all your troubles and that you neither would nor could ever emerge from them until you had shaken yourself free of it. This everlastingly unfinished thing exhausted

---

* Franziska Kugelmann, aged 8, the daughter of the house where Marx was staying. A correspondence started, though they were not to meet for some years, and Dr. Kugelmann became a regular contributor to Eleanor's stamp collection from now on.

you physically, mentally and financially, and I can very well conceive that, now you have rid yourself of this incubus, you will feel a different fellow altogether, more particularly since the world, when once you go into it again, does not look so dismal as it did before. . . ."

In reply, despite complaints about the printer who had been held up over the Easter holiday, thus making it impossible after all for him to see the proofs as they came off the press, Marx expressed great optimism. "I confidently hope and believe," he wrote, "that in a year's time I shall be able to make a fundamental change in my economic circumstances and stand on my own feet again at last. Without you I could never have finished the work and I can assure you it has always lain as a deadweight on my conscience that your splendid powers were left to waste and rust in commerce mainly for my sake and that, into the bargain, you had to share the experience of living through all my petty miseries. . . ."

Nevertheless, he dreaded his homecoming, where the "Manichaeans"* were waiting to pounce and the accumulation of debt was truly imposing. He also foresaw domestic wailings, clashes and hounding, whereas all he wanted was to settle down, fresh and unhampered, to work. He had, however, hopes of raising £100 before he left for London.

He travelled from Hanover to Hamburg on 15 May and a day or two later crossed to England. His homeward journey was diverted, in both senses, by a young lady of military bearing whose imperious wish to travel straight on from London to Weston-super-Mare none but the British railway system could have gainsaid. It was a Sunday and as there were no porters on duty Marx gallantly took charge of operations, escorting her and her mighty baggage to the wrong railway station, then to the right one on the other side of London, only to find that the next train for Weston-super-Mare would not leave for another six hours. They spent the long afternoon in affable conversation, strolling about Hyde Park and eating ices, quite charmed by each other. Long before he saw her off at 8 o'clock that evening the truth was out: he had been consorting with Fräulein Elisabeth von Puttkamer, Bismarck's niece,† she

---

* His creditors.　　　　† Bismarck married Johanna von Puttkamer in 1847.

with the most abhorred of all the Reds in Europe. They parted
on the best of terms at Paddington Station.

Matters at home were much as he had anticipated and he
speedily left again for Manchester to spend a fortnight with
Engels. It was only after he had picked up life again inMaitland
Park that the familiar torments started in earnest. "I hope that
as long as it lasts the bourgeoisie will remember my carbuncles",
he wrote on 22 June. He grumbled that the girls planned to
give a dance on 2 July, as they had done no entertaining at all
that year and were afraid of losing caste. Even less enchanting
was the prospect of a visit from Lina Schoeler, to whom Mrs.
Marx would again have to repay the money she had borrowed
from her guest during the last stay. Having taken defensive
action against the first assault of creditors, Marx did not know
how this was to be done. He had heard nothing from the various
people on the Continent who had promised to raise money for
him.

Engels sent £100 before going abroad in early July. While
he was away and Marx thereby cut off from the source of
supplies, the three girls received an invitation from the Lafargues
to spend a holiday in France at the seaside. They were to
travel with Paul to his home in Bordeaux and he offered to pay
for the journey, but this Marx could not allow. The return
fares cost £30 and—concomitant with every excursion—there
were watches and clothing to be taken out of pawn. Reflecting
that the girls' health would benefit by this change—"the
seaside" was, in medical as in lay opinion, a panacea only
second to alcohol—Marx quite simply used the £45 he had
set aside for the rent.

Unfortunately Eleanor has left no account that can be traced
of this, her first conscious experience of foreign travel, though
it is unlikely that in the seven weeks she spent with her sisters
at Royan* she did not communicate her impressions of life
abroad in the family of a prosperous wine merchant.

It was now, while the girls were away, that Marx received
the forty-ninth and last sheet of his proofs and during the night
of 16–17 August he wrote to Engels: "It is thanks to YOU
alone that this has been possible. Without your self-sacrifices
for me I could never possibly have done the enormous work

* At the mouth of the Gironde estuary. They stayed from 21 July to 10 September.

for the three volumes. I embrace you, full of thanks!* . . . I salute you, my dear, beloved friend! . . ."

The second IWMA Congress, with 64 delegates, was held in Lausanne from 2 to 8 September. Paul Lafargue drew up the French version of the Report, edited by Marx, though neither of them attended. Paul brought the girls home and then planned to visit Engels in Manchester, hoping Marx would accompany him. Marx could think of no plausible excuse for refusing, but he could not afford the fare and, naturally, Paul was not "in the secret" of his financial state. Engels sent £5 to cover up for him and enable Mrs. Marx to meet household expenses in his absence.

Thus it was that Marx was not at home but, perhaps where it was most proper that he should be, with Engels, when at last, on 14 September 1867 the first edition of Volume I of *Das Kapital* was published.

It was for this that not only Marx's health but also that of his wife had been ruined; for this that Helene Demuth had slaved and skimped to keep the family going; for this that Jenny and Laura had forgone the little vanities and sweets of adolescence, each in her turn acting as a part-time secretary or devilling for Marx at the British Museum.

Only for Tussy, now twelve, was no other way of life conceivable. For ten years Marx had been working on the preparation of this book.[65] To write *Capital* was the most natural, indeed the only thing a father might reasonably be expected to do. *Capital* had, as it were, grown up with her—or she with it— and she was not conscious that this activity, whose end-product would change the world, had meant inordinate pain and sacrifice to all those she loved, or that hers had been in any way an unusual childhood.

* This phrase in English.

§ 7

By chance Marx arrived in Manchester at a time of tumultuous excitement.*

Two Fenian officers, Thomas Kelly and Timothy Deasy, seconded for duty in Lancashire after evading the Irish constabulary for their part in the abortive March rising of that year, had been arrested in dubious circumstances on 11 September 1867. Tracked down and denounced by a Crown spy, John Joseph Corydon, they were remanded in custody and lodged in the old Manchester city gaol. They were brought before the magistrates on 18 September and again remanded, when they were driven with convicted prisoners in a Black Maria from the Bridge Street court to Belle Vue prison in Gorton, then a separate small township surrounded by brickfields. As the police van, drawn by two horses and followed by a cabful of constables, passed under a railway viaduct on the Hyde Road it was ambushed by a posse of armed men. One horse was wounded and both were cut loose, the roof panel was hammered open with a stone, while a shot fired either at the lock of the door or into the ventilator grille immediately above it fatally wounded a 51-year old police sergeant, Charles Brett, standing just inside the van. In the general confusion Kelly and Deasy escaped, never to be recaptured, but a ferocious man-hunt began, ending in the arrest of over 30 Irishmen and the later identification of five who stood trial for the murder of Brett.

On Saturday, 21 September, Engels took Paul Lafargue to the scene of the attack on the van: the railway bridge which, until its rebuilding nearly a century later, was a brick structure that became known as Fenian Arch.

Though Marx and Paul had left Manchester before the trial

* Another chance visitor in Manchester at the time was young Annie Wood, the future Mrs. Besant, staying with the family of the radical lawyer, W. P. Roberts, known as "the pitmen's advocate".

opened in October, passions were aroused throughout the land, inflaming everyone from the highest to the lowest. Queen Victoria, howling and drunken hordes of whose English subjects were to spend the night a few weeks later under the prison walls below the gallows to witness the killing of three fellowmen, wrote to Sir Stafford Northcote on 2 October: "These Irish are really shocking, abominable people—not like any other civilised nation",[66] while monster demonstrations, petitions and questions in the House greeted the pronouncement on 1 November of the death sentence on all five prisoners. One of the men was subsequently pardoned, without redress for his wrongful conviction and sufferings, while another had his death sentence remitted to penal servitude for life but, as a citizen of the United States, was released after eleven years.

The remaining three men, William Philip Allen, Michael O'Brien and Michael Larkin, the "Manchester Martyrs", were publicly hanged on 23 November.*

Engels described the courageous demeanour of the three as they went to the gallows where the public hangman, Calcraft, bungled his work, despatching only one man by means of the rope and the "long-drop" method he had humanely devised.

While all the "Martyrs" protested their innocence to the end, none disclosed the name of their companion—Peter Rice—who had fired the mortal shot. On the day, a Sunday, following the executions and in defiance of rabid English feeling, every Catholic priest in Manchester—where with the influx of unemployed Irish the hierarchy had been restored in 1850 for the first time since the Reformation—denounced the "murder" of the hanged men from their pulpits. Masses were said throughout the country, processions marched through the streets playing the Dead March on black-draped instruments, while in Hyde Park a vast concourse of people gathered to kneel and pray. The Irish Question had become an English question and few were left untouched. "All the Fenians lacked was martyrs", wrote Engels. "These they have been presented with . . . through the execution of these men, the liberation of Kelly and Deasy has been made an act of heroism which will now be

---

* This gruesome gala was among the last public executions in England. Ten more were to take place before, by Act of Parliament, executions were carried out behind prison walls.

sung over the cradle of every Irish child. . . . The Irish women will see to that."

From that time Jenny took to wearing black and the cross, given to her by the Polish patriots on her 23rd birthday earlier that year, she hung on a green ribbon to honour the Irish Brotherhood, while Tussy became emotionally involved for the first time in a political issue whose interest for her was never to abate.

Marx was in something of a quandary: anxiously awaiting the first reception of *Capital* and fidgety because as yet there had been no word of comment, his views on the Fenian affair were being sought on all sides. He had promised Meissner Volume II of *Capital* by the late autumn, the third volume by the winter of 1867,* so there was no change either in his circumstances or occupation as a result of this first major publishing event. The IWMA General Council had sent a Memorial to the Secretary of State (Gathorne-Hardy) on 20 November declaring that the forthcoming executions bore the stamp "not of a judicial act, but of political revenge", and the Council debated the Fenian question on 26 November[67] but failed to reach agreement, the resolution proposed being described by Marx as "absurd and meaningless". He thought that a great deal of rubbish was being talked: that, on the one hand, the significance of Irish emancipation was imperfectly understood and that, on the other, some misguided Fenian tactics were unlikely to lead to a better understanding. In the circumstances he was not willing to "hurl revolutionary thunderbolts" on the Irish question and gratuitously present reviewers of his theoretical work with the means to dismiss him as a demagogue. He was incensed by the "melodramatic folly" of the Clerkenwell Explosion: an event which took place on 13 December, barely three weeks after the execution of the Manchester Martyrs, whereby, in an attempt to release two Fenians held in the House of Detention,† a 548-lb. barrel of gunpowder

---

* Volume II appeared in 1885, Volume III in 1894, both posthumously, assembled and edited by Engels from the mass of papers Marx had left.

† The gaol stood on the site of what is now Mount Pleasant post office. In 1887 the parcel post service was installed in the former treadmill house, bakery and other outbuildings of the prison. By 1900 the old structure had been entirely replaced and then accommodated the London letter post office, transferred from the G.P.O. in St. Martin-le-Grand. Clerkenwell gaol was the Middlesex

was ignited, blowing up the prison wall and wrecking a number of nearby working class houses with dire consequences to their inhabitants.*

Marx justly concluded that this exploit would alienate the wide public sympathy displayed by the London workers at, among other demonstrations, a massive torchlit meeting held in defence of the Manchester Martyrs on nearby Clerkenwell Green so short a time before.

Stirring as were the events of that autumn, the family had nevertheless to cope with its own affairs, among which Laura's forthcoming marriage, arranged for the following April, presented a problem different for each of the bride's parents. To Marx it was a matter of finance. Paul was more or less living in the house—though officially lodged at 35 Kentish Town Road—and expenses soared, since he must not be allowed to feel nor even to detect the pinch. Now a trousseau was to be added to the burden. "After all, she can't be sent out into the world like a beggar." Marx's borrowings became frantic. At last, in December, with Engels as security, he applied to a life insurance society, submitted himself, reluctantly, to a medical examination for actuarial assessment and, rather to his surprise —for his body was scarred with the evidence of past and aflame with present carbuncles—came through with credit, in both senses, for his deep chest-barrel impressed the doctor and he obtained a loan forthwith.†

House of Correction, otherwise known as Coldbath Prison. The change of name to Mount Pleasant—an earlier 17th century designation—was officially made in 1888.[68]
* According to *The Times* of 29 April 1868: "Six persons were killed outright, six more died from its effects according to the coroner's inquests; five in addition owed their deaths indirectly to this means; one young woman is in a madhouse, 40 mothers were prematurely confined, and 20 of their babes died from the effects of the explosion on the women; others of the children are dwarfed and unhealthy. One mother is now a raving maniac; 120 persons were wounded; 50 went into St. Bartholomew's Gray's Inn Lane, and King's College Hospitals; 15 are permanently injured, with loss of eyes, legs, arms, etc.; besides £20,000 worth of damage to persons and property." The melodramatic folly of this report, with its dwarfs and raving maniacs, is evident. More sober accounts of the outrage put the figures at twelve killed and 20 seriously injured, though it is not disputed that women and small children were among the victims. As Marx commented, English workers could hardly be expected to regard being blown up by Fenian emissaries as an honour. Moreover, the breach made in the prison wall would have killed those it was intended to deliver had they been, as their rescuers supposed, at exercise in the yard rather than in their cells. The hanging of Michael Barrett in May 1868 for his part in the outrage was the last public execution in England.
† This was not strictly a life insurance policy, but a straight loan given against a

Mrs. Marx's preoccupations were of a more delicate but no less troubling nature: how to conceal the scandal of a civil marriage? She was in a great taking and Engels was asked to consult Ernest Jones, the old Chartist, on the necessary formalities. It is not quite clear why Jones was to be consulted, for, ten years earlier, both Marx and Engels had broken off relations with him on political grounds and the friendship had not been renewed until 1864, when it took on a socially pleasant but by no means intimate character.* However, Jones responded. He had recently emerged from graver considerations, having figured prominently not only in the activities of the Reform League but also in the defence of the Martyrs.†

Engels passed on the vital information regarding civil marriage, adding: "Your wife can tell her Philistine neighbours that this course has been elected because Laura is a Protestant and Paul a Catholic." Whether Mrs. Marx was appeased by this advice is not known.

That year, 1867—a year which, incidentally, saw the passing of the Second Reform Bill, the founding by John Stuart Mill of the London National Society for Women's Suffrage and the demolition of the old St. Martin's Hall of IWMA fame—ended, like most years for Mrs. Marx, with a dismal Christmas. It was not, however, without its heavy humour, for on Christmas Eve, while Marx, unable to lie on his back and groaning with pain, tossed from side to side and the females were busy making the Christmas pudding below stairs, there arrived a tremendous bust of Jupiter Tonans, which daunting gift, slightly chipped *en voyage*, had been sent by Dr. Kugelmann as a conspicuous token of his friendship.

bond, for a fixed term, to be cancelled in the event of death occurring before the term expired but otherwise to be repaid at enormous interest. "The worst and most expensive way of raising cash", as Marx said.

* It will be recalled that he was a guest at Jenny's 21st birthday party in 1865. On his death in January 1869, when a vast concourse followed his bier to the cemetery, Engels said of him: "He was the only educated Englishman who was at heart entirely on our side".

† After an initial outburst of justified but, in the circumstances, unhelpful indignation, he had thrown up his brief at the preliminary hearing. He objected not only to the presence of troops stationed inside the magistrates' court but, more vigorously, to his clients entering the dock handcuffed and, when the magistrates refused to unfetter the men, Jones declared he would not appear in a court room under police rules and swept out. At the Grand Jury trial, however, he was again briefed by W. P. Roberts to defend Allen and O'Brien, who were hanged, and the American, Condon, whose death sentence was remitted.

Laura's marriage was solemnised on 2 April 1868 before Messrs.
Matthews and Ivimey, the St. Pancras Registrars, in the
presence of Marx and Engels. It was followed by a luncheon
at Modena Villas* when, as Laura recalled 25 years later,
Engels "cracked a lot of silly jokes at a very silly girl's expense
and set her a-crying".[70] The young couple then spent a brief
honeymoon in Paris, where her father sent Laura a letter
rejoicing that "the spring and sun and air and Paris jollities
conjure in your favour", followed by requests for catalogues
and journals which, acknowledged as untimely, he excused
by saying: "I am a machine, condemned to devour books and
then throw them, in a changed form, on the dunghill of
history."[71] †

Laura and Paul were back in London in time for Marx's
fiftieth birthday (5 May), which he spent—"still a pauper"—
tortured by carbuncles and distracted by debts, the most pressing of which appeared to be those for Tussy's school fees and her
course of private gymnastic lessons with a Mr. Winterbottom.

Meanwhile, after spending a few extra days in London,
Engels had gone back to Manchester to toast the bride and
groom *in absentia* with such a will that even his pet hedgehog,
referred to as "The Right Honourable", got fuddled and, as
Engels informed Tussy, suffocated itself in a blanket. Tussy
herself was soon to experience at first hand the joys and sorrows
of Engels' home life, so different from her own, for at the end
of May, advised to travel "by the new Midland line from King's
Cross",‡ she accompanied her father to Manchester for a fortnight.

* On 1 May 1868 it was renamed No. 1 Maitland Park Road.[69]
† Strangely enough, the other great man of that epoch, Charles Darwin, writing
in 1876 described his function in almost the same terms: "My mind seems to have
become a kind of machine for grinding general laws out of large collections of
facts."[72]
‡ The new Midland line, "the picturesque and favourite route between London
and Manchester via Matlock and the Peak of Derbyshire", started in fact from

During their stay—Marx seems accidentally to have timed his visits to Manchester to coincide with significant happenings —a conference of 34 delegates took place at the Mechanics' Institute in David Street. This was the first Trades Union Congress, held in Whit Week from 2 to 6 June 1868. The invitation to attend had been issued on 21 February by the President and Secretary of the Manchester and Salford Trades Council, the compositors Samuel Caldwell Nicholson and William Henry Wood, whose names do not appear in the index to the Webb's *History of Trade Unionism* where this first Congress is accorded two modest sentences in a footnote.

It was not in itself a world-shattering event: boycotted by many of the most powerful Associations and representing fewer than 120,000 organised workers, it was nevertheless a landmark in the peculiarly British development of the working-class movement and one which, in days to come, was to prove both a stepping-stone and a stumbling-block in Eleanor's path.

At the time she was oblivious to it, passionately engaged in the Irish cause with the example and encouragement of Lizzie (Lydia) Burns* who, added to the distinction of being Irish herself, had on more than one occasion given asylum to Fenians on the run. These dazzling exploits and the warmth of her partisanship fired the young Eleanor with such fanatical enthusiasm that, on her return home, she earned herself the nickname of "the Poor-Neglected-Nation", so constantly was this phrase on her lips, and, transferring her allegiance from the much-wronged Emperor of China, she declared: "Formerly I clung to a man, now I cling to a nation." She took to buying *The Irishman*,† reporting back to Lizzie such items of news as that the Fenians had held a Congress lasting 19 hours. Splendid as a proof of stamina, it aroused in Eleanor the compassionate reflection that it must have left them very tired. She also sent Lizzie the words of a revised version of the National Anthem—

the terminus of St. Pancras, opened in 1868. The journey took roughly five hours. There were no corridors on the trains.

* 1826–1878, with whom Engels had lived since shortly after the death of his early love, her elder sister Mary (1823–1863).

† The organ of the Irish Nationalists, published first in Belfast and then in Dublin from 1858 to 1885. In 1867 the editor, Richard Piggott (1828–1889) was imprisoned for his support of the Fenian cause.

"God Save Our Flag of Green"—and signed herself "Eleanor, F.S." (Fenian Sister).

Back in London, her panegyrics upon the delights of Manchester and her intention to return there as soon as might be, stirring up bad blood, as Marx recorded, were temporarily halted by an attack of scarlet fever to which both she and Jenny succumbed in June.* Her case was more serious than her sister's but she had the good fortune to be attended by an Irish doctor named Korklow who, in addition to his meritorious nationality, was a close neighbour and a "scarlet fever man", recommended to the Marxes as physician to the South Hampstead College for Ladies. This was not the only thing Tussy owed to the school, for she had caught the infection from a fellow pupil: no less a person than the daughter of Professor Frankland,† as Marx was at pains to point out when Lizzie Burns reproached herself in the belief that the illness had been picked up in Manchester.

Marx now played two curiously conflicting roles: he was both a notability while remaining a notable debtor. He was invited to such functions as the annual conversazione of the Royal Society of Arts, a function to which Jenny accompanied him.‡ He and his family were looked upon as among the distinguished patrons of the Maitland Park Orphan Working School at a time when he was still borrowing from the baker to pay the cheesemonger and could not meet the rent or rates.

---

* They were put on a diet of Liebig's beef-tea laced with port.

† Sir Edward Frankland, F.R.S. (1823–1899), Professor of Organic Chemistry at the Royal Institution, where he succeeded Faraday in 1863. With Sir Joseph Lockyer, the astronomer, he discovered helium in the sun's chromosphere in 1868, when he also became a member of the Royal Commission on the Pollution of Rivers and, as Superintendent of the Royal College of Chemistry, made monthly reports from 1865 onwards to the Registrar-General on the character of the London water supply.

‡ Jenny commented on the occasion: ". . . of the works of art (the Queen has sacked all the museums of the people, in order to carry off their treasures to this aristocratic and favourite resort of the 'belated lamented') it was next impossible to get a glimpse . . . My impression of the Society of Arts is that it is a Society of Snobs . . ."[73]. This is one of the rare, and not illuminating, references to the visual arts in the entire available correspondence of the Marx family. While literature and music played a formative part in their cultural environment, drawing, painting and sculpture—despite the art lessons enjoyed by Jenny and Laura—do not so much as figure among the tastes and preferences in the "Confessions" of Marx, Jenny, Laura or Eleanor. It comes as something of a shock to realise that, though Eleanor grew up in the England of Leighton, Holman Hunt and Alma-Tadema, her contemporaries included Manet, Degas, Cézanne, Monet, Gauguin, Renoir, Van Gogh and Seurat. Almost her only reference to painting occurs in 1881 when she likened one of her little nephews to a portrait "of" Murillo.[74]

This double life reached its final absurdity when he was simultaneously elected Constable by the vestry of St. Pancras and summoned by the same body to "show cause why his goods and chattels should not be distrained". The former mandate—"an honour much valued by the Philistines of St. Pancras", according to Dr. Korklow—he evaded by going to Manchester when he should have been taking his oath of office, with the remark: "They can kiss my arse". Engels was vastly amused by the whole medieval nonsense,* apostrophising him: "*Salut, ô connétable de Saint-Pancrace*", and suggesting that Paul, suitably accoutred, should act as Squire.

While the invalids made slow but satisfactory progress it was planned that in July they should go to the seaside: not only they, but Laura, now four months pregnant, Paul, his parents and also Mrs. Marx, who was anxious not to be parted from Laura in these last weeks before the young couple left to make their home in France.

From week to week, while Marx fumed over the delay, the holiday was postponed. Paul, who had finally taken his MRCS degree and was now qualified "to kill men and beasts", had still to finish his term of duty as House Surgeon at the hospital and Mrs. Marx, though anxious to be off, was perturbed by the necessity of finding at least £20 for Laura's household linen at a time when Marx was already driven to distraction by the debts he had incurred in the past twelve months, now coming home—with interest—to roost.

At last, on 5 August, Mrs. Marx having forayed to find lodgings, the holiday party set out for Ramsgate, with watches redeemed from pawn and clothing suitable and respectable enough for a seaside resort packed in the battered portmanteaux.

In the absence of the family, whose noise about the house he strangely missed, Marx wrote to Engels in despair: it had come to a matter of life and death; there had been no response to his bids for loans from abroad; everyone was away from home at this season so it was useless for him to go in person to the Continent; his insurance society loan was falling due and, more immediately, unless he could raise the money the children could not stay at the sea. When Mrs. Marx came back after

---

* Instituted in the reign of Edward I, 1285. Parish Constables fell into desuetude by an Act of August 1872.

a fortnight she found her husband so ill with worry that she insisted upon his joining the others for a few days, which he did, returning with his daughters on 25 August.

A new note of panic had crept into Marx's appeals for money. Domestic rather than political economy obsessed him, despite his preoccupation with the IWMA Congress to be held in Brussels from 6 to 13 September.

On 15 October, by which time the money for the necessary equipment had been provided by Engels, the young Lafargues departed for Paris—to live in furnished rooms for a month before moving into a flat—where Paul found that his British degree was not recognised and that he would have to sit five further examinations to practise in France.* The news did little to cheer Marx who had counted upon his son-in-law, with student days behind him, assuming the responsibilities of a career and the support of a wife and family. This circumstance moved Jenny in the late autumn stealthily to seek a post as a daily governess to the children of a Scottish doctor named Monroe.† Her father, confronted by the *fait accompli*, did not oppose it, though, as if to confirm his opinion of such sorry undertakings, her employers failed to pay Jenny's salary for six months, and then had to be dunned for it. But, as he explained in words that he confessed he would rather have spoken than written, he thought it no bad thing that Jenny should have interests outside the home where Mrs. Marx's snappish temper had been for years a trial to the girls, no less vexatious for being both understandable and understandingly borne.

At the same point of time, at the end of November 1868, Engels began to take practical steps, long foreshadowed, to quit the firm of Ermen & Engels for good. His life as a business-man had never ceased to irk him, while his relations with God-frey Ermen, whose partner he had been since 1864, progres-sively deteriorated. He now asked Marx to tell him how much he actually owed and, if he were able to make a clean start free of debt, whether he thought he could live on £350 a year—

---

* He was in fact excused three of the examinations but intended, and promised his father, to take the other two at Strasbourg University.
† This arrangement, which entailed working five mornings a week, lasted for nearly three years, until, in 1871, the Monroes made "the terrible discovery that I am the daughter of the petroleum chief who defended the iniquitous Communal movement".[75]

illness and other unforeseen contingencies apart—for this was the regular income Engels proposed to guarantee him for the next five or six years, to start in 1869.

Marx was overwhelmed. The outstanding bills—omitting Dr. Korklow's fees, not yet claimed—presented a total of over £275. The account was drawn up by Mrs. Marx who, with the futile cunning of the innocent, since it was bound to come out sooner or later causing embarrassment all round, knocked off £75. With "strict administration" Marx believed that they could manage on £350, though he could not claim that they had done so in the past few years.* This he attributed in part to their perennial insolvency, compelling them to spend more than they could afford on daily necessities since the credit and patience of the small shopkeepers had been exhausted.

Christmas 1868, then, was in every way a time of high optimism, though, as Eleanor wrote ruefully to Laura, the dinner was "neither goose nor turkey, but a hare", which "shameful treatment" was owed to the fact that they were to sup with friends† later in the day, when, *en travesti*, Eleanor scored a success in *Beauty and the Beast* and the evening was passed with much merriment.

On 1 January 1869 two events of great importance to the family occurred: Charles Etienne Lafargue was born at 47 rue du Cherche-Midi in Paris and the first quarterly instalment of a regular private income was deposited for Marx at the Union Bank of London.

The three sisters were now launched on their several ways: Jenny embarked upon earning her own keep; Laura, a wife and mother, temporarily moored in foreign parts; and the voyage of Eleanor's childhood, her formal schooling virtually at an end, was over.

---

* It is estimated that this would be equal to something over £1,750 in terms of a century later. Indeed, all sterling amounts in the period 1865–1875 may be multiplied by at least five to equate them to the values of our own time. This sheds some light on the magnitude of Engels' generosity, Marx's debts and the standards observed by his wife (e.g. the sum equal to about £2,500 spent on the move to Modena Villas, see p. 57). Bowley estimates the weekly wages of the London artisan in 1867 at 36s., those of the skilled worker in the provinces at 27s., the lower skilled earning 20s. and the agricultural labourer 14s. (i.e. respectively £9, £6 15s., £5 and £3 10s. at approximate 1968 values).[76] These figures take no account of the inflation raging while this book was being written: official Cost of Living Index 1968 average = 100, mid 1971- = 124.
† A French family called Lormier.

REFERENCE NOTES

Abbreviations

Andréas   *Briefe und Dokumente der Familie Marx aus den
                   Jahren 1862–1873* by Bert Andréas in *Archiv
                   für Sozialgeschichte*, II. Band, 1962. Verlag für
                   Literatur und Zeitgeschehen, Hanover.
BIML   Institute of Marxism-Leninism, Berlin.
Bottigelli Archives Letters in the custody of Dr. Emile Bottigelli,
                   Paris.
ELC   *Frederick Engels Paul and Laura Lafargue:
                   Correspondence* Volumes I–III. Lawrence &
                   Wishart, 1959–1963.
IISH   International Institute of Social History,
                   Amsterdam.
IWMA   *Documents of the First International*, Volumes I–V.
                   Lawrence & Wishart, 1963–68.
Liebknecht   *Wilhelm Liebknecht Briefwechsel mit Karl Marx
                   und Friedrich Engels*. Edited by Georg Eckert.
                   Mouton & Co., The Hague, 1963.
MEW   *Marx Engels Werke*. Dietz Verlag, Berlin,
                   1956–1968. Unless otherwise stated Volumes
                   27–39.
MIML   Institute of Marxism-Leninism, Moscow.

(1) Compton Mackenzie, *My Life and Times, Octave 7 1931–1938*,
    Chatto & Windus, 1968.
(2) Privately communicated.
(3) IISH.
(4) Jenny to Eleanor, 23 March 1882. IISH.
(5) *The Parish of St. Anne, Soho, Survey of London*, Volumes 33 and
    34, Athlone Press, 1966. This provides the most splendid
    factual matter concerning the neighbourhood. It is a pity
    that it should sink to the vulgarity of assessing Karl Marx's
    work in a particularly silly footnote.
(6) *Madeleine*. 2nd edition. Bentley 1851.
(7) Quoted in *Edwin Chadwick and the Public Health Movement
    1832–1838*, R. A. Lewis, Longman, Green & Co., 1952.
(8) Originally published in the *New York Daily Tribune* and later
    forming part of the volume known as *The Eastern Question*,
    edited by Eleanor and Edward Aveling, Swan Sonnenschein
    & Co., 1897.

(9) Also written for the *New York Daily Tribune* and collected under the title *The First Indian War of Independence*, Lawrence & Wishart, 1960.

(10) Andréas.

(11) District Surveyors' Returns. Office of Metropolitan Buildings. G.L.C. Records. (See also "The Metropolitan Buildings Office: A missing chapter in the History of the Development of London" by Ida Darlington in *The Builder*, 12 October 1956.)

(12) *London Labour and the London Poor*, Volume I, Henry Mayhew. Chas. Griffin & Co., n.d., probably 1861.

(13) Mrs. Marx to Luise Weydemeyer, 11 March 1861. MEW.

(14) Metropolitan Board of Works, G.L.C. maps 1280 and 4121.

(15) *My Past and Thoughts*, Volume 5, translated by Constance Garnett. Chatto & Windus, 1924–1927. Herzen himself came to London in August 1852.

(16) Gustav Mayer, *Friedrich Engels*. Chapman & Hall, 1936.

(17) To Kautsky, 19 June 1897. IISH.

(18) Eduard Bernstein, *Die Neue Zeit*, No. 30. 1898.

(19) To Kautsky, 1 January 1898. IISH.

(20) Mrs. Marx to Mrs. Markheim, 6 July 1863. Andréas.

(21) *Österreichischer Arbeiter-Kalender für das Jahr 1895.*

(22) Jenny to Marx, November/December 1860. IISH.

(23) To Frank Van der Goës, 31 October 1893. IISH.

(24) Marx to Weydemeyer, 1 February 1859. MEW.

(25) Mrs. Marx to Marx from Manchester, November 1877. MIML.

(26) Mrs. Marx to Marx from Manchester, 1877 (probably November). MIML.

(27) Mrs. Marx to Mrs. Liebknecht, April 1866. BIML.

(28) 26 May 1872. MEW.

(29) Quoted in Volume I of *Capital* (3rd German edition 1883) from the opening address to the Sanitary Conference at Birmingham by Joseph Chamberlain, then mayor, on 15 January 1875.

(30) *Geschichte des sozialdemokratischen Parteiarchivs und das Schicksal des Marx-Engels-Nachlasses* by Paul Mayer in *Archiv für Sozialgeschichte*, VI./VII. Band 1966/7. Verlag für Literatur und Zeitgeschehen. Hanover.

(31) Published in book form, together with Engels' writings on the same subject, under the title *The Civil War in the United States*. Lawrence & Wishart. n.d.

(32) Andréas.

(33) Mrs. Marx to Mrs. Markheim, 6 July 1863. Andréas.

(34) For this and other medical diagnoses made on the basis of the

symptoms described in contemporary letters, I am indebted to Dr. Edwin Clarke, Senior Lecturer in the History of Medicine at University College, London.

(35) According to Werner Blumenberg's calculation (*Karl Marx*, Rowohlt, Hamburg, 1966), which converts the thaler into marks, though the mark did not become German currency until 1875. (14,000 marks= 4,667 thaler. The thaler was worth 6.20 to the £ sterling in 1863–1864. *Exchanges on London*, Soetbeer 1886.)

(36) 100 gulden were worth about £9 at the time.

(37) *Karl Marx zum Gedächtnis*, Nuremberg, 1896. To be found in English in *Karl Marx Selected Works*, Vol. I. Lawrence & Wishart, 1942.

(38) IISH.

(39) Karl Marx. *Manuskripte über die polnische Frage*, edited by Werner Conze and Dieter Hertz-Eicherade. Mouton, The Hague, 1961.

(40) Reproduced by kind permission of the IISH.

(41) To Ernestine Liebknecht, 10 December 1864. BIML.

(42) Collected and edited by Dona Torr under the title *Marx on China*. Lawrence & Wishart, 1951.

(43) Blumenberg. *International Review of Social History*, Volume I, Part I. Amsterdam 1956.

(44) 16 July 1864. MIML.

(45) 10 December 1864. BIML.

(46) 13 February 1865. IISH.

(47) 16 February 1865. IISH.

(48) MIML.

(49) *The Bee-Hive* was founded by George Potter in 1861. He was the sole proprietor from 1868 until 1873. A weekly which appeared until 1876, it was adopted as the organ of the IWMA from November 1864, which connection it retained until 1870.

(50) George Allen & Unwin Ltd. It has also appeared in subsequent editions as *Wages, Price and Profit*.

(51) A more elaborate though equally imprecise way of arriving at much the same result has been calculated on the basis of the cheapest retail commodities and services advertised in the *Camden & Kentish Towns Gazette* over the years 1866–1870 and in the local Directories 1862–1870; food prices given in the first edition (1861) of Mrs. Beeton's *Book of Household Management*; contemporary Ratebooks; the known rent, school fees, doctors' expenses and other items specifically mentioned in Marx's correspondence of the period and by examining the

cost per head of certain basic items consumed by the inmates of the Orphan Working School for the years 1863–1867 whose accounts were kept in great detail. The calculation assumes that Helene Demuth's wages were paid, does not include travel abroad or seaside holidays, interest on loans, or drink, the last being relatively the cheapest single item in any budget of the period (the duty on French wines having been repealed in 1860) and, in the case of the Marxes, supplied by Engels. This leaves a large margin of guesswork. In 1969 prices the equivalent annual income would have been in the region of £2,250.

(52) Early 1866. Liebknecht.

(53) Original English MIML. A German version appears in *Familie Marx in Briefen* (Dietz Verlag, Berlin, 1966) and in Vol. 31 MEW.

(54) Reproduced by kind permission of the Public Record Office.

(55) Bottigelli Archives.

(56) March 1866. Bottigelli Archives.

(57) To Natalie Liebknecht, 1 March 1898. Liebknecht.

(58) Early April 1866. IISH.

(59) Marx to Annenkov, 28 December 1846. MEW.

(60) n.d. (August/September 1866). IISH.

(61) October 1866. This last sentence originally written in English. Liebknecht.

(62) 14 October 1866. IISH.

(63) *Die preussische Militärfrage und die deutsche Arbeiterpartei* (The Prussian Military Question and the German Workers' Party). Published anonymously in the *Berliner Reform* on 3 March 1865.

(64) Bottigelli Archives.

(65) Including the *Grundrisse der Kritik der Politischen Ökonomie* (*Rohentwurf*) written in 1857 and 1858 but not published in full until 1953, and *Zur Kritik der Politischen Ökonomie*, written in 1858 and 1859, published in June 1859 by Franz Duncker, Berlin.

(66) Quoted in *High Upon the Gallows Tree*. Anthony Glynn. Anvil Books. Co. Kerry, 1967.

(67) IWMA, Vol. II.

(68) Post Office Records. HS No. 9A.

(69) Metropolitan Board of Works G.L.C. map 742.

(70) Laura to Engels, 6 March 1893. ELC Vol. III.

(71) 11 April 1868. Original English. MIML.

(72) *Autobiography of Charles Darwin*, edited by Nora Barlow. Collins, 1958.

D

(73) Jenny to Engels, 2 July 1869. IISH.
(74) Letter to Natalie Liebknecht, 12 February 1881. Liebknecht.
(75) Jenny to Kugelmann, 21 December 1871. Andréas.
(76) A. L. Bowley. *Wages in the United Kingdom in the Nineteenth Century.* C.U.P., 1900.

PART II

SHADES OF THE PRISON HOUSE

Although well versed in politics and literature, subjects fostered in the home, Eleanor at 14 years of age had picked up only twittercrumbs of learning. She spoke German as a matter of course but wrote it poorly; her French was weak, her spelling of English eccentric and her scholastic attainments low. This is no reflection upon the Misses Boynell and Rentsch of the South Hampstead College: there was scant demand for anything more than they could supply.

As late as the '60s the majority of middle-class girls were still sent to the innumerable private establishments set up and staffed by amateur tutors of both sexes, who, harking back to the 18th century, directed their efforts towards turning out commodities for a marriage market where now even the rudiments of domestic—let alone of any other—science were not an essential stock-in-trade. There was no fixed curriculum nor qualified teaching. Isolated alternatives were of course in existence,* and in this year of 1869 the battle for women's higher education was marked by two signal victories: girls over 17 were permitted to sit for the equivalent of London matriculation and Hitchin College—the forerunner of Girton—was inaugurated. But the first Education Act had not yet been passed† and female secondary education was not generally available to the middle class until the Girls' Public Day School Company— the mother of the High Schools—was formed in 1872.

Eleanor, far from bracing herself to take some formal examination or qualify for future academic excellence, as her

---

* As far as London was concerned certificated teachers had been trained for the charity schools by the Home and Colonial Infant School Society since 1836 and by the National Society for Promoting the Education of the Poor in the Principles of the Church of England since 1842. Queen's College for Women in Harley Street, originally intended to improve the standards of professional governesses on principles devised by the Christian Socialist, the Rev. Frederick Denison Maurice, was opened in 1848 and Miss Frances Mary Buss established her North London Collegiate School for Ladies in Camden Town in 1850.

† It received the Royal Assent on 9 August 1870. Board School education was not compulsory until 1880 and fees not altogether abolished until 1918.

coevals of a century later are condemned to do, spent her
fourteenth year gadding about—to Paris, to Manchester, to
Ireland—with never a textbook to hand. Not that her education
ceased: in some senses it may be said to have started in earnest
now; but it took an outlandish form, while in her unbounded
leisure she confected little gifts of a tendentious nature: tatting
a collar threaded with green ribbons to fasten with an Irish
harp and a "steal" (*sic*) cross to hang upon a challenging green
neckband.

In the early spring of 1869 Marx wished to go to Paris to
discuss Charles Keller's French translation of his work* and
to visit Laura, who had been unwell for many weeks before
and ever since the birth of her baby. He announced his intention
by letter to the Lafargues who were promptly called upon by a
gentleman asking whether Monsieur Marx had yet arrived.
Forewarned by this vigilance Marx thought better of the plan†
and it was decided that Jenny and Eleanor should go instead.
They set out on 26 March—Good Friday—to stay in the rue
du Cherche-Midi. The streets in that quarter had not changed
much since Laurence Sterne a century before had pronounced
them so villainously narrow that "there was not room in all
Paris to turn a wheelbarrow", and in summer they stank.
Nevertheless it was to Haussmann's Paris that Eleanor came
and at the moment of its progenitor's fall from grace.‡ This was
a Paris of nearly two million inhabitants, with the straight

* Immediately on the German publication of *Capital* in 1867 Elisée Reclus and
Moses Hess attempted and then abandoned a French translation. Two years
later a second, equally unsuccessful, start was made. In the event the work did
not appear until 1872, translated by Joseph Roy and published by Lachâtre.
† The *loi des suspects* passed in 1858 after Orsini's attempt on the Emperor's life
gave Napoleon III and his government unlimited powers to banish, expel or im-
prison any person suspected of opinions hostile to the Empire. The interception of
his letter, spelling out the risks he would run in France, made Marx toy with the
idea of acquiring British citizenship. He did not pursue the matter for another five
years but went to Paris in July 1869 under the name of "A. Williams", staying
in the rue St. Placide, near to the Lafargues, for six days. He was unmolested by
customs officers and police.
‡ Georges Eugène Haussmann (1809–1891), whose family originated in Alsace,
studied singing at the Conservatoire as a youth but abandoned this career for the
law and politics. He became Prefect of the Gironde in 1851 and, as a result of the
impressive demonstrations he organised in Bordeaux in the following year to
honour the visit of the newly proclaimed Emperor, Napoleon III, he was called
to Paris where he became Prefect of the Seine in 1853. The malpractices which
flourished under cover of his ambitious town-planning were brought to light in
1868 and he was forced to submit the budgets to the Chamber of Deputies. As a
result he was deprived of office in January 1870, whereupon he retired to Nice on a
modest pension.

avenues, wide boulevards, handsome streets and public parks
that, together with 40,000 new houses, had been built between
1853 and 1865 at a cost equivalent to £35 million. The
reconstruction of the city's centre had given rise not only to
furious and corrupt speculation in land but also to such inflated
rents that working class families, spending a third of their wages
to keep a roof over their heads, were driven out to huddle in the
slums still festering on the outskirts, for the most part, as in so
many capitals, to the east. It was estimated that those employed
on the reconstruction had to walk an average of three hours a
day to reach and return from their work.[1] Twenty thousand
houses had been demolished to make way for modern Paris,
whose *arrondissements* were increased from twelve to twenty,
while the glory of the Étoile, with its twelve radiating avenues
strategically designed for the containment of disaffected mobs,
was Haussmann's answer to that half of the Paris population
which, on his own admission, lived in a state of poverty
bordering upon destitution.*

Jenny could not stay long in Paris. She had to return to her
job on 14 April, but Eleanor was there for seven weeks. All
that spring she went "bockomanning" the boulevards: a
portmanteau term of Laura's invention[2] for sightseeing strolls
punctuated by small glasses of beer. The Second Empire in
this its last year of carnival, far from presenting itself to the
young visitor as "gorgeous, meretricious and debased"[3], seemed
a place of simple and continuous delights. She saw Sardou's
Séraphine at the Gymnase, and went to what she called "the
fair of the pain d'épis"; she watched the open-air puppet-
shows and gazed at the marvels displayed by the novel great
department shops, pleased and amused by everything, but,

* In the years 1855 to 1869 prices had risen by some 45 per cent. The average
wage of a man working 11 hours was 5 frs. a day (approximately 4s.). "Real"
wages, i.e. purchasing power, may be measured by the price of bread which was
50 c. a kilo. Almost 60 per cent of wages was spent on food alone. Women, of
whom some 17,000 were employed in the Paris of 1869, earned roughly half the
male rate, while several thousand children were put to work at the age of eight
at half the female rate. There had been no legislation governing children's working
conditions since 1851: none, that is, under the Second Empire. Thus an entire
family of four persons gainfully employed might earn less than 9 frs. a day. Contemporary economists estimated that such a family needed 1,700 frs. a year in
order to subsist. This was not achieved by the average family, not all of whom could
be wage earners, since most trades had a high incidence of seasonal unemployment:
in the case of building workers—among the best paid—it was not uncommon to
be laid off for as long as from four to six months in the year.

above all else, she doted on her tiny nephew, known as Fouchtra and later in his short life as Schnaps or Schnappy. She had "never seen such a lovely child": his nose, his noble forehead—as immense as his grandfather's—his wonderfully good temper and his astonishing precocity in teething wrung from her paeans of praise cut short only by the need to attend to him. Her letters home, forwarded to Engels, bubbled over with gaiety, aberrant spelling and a relish for the absurd, as when she described the gentleman who, on the stormy Channel crossing, had worn spectacles for the prevention of seasickness. "Did you ever hear of such a think?" she brilliantly asked.*⁴

In reply Marx, after promising that Lenchen would regularly send her *The Irishman*, gave her a full report upon the conduct of her pets: Blacky, who behaved "always like a gentleman, but a very dull one"; the misnamed Tommy who had just presented the world with a large litter again and "done everything in her power to prove the truth of the Malthus theory"; the dog Whiskey, "a great and good personage" who repined in his mistress's absence, exhibiting the sufferings of a lofty soul, unlike the bird Dicky who profited by the occasion to develop a fine voice, and so on.⁵

While Marx was regaling Tussy with news of her menagerie he was growing more and more uneasy about his son-in-law's position.

Paul Lafargue had finished his translation of *The Communist Manifesto* for Jenny to take back with her to London. Despite his promises, he appeared to have discarded all notion of finishing his medical studies and was deeply involved in French politics. Marx disapproved. He feared that Lafargue *père* "should suspect me to push his son to premature political action. . . . As it is, he has not much reason to delight in his connexion with the Marx family".⁶ He thought Paul ought to qualify in France first; moreover he did not favour the political company Paul kept—"a pack of Blanquists"—which could only lead to trouble. Despite earlier quarrels and their fundamental differences, Marx was quite willing "to oblige" Blanqui,† as he wrote to Paul, by contributing to his projected

* In the same letter Eleanor deemed that a former acquaintance (Sassonov) had remarkably improved in looks and was now "hansom".
† Louis-Auguste Blanqui (1805–1881) though not a socialist was a genuine revolutionary firmly wedded to what Engels called "the fantasy of overthrowing an entire

journal *La Renaissance*,* but he was averse from Laura's husband courting unnecessary dangers in that well-organised police state, the Second Empire.

Nothing, however, could immunise Paul against the election fever that swept France in April with the dissolution of the Legislative Assembly. Over a month before Eleanor's arrival in Paris the Government had intensified its repressive measures to paralyse the Republican and working-class movement in anticipation of the elections. When these measures proved ineffective and riots—said to have been instigated by the police —broke out, wholesale and illegal arrests were made both in Paris and the provinces. Charles Louis Napoleon Bonaparte, the putative nephew and step-grandson of Napoleon I—none of whose titles to fame he seems to have inherited—had staged a *coup d'état* in 1851 and was proclaimed Emperor Napoleon III in December 1852 "after 20 years' vagabondage and a number of preposterous adventures".[9] These had included enrolment as an émigré in England among the 150,000 special constables assigned to protect the banks and other seats of power against the Chartists' procession to Westminster on 10 April 1848. He had not changed his spots and though he was shortly to meet his Waterloo—its name was Sedan—his manoeuvres to retain what amounted to a personal dictatorship were supported by every reactionary section of the population whose luxurious greed his reign had fostered. Paul was 27 years of age, with a record of student revolt behind him and married into the Marx family. It was too much to expect him to stand aside not merely from the increasing opposition to the régime but, more importantly, from the militant socialist wing within the Blanquist party now emerging under such people as Jules Guesde and Edouard Vaillant. Paul plunged into the campaign. Eleanor's unorthodox education progressed.

society through the action of a small conspiracy".[7] Politically active at a time before organised workers' parties had emerged, he never recognised that "the time for surprise attacks, of revolutions carried through by small conscious minorities at the head of unconscious masses, is past".[8] Blanqui had a passionate faith in insurrection and none in working class organisation, nor was he much interested in the nature of the society that would succeed the overthrow of capitalism. He spent in all over 33 years of his life in gaol for his beliefs. Elected to the Executive Committee of the Commune while serving his last sentence, he was not released until towards the end of his life when, in April 1879, he was elected deputy for Bordeaux.

* It never appeared.

Her mother came to Paris for a fortnight and they left for home just before the elections took place.* No sooner had Eleanor reached London on 19 May than she learned that she was to set out on her travels again.

In her absence there had been a recurrence of the Marxist syndrome (carbuncles and liver trouble). Engels was sure that a change of air, combined with a brisk daily walk and treatment by Dr. Gumpert in person, would enable Marx to do in a week more work than now took him a month in his debilitated state. Marx was persuaded to go to Manchester; but, apart from urgent IWMA business, he was not willing to deprive Jenny of her pleasure in his undivided company while the rest of the family was abroad and he waited until Mrs. Marx's return, when he wrote proposing to bring Tussy with him. There was great rejoicing at this plan and Engels made it clear that there would be no getting out of it. Indeed, father and daughter would have started off at once had there not been certain obstacles to paying for the railway tickets. Marx had been giving and lending money to those in greater need than himself—a fresh and agreeable experience—but ancient debts had an uncomfortable way of catching up with him just when he had lavished his funds, on Lessner,† on Liebknecht and on Eugène Dupont, a member of the IWMA General Council, and on his family's jaunts to Paris. Naturally Engels sent the fares and on 25 May Eleanor and Marx left for Manchester, where he stayed for some three weeks and she for five months.

Only a short time before, in April that year, had Engels finally "cut the navel cord" with his life in the "gloomy city", giving up his rooms in Dover Street and moving finally into 86 Mornington Street, Stockport Road, Ardwick, where his household consisted of Lizzie Burns, now 43 years of age, her nine-year old niece Mary Ellen, known as Pumps, and the servant Sarah Parker.

Eleanor's relations with Engels had always been close. She

* The first ballot was held on 23 and 24 May, the second on 6 and 7 June. The Republican opposition polled three million votes—against 4,300,000 for the Government—and more than trebled their seats in the new Assembly which first met on 26 June 1869.

† Frederick Lessner (1825–1910) was a tailor by trade who, after a revolutionary career and imprisonment in Germany, emigrated to England in 1856. One of the closest friends of both Marx and Engels, he remained in touch with Eleanor to the end.

ELEANOR AT ABOUT 14
One recognises the adolescent's hope that a graceful pose
and a soulful gaze will proclaim to the world that there
is more to this rather plain young person than meets the
eye

ENGELS, COTTON MANUFACTURER, IN 1864

looked upon him as a second father: the giver of good things. From him had flowed wine and stamps and jolly letters all her childhood. She may not have been aware that to him she owed not only every holiday by the sea, all minuscule treats and luxuries, but the very food she ate: she knew that he was the soul of loyalty and generosity to her family and that his beneficence embraced herself.

Not every member of the family was on terms of equal intimacy with him. After 25 years of friendship, during the greater part of which she had lived at his expense, Mrs. Marx still addressed him as *lieber Herr Engels* in her far from effusive letters. Though invited to do so, Jenny had never once stayed with him in Manchester and there is no evidence that Laura went there either. Only once, in the spring of 1855, following the death of her son Edgar, did Mrs. Marx visit Engels with her husband. But to Eleanor he had been "My dear Frederick" from her earliest years. Their correspondence, referred to though not apparently preserved, had been at its liveliest when she was eight, but it never ceased and she was said to know by heart the six letters he wrote to her when she was ill in 1868. He had also impressed upon her early in life that not to answer letters was "unbusinesslike" and occasionally she had acknowledged his letters to her father. Thus it had come to her knowledge that he sometimes sent Marx five-pound notes (cut in two halves).

§ 2

Engels was now 48 years of age. Well over six feet, this handsome, fair, strongly-built Westphalian was neatly characterised when addressed by Paul Lafargue as "my ever-laughing Engels".[10] An enthusiastic rider to hounds, a mighty walker and a deep drinker, Engels was of an equable temper, a man with a tender and chivalrous regard for women, turning a blind eye to the imperfections of those who successively held the reins of his household. He took things in his stride and constantly found in people with whom he had otherwise nothing in common qualities that were "jovial" or "genial", detecting in them a kindred streak.* It was indeed the ease and grace of his style that gave harmony to his many-sided life as active revolutionary, astute businessman and a master of political, economic, scientific, historical and military theory. His erudition owed nothing to a university education. Though in his private correspondence he was capable of criticising with brutal frankness the stupidities and ineptitudes of others, he used the rapier rather than the bludgeon in his polemical writings and, large in all things, he never descended to petty malice. He suffered fools patiently provided their hearts were in the right place. His venial tolerance was sometimes interpreted as lack of judgment. He scorned to misuse his superior intellect to browbeat or discourage and he took infinite pains with the tiresome and the bungling, the jejune and the wrongheaded, so long as they did not positively harm the cause of revolution, though he had no illusions about their capacity to learn and shrewdly estimated those who were and those who were not fitted to interpret and disseminate Marx's theories correctly. If lack of judgment means that to attain a human end one must accept and work with such fallible human material as offers itself, then Engels was guilty; but he could be a stern teacher of tactics and few came up to his standards.

* See Appendix 3, p. 300.

Life never gave him much opportunity to "take it aisy", in the words of his own favourite maxim, but like most people of imperturbable temperament who have too much work to do, he found time for everything and did it with zest, whether translating Humpty-Dumpty into Latin, *The Vicar of Bray* into German, annihilating the pretensions of others,* writing his outstanding works on science, philosophy and economics, his articles on current political and military matters, or, during the last twelve years of his life, devoting himself to the immense task of ordering the endless pages of manuscript which were to become the second and third volumes of *Capital* left unfinished when Marx died.

It was during Eleanor's stay with him in 1869 that Engels finally threw off the servitude to commerce he had voluntarily entered upon 19 years before in order to support and further Marx's work.

In 1837 Engels' father had become a partner of the three Ermen brothers—Peter, the founder of the cotton manufactory in Lancashire, Anthony and Godfrey—one mill operating in Engelskirchen near Cologne, the other in Eccles near Manchester. In 1842, at 22 years of age, the young Engels had been sent to England to learn the business, arriving a few months after a general strike of the Lancashire cotton workers. He was employed at the Victoria Mills in what was then known as Pendlebury Without in the parish of Eccles[12] where he met and fell in love with Mary Burns, a mill-hand then aged 19, whose father, recently emigrated from Ireland, followed the trade of dyer. The product of Engels' two years' apprenticeship was *The Condition of the Working Class in England in 1844*, that earliest and still most telling social survey. Dedicating the 1st edition of 1845 to "The Working Classes of Britain", he wrote:

> "I have tried to lay before my German countrymen a faithful picture of your condition, of your sufferings and struggles, of your hopes and prospects. . . . I have . . . devoted my leisure hours almost exclusively to intercourse with plain working men; I am both glad and proud of having done so. . . . Having, at the same time, ample opportunity to observe the middle-

---

* A curious instrument called the rhigometer Engels demolished with the phrase that it served as "a measure not of temperatures either high or low but simply and solely of the ignorant arrogance of Herr Dühring".[11]

classes, your opponents, I came to the conclusion that you are right, perfectly right in expecting no support whatever from them . . . What have they done to prove their professed goodwill towards you? . . . Have they even done as much as to compile from those rotting Blue Books a single readable book from which everybody might easily get some information on the condition of the great majority of 'freeborn Britons'? Not they . . . . They have left it to a foreigner to inform the civilised world of the degrading situation in which you have to live. A foreigner to *them*, not to *you*, I hope. Though my English may not be pure, yet I hope you will find it *plain* English. . . ."[13]

The Manchester experience, his introduction into the world of Mary Burns, had given Engels a new and poignant awareness of "the cause of contemporary class antagonisms" and of the economic factors that made capitalism a scourge to the majority of men and women. He left England a confirmed revolutionary, pledged to the abolition of private property and to the violent overthrow of the ruling class. He was ripe for the most important event of his life which now occurred.

On his way back to Germany in 1844 he stopped in Paris for ten days (28 August to 6 September) and these he spent with Marx. The two men had met briefly in Cologne a couple of years earlier, but at a time when Engels was freshly caught up by the Young Hegelians and their club of "The Free" while Marx had outgrown that philosophy and was disenchanted with its adherents. The encounter had meant little to either Engels or Marx. Now, however, there was a fusion of interests, outlook and objectives. They began to work together on *The Holy Family* and so the basis was laid for that friendship and collaboration which were to determine Engels' entire future.

In the following year, 1845, he rejoined Marx in Brussels, where they collaborated on the writing of *The German Ideology* and spent the summer in England. Engels was able to initiate Marx into the workings of the most highly developed industrial country. On their return to the continent Engels took Mary Burns back with him. He now threw himself into political and revolutionary activity, writing *The Communist Manifesto* with Marx, contributing articles on France and Germany to *The*

Northern Star and, again with Marx, starting the publication of the *Neue Rheinische Zeitung* in Cologne.* In 1849 Engels took part in the armed uprising in defence of the German Constitution—voted but not put into effect—and directed the defences of Elberfeld. He fought in the campaigns in Baden and the Palatinate, crossing into Switzerland with the last of the defeated insurgent armies when the order for his arrest was out. After a short holiday in Italy he again rejoined Marx, now settled in London. There he stayed for a year, living at No. 6 Macclesfield Street,† within a stone's throw of the Marxes.

As the revolutionary wave of 1848 subsided it became clear to both men that the paramount need of the time was to broaden and deepen the theoretical principles of revolution, as a guide to future action, and that Marx was best fitted for this task. Thus, in November 1850, in deference and homage to Marx's gifts, Engels took the hard step of going back into the firm of Ermen & Engels in Manchester. As corresponding clerk and "general assistant" his salary was not large: £100 a year with 10 per cent of the firm's net profits, yet out of this he managed to provide for the Marx family. After ten years, following his father's death, he became the general representative of the Manchester branch and in 1864 a full partner. During all those years, despite long hours of hated work, he produced pamphlets, pursued researches into linguistics and military history, kept abreast with the new developments in science and technology, wrote articles for the *New York Daily Tribune* when Marx's English was still too imperfect and maintained by almost daily correspondence that friendship which had become his *raison d'être*, his life's blood.

His own part he considered negligible save in so far as it enabled Marx to work: this was the sole justification for remaining in commerce, that most senseless misapplication of human effort in his view. When at last he was within sight of his freedom, he wrote to Frederick Lessner in gentle rebuke for

* The organ of the Communist League, it appeared from June 1848 until May 1849 when proceedings were taken against it and Marx was expelled from Prussia. Thereafter six numbers, which published in 1850 Marx's *Class Struggles in France 1848 to 1850* and Engels' *The Peasant War in Germany*, were edited in London and printed in Hamburg.
† Macclesfield Street runs from Gerrard Street to what was then King Street, now Shaftesbury Avenue: the southern extension, as it were, of Dean Street. No. 6 was roughly in the centre of the west side.

compliments which were "the more embarrassing to me insofar as in the past 18 years I am afraid I have been able to do
practically nothing *directly* for our cause and have had to devote
all my time to bourgeois activity. Now, I hope, that will soon
be otherwise . . . and then I shall certainly do my part to deserve
your compliments, for it will always be a joy to me to fight at
the side of an old comrade like yourself on the same battle-
ground and against the same enemy."[14] He was resolved to
dedicate the rest of his days to the revolutionary movement.
"You have always known", he wrote to his mother with whom,
until her death in 1873, he maintained a loving and frank
relationship, "that I have never in any way changed the
views I have held for nearly 30 years and it can come as no
surprise to you that, when occasion demands, I should not only
speak out but do my duty in other respects. You would need to
feel ashamed of me if I did not. Were Marx not here, if he
did not exist at all, it would not alter the situation by one
jot."[15] Many years later, looking back, he corrected this assessment and said with dignified and reasonable modesty: "All
my life I did what I was made for, that is, played second fiddle
and I believe I acquitted myself tolerably well. And I was
happy in having so excellent a first violin as Marx."[16]

Now, in the May of 1869, on Eleanor's arrival in Manchester,
Engels was still tied to the firm. Since January he had been
negotiating the legal and financial terms of his release which
eventually took place on 1 July. Recalling that summer day
twenty-one years later Eleanor wrote: "I was with Engels
when he reached the end of this forced labour and I saw what
he must have gone through all those years. I shall never forget
the triumph with which he exclaimed 'For the last time!'
as he put on his boots in the morning to go to his office. A
few hours later we were standing at the gate waiting for him.
We saw him coming over the little field opposite the house
where we lived. He was swinging his stick in the air and
singing, his face beaming. Then we set the table for a celebration and drank champagne and were happy. . . ."[17]

§ 3

"Then we . . . were happy": Eleanor could have said this of her whole stay with Engels. Though there is little evidence for it, Marx was under the impression that her Paris life had been one of restraint. "Here," he wrote to Jenny from Mornington Street, "she feels quite at her ease, like a new-fledged bird"[6] and, a week later: "She looks quite blooming . . . a little longer stay will do her good."[18] If a round of pleasure does one good—as Engels for one firmly believed—then Eleanor was much benefited. There were fireworks at Belle Vue, an excursion to Bolton Abbey—including a stay at the Devonshire Arms— a week-end house party with friends of Sam Moore*; there were picnics and shopping expeditions, an evening at the theatre and tea-parties of bread and treacle. There was even a glimpse of the Prince and Princess of Wales when they came, the guests of the Earl of Ellesmere, to visit the Royal Agricultural Show at Old Trafford, on which occasion Eleanor hoped the children would greet the royal pair by singing "The Prince of Wales in Belle Vue jail for robbing a man of a pint of ale".[19]

Running through it all, like the green ribbon of the collar Tussy had made for her, was Lizzie Burns with her Irish lore; not only the old folk tales which Mary Ellen, her niece, recited, but more stirring stuff, for Lizzie now took Eleanor to the market and showed her the very stall where Kelly—one of the Fenian prisoners rescued from the police van two years before—had once sold pots. She saw the house where he had lived and heard "a great many amusing things about Kelly and 'Daisy'† whom Mrs. B had known quite well having been to their house and seen them three or four times a week".[19]

That the "so-called liberty of English citizens is based on the

---

* c. 1830–1912. An English lawyer, one of the oldest friends of Marx and Engels, the translator of *The Communist Manifesto* and co-translator of Volume I of *Capital*.
† Lizzie's way of referring to Deasy, the second rescued prisoner.

oppression of the colonies",[20] of which Ireland was the first with a history of 700 years of disaffection under "the most abominable reign of terror and the most reprehensible corruption"[21], was an article of Lizzie's faith. Like Engels in his youth, now Eleanor saw with her own eyes the conditions of the immigrant Irish in Manchester. A quarter of a century earlier Engels had written:

> "The rapid extension of English industry could not have taken place if England had not possessed in the numerous and impoverished population a reserve to command. The Irish had nothing to lose at home, and much to gain in England.... These Irishmen ... migrate for 4d. to England, on the deck of a steamship in which they are often packed like cattle.... The worst dwellings are good enough for them; their clothing causes them little trouble ... shoes they know not; their food consists of potatoes and potatoes only; whatever they earn beyond their needs they spend on drink. What does such a race want with high wages?"[22]

Since then the number of immigrants, and their distress, had been balefully multiplied by famine and evictions. Between 1846 and 1851 nearly a million Irish emigrated and, though Manchester was by no means their main destination, it is recorded that in one week during November 1847 the city paid out relief to 5,000 Irish paupers,[23] while in the decade 1851–61 "one-sixth of [Hibernia's] toiling sons and daughters perished by famine and its consequent diseases, and a third of the remainder were evicted, ejected and expatriated by tormenting felonious usurpers".[24]

Lizzie Burns exercised a lasting influence on Eleanor. "She was quite illiterate ... but she was as true, as honest and in some ways as fine-souled a woman as you could meet. She was the staunchest of friends", Eleanor wrote many years after Lizzie's death and but two weeks before her own.[25] What Lizzie meant to Engels he himself recorded in a letter to August Bebel's wife: "She was of genuine Irish proletarian stock and her passionate, innate feeling for her class was of far greater value to me and stood me in better stead at moments of crisis than all the refinement and culture of your educated and aesthetic young ladies."[26]

There was also another side to Lizzie: a freedom of conduct unknown in the Marx household and very stimulating to the young guest. As the summer advanced, the ladies, overcome by the heat "laid down on the floor the whole day, drinking beer, claret, etc.", which was how Engels found them in the evening when he came home: "Auntie, Sarah, me and Ellen . . . all lying our full length on the floor with no stays, no boots and one petticoat and a cotton dress on and that was all."[27] Drink, indeed, played an overflowing part in the Engels environment. Carl Schorlemmer, the distinguished chemist,* was a frequent visitor and, according to Eleanor, on one occasion "got so 'screwed' that we had to make a bed for him and he slept there too, for he couldn't get home", while in the same letter Engels was reported as having returned from a party "as drunk as jelly".[27] Inebriated men—and women—did not trouble Eleanor in the least: she accepted the current view that they were screamingly funny.

However, life in Manchester was not all uncorseted bliss and alcohol. Engels relinquished to Eleanor the task of teaching Mary Ellen to play the piano and he also set her a stiff course of reading. Starting with the Young Edda,† she went on to 14th century Serbian folk ballads, translated by Goethe, and then graduated to Goethe himself—*Herrmann und Dorothea*, *Goetz von Berlichingen* and *Egmont*—and by midsummer she was engrossed in Firdousi‡ though Engels doubted that she would get through the enormous tome.

Eleanor at this age, having always been the baby of the family, was still in many ways a child. Engels and Lizzie insisted upon addressing her as "Miss Marx", to cure them of which teasing habit she dropped the formal "Mrs. Burns" and called the couple "Uncle" and "Auntie", making them repeat "Tussy, Tussy, Tussy" 24 times until they—and Sarah Parker—had mended their ways. But while Engels devised such

---

* 1834–1892. Engels had known him for some years and wrote of him later to Bernstein (27 February 1883): "After Marx, Schorlemmer is undoubtedly the most eminent man in the European Socialist Party. When I got to know him . . . he was already a Communist." In 1874 the Chair of Organic Chemistry was specially created for him at Owen's College, Manchester, and he became an F.R.S.

† In the text of Frantz Eduard Christoph Diotrich's *Altnordisches Lesebuch*, Leipzig 1864.

‡ Author of the 10th century Persian national epic *Shah-nameh* (The Book of Kings), consisting of 60,000 couplets of which selections had been translated into German by both Adolf von Schack and Friedrich Rückert at that period.

playful mystifications as sending her a letter in a disguised
hand, to be posted by Marx from some improbable place, he
also went out for a walk with her each day and they enjoyed
a true companionship. They were in fact temperamentally
alike, sharing a sense of humour, gaiety, consideration for
others, good temper and commonsense.

The days and the weeks sped by so congenially that when, in
August, Marx wrote to say that the Lafargues were coming to
London he feared that Tussy would be on the horns of a great
dilemma: if she were not told that her nephew was there she
would have good cause to reproach Marx but would be torn
between her longing to see the baby and the delights of Manchester. Engels was not one to make heavy weather of such a
problem. "I have cut the Gordian knot over Schnaps", he
wrote, "and simply informed Tussy of the fact." Whether it
had caused her a tragic conflict he really could not say, but in
any case she had other things on her mind at the moment,
being distracted by toothache.

Eleanor elected to stay on and bear Lizzie company while
Engels went abroad for a fortnight in August. The day after
his return the three of them went to Ireland for a week, visiting
Dublin, the Wicklow mountains, Killarney and Cork. It
was thirteen years since Engels had been to Ireland with Mary
Burns* and great changes had taken place since 1856. He
would not have recognised Dublin harbour, he said; while
at Queenstown, formerly the insignificant Cove of Cork, which
had vastly expanded during the American Civil War, he
heard every conceivable language spoken on the quayside.

It was Eleanor's first visit to Ireland and it coincided with a
new upsurge of the national liberation movement. The immediate cause of this ferment in the summer and autumn of
1869 was the demand for the Fenian prisoners to be amnestied.
There were monster demonstrations: 30,000 people turned out
in Limerick, 200,000 in Dublin. The English government was
flooded with petitions demanding the release of the prisoners
whose treatment had long been a matter of public scandal.
Two years earlier Parliament had been forced to appoint a
commission of investigation whose report[28] drew from Marx

* On that occasion he had journeyed from Dublin to Galway and Limerick, then
down the Shannon to Tarbert and on to Tralee and Killarney.

the furious comment: "These filthy swine boast of their English
humanity because they do not treat their political prisoners
any *worse* than murderers, footpads, forgers and paederasts."[29]
Now, as Engels, Lizzie and Eleanor travelled through this
country whose ruinous depopulation was only too manifest,*
they found troops swarming everywhere, and everywhere, in
battle order, the Royal Irish Constabulary, armed with short-
swords, truncheons and revolvers. A field battery clattered
through the centre of Dublin. The whole of Ireland appeared
to be on a war footing. Although Engels' interest in the
subject had never ceased since his early encounter with that
"most horrible spot" in Manchester known as Little Ireland,
it was now that he decided to write a social history of Ireland
which, in Marx's view, would be a pendant to his *Condition
of the Working Class in England*.†

At last, on 12 October, Eleanor came back to London in
time for a brief family reunion: the Lafargues were there for
another six or seven days, having had to prolong their stay
because the baby had been ill and Laura, pregnant again, was
also far from well, while Marx and Jenny had returned only a
day before from their stay with the Kugelmanns in Hanover.
"Tussy has returned from Ireland a stauncher Irishman than
ever", Jenny reported to the Kugelmanns[32] and when the
petitions for the release of the Fenians had been refused by
Gladstone, Eleanor not only went but insisted upon her father,
mother and Jenny going to Hyde Park, where on 22 October
some 100,000 demonstrators protested. Jenny described the
event to the Kugelmanns: the vast crowds, the red, green and
white banners, the defiant placards—"Disobedience to Tyrants
is a Duty to God", "Keep your Powder Dry"—the "profusion
of red Jacobin caps" hoisted higher than the flags to the strains
of the *Marseillaise*, were all impressive and profoundly stirring.
Except to the press, which dismissed the whole affair as "an utter
failure". It was Marx who pointed out its real significance:
"The main feature of the demonstration had been ignored,
it was that at least a part of the English working class had lost

---

* "Since 1841 the population has dropped by two and a half millions, and over
three million Irishmen have emigrated. All this has been done for the profit of
the large landowners of English descent, and on their instigation."[30]
† Engels collected material for this work for a period of two years but was unable
to complete it.[31]

their prejudice against the Irish."[33] Eleanor had been excited
by the crowds, and this was perhaps why she turned out to
mingle with them when Queen Victoria opened Blackfriars
Bridge and Holborn Viaduct on 6 November.* This, she found,
was a very different and a sullen crowd, "staring sourly at
Madame". It was put about that handbills had been distributed
in the East End calling upon the famished workers to present
themselves *en masse* before their sovereign on this public occasion. It may have been a hoax, but the police were taking no
chances and by sheer force of numbers crushed the breath out
of the spectators, thus stifling their loyal cheers.

Fresh from her Manchester training Tussy tried to persuade
Marx to take a daily walk with her. He neatly turned the tables
by giving her the alternative exercise of putting his chaotic
study to rights, which at least served the purpose of giving them
much time together at a moment when, for the newly founded
Land and Labour League and for the General Council of the
IWMA, Marx was drafting material on the Irish situation. In
the midst of this, on 25 November, Jeremiah O'Donovan
Rossa,† one of the leading Fenians serving a life sentence in
Chatham gaol, was elected M.P. for Tipperary. Eleanor was
not the only one to go "mad with excitement" over the success
of this convicted felon who, though ineligible to take his seat
in the House of Commons, changed the whole nature of the
campaign. "It forces the Fenians to abandon their conspiratorial tactics and the staging of minor *coups* in favour of practical
activities which, though seemingly legal, are far more revolutionary than anything they have done since their unsuccessful
insurrection", wrote Engels.[34] Even before the Tipperary results
Marx had proposed a resolution to the General Council of the
International which was passed on 2 December saying that
Gladstone "had deliberately insulted the Irish nation; that he
clogs political amnesty with conditions alike degrading to the

---

* The 18th-century bridge, fast sinking, was demolished in 1864 and a temporary
structure took its place. The new bridge, built at a cost of £400,000, was designed
by Joseph Cubitt. Since the name is not unknown in modern times it is of interest
to record that an earlier Cubitt—William, the father of Joseph—was the inventor
of the prison treadmill. He also drew up plans to house the 1851 Great Exhibition
in Hyde Park. His plans were never adopted but he was knighted for his pains.
† The business manager of *The Irish People*, a paper issued in Dublin from November
1863, he had been arrested together with the editors, Thomas Luby and John
O'Leary, on 15 September 1865.

victims of misgovernment and the people they belong to" and expressing "admiration of the spirited and high-souled manner in which the Irish people carry on their amnesty movement".[33] Before the year was out this resolution was communicated to all branches of the IWMA in Europe and America and was published in London, Leipzig, Geneva and Brussels.

Gradually and grudgingly, under the pressure of the swelling movement inspired now by the IWMA and O'Donovan Rossa's unprecedented situation, Gladstone granted a shabby conditional amnesty to the Irish patriots at the end of 1870.

Living at the heart and centre of the campaign, endlessly discussing the subject with her two great masters and listening to discussions between those better informed than herself, Eleanor, too, shifted her slightly romantic Fenianism on to the basis of political realities. She began to understand the import of Marx's words to Kugelmann: "The English working class . . . can never do anything decisive here in England until it separates its policy towards Ireland in the most definite way from the policy of the ruling classes . . . not as a matter of sympathy with Ireland, but as a demand made in the interests of the English proletariat", [35] and his pronouncement that "any nation that oppresses another forges its own chains".[33]

"Here, at home, as you are fully aware, the Fenian sway is paramount. Tussy is one of their head centres. . . ." So wrote Marx to Laura and Paul early in March 1870.[36] Though Home Rule for Ireland was a question insular only in the literal sense, Eleanor in the next two years was to become personally involved in Continental politics and the Fenians, though never banished, yielded pride of place to the French. She and her sister Jenny were infatuated with what Mrs. Marx called *"la grrrrande nation"*, adding that they would soon get over it. But they did not.

Engels had decided in February to move permanently to London by the autumn. He was influenced partly by Lizzie's wish to leave Manchester, where she was squabbling with her relatives, and partly, it may be, by a confession wrung from Mrs. Marx at the cost of two points of exclamation. "How often over the years, *lieber Herr Engels*, have I silently wished you were here!! Many things might have been different." She was referring to Marx's ill health, caused by the incessant overwork that she was powerless to restrain and to which, at the age of 51, he now added learning the Russian language. With more than goodwill Mrs. Marx set about househunting for Engels.

Tussy's visit to the Manchester *ménage* in 1870 was thus her last, nor was it a long stay, for she was supposed to be at school again and this must have been regarded as a mere fortnight's mid-term break. Engels for his part seemed to have thought it a fine joke to propose that the time had come for her to be gainfully employed. "I am *very* much obliged to you for sending that advertisement", she wrote to him. "The situation is one that will suit me very well, so I shall lose no time in applying for it. You will I am sure give me a reference."[37]

Shortly before she went to Manchester in May, a plebiscite was held in France to test the support for Napoleon III and

his "liberalised" Constitution, the questions being so framed
that to vote against the Bonapartists was in effect to dissent
from any measure of democratic reform. The result was a foreseen victory for the Emperor in all the constituencies except
Paris, where the opposition won a small majority of 45,000.*
Laura reported that the excitement was intense: the smell of
war was in the air.

The reality was not long delayed. Napoleon III announced
war on the Prussians on 15 July, the declaration was delivered
to Berlin on the 19th and on the 29th hostilities opened.
Between these latter dates Marx had written the General
Council's *First Address on the Franco-Prussian War*, including the
words:

> "Whatever may be the incidents of Louis Bonaparte's"
> [Napoleon III] "war with Prussia, the death knell of the
> Second Empire has already sounded in Paris. . . . On the
> German side, the war is a war of defence, but who put Ger-
> many to the necessity of defending herself? Who enabled
> Louis Bonaparte to wage war upon her? *Prussia!* It was
> Bismarck who conspired with that very same Louis Bona-
> parte for the purpose of crushing popular opposition at
> home and annexing Germany to the Hohenzollern. . . .†
> If the German working class allow the present war to lose
> its strictly defensive character and to degenerate into a war
> against the French people, victory or defeat will prove alike
> disastrous."38

This penetrating analysis was reflected quite soon in British
public opinion. The popular enthusiasm for the Prussians
was dissipated as they crossed the frontiers, 200,000 troops
advancing before August was out, systematically sacking, burning and plundering French villages and shooting all *francs-
tireurs*. Among English crowds the singing of the *Wacht am
Rhein* was drowned by that of the *Marseillaise*. "Of course",
commented Marx in a letter to Kugelmann, "the English did
exactly the same in India, Jamaica, etc., but the French are
not Hindus, Chinese or Negroes nor are the Prussians heaven-

---

* The total vote for the Bonapartists was 7½ million with 1½ million against, but
there were close on 2 million abstentions.
† On 18 January 1871 Wilhelm I, the Hohenzollern King of Prussia since 1861,
became the first Emperor of Germany.

born Englishmen . . . Whatever the outcome of the war", he went on, "it has trained the French proletarians in the use of weapons and that is the best guarantee for the future."[39]

On 2 September 1870 at Sedan, an unimportant little town in the Ardennes noted only for its manufacture of black cloth,* the decisive battle of the war was fought. It raged from dawn until dusk, ending with the capture of Napoleon III, 39 of his generals, some 3,000 officers, 28,000 men, the destruction of MacMahon's army and the downfall of the Second Empire.

Two days later, on 4 September, the Third French Republic was proclaimed. Although it marked the end of nearly two decades of the imperial rule that had produced unprecedented riches for the rich and poverty for the poor, the new Republic was not in any sense a progressive administration being almost entirely in the hands of those who had shamefully betrayed the 1848 rising.

The *Second Address on the Franco-Prussian War* was written between 6 and 9 September, that is, in the days immediately following Sedan when, in Engels' view, the war was over to all intents and purposes. It was again an accurate assessment of the situation, penned when the English newspaper reader had barely caught up with the events themselves. Indeed, the political journalist, or "commentator" as he is often called today, who devotes so much energy to stoking hatred of Communism could well take a lesson from its founders who were also masters of his meaner trade.

Though Marx wrote this document Engels had provided much material for it. Since the end of July he had been contributing regular articles to the *Pall Mall Gazette*† under the title "Notes on the War", many of which were plundered, without acknowledgment, by the other London papers: perhaps as an honorary tribute to the leading military theorist of the time.

It was these articles, for which he received 2½ guineas apiece —half of which he declared he owed and therefore paid to Marx, while Eleanor, "the ferocious girl", and Jenny laid claim to the "first spoils of the war as brokerage"—that earned Engels the nickname of "General" by which he was known to his

---

* It was also the centre of the German armoured breakthrough on 14 May 1940.
† Founded in 1865.

intimates for the rest of his days. Originally it had been "General Staff" and arose from "a comical mistake of *Le Figaro* which paper showed its gross ignorance by speaking of the General Staff as if it were an individual",[40] meaning General von Moltke.

Though he continued to write his articles until February of the following year Engels was now actively preparing his move to London. From Ramsgate, to which the Marxes and Lenchen travelled by sea to spend the last three weeks of August, Tussy wrote to him: "I suppose you know that last Tuesday Mohr and Jenny went to look for houses."[41]

They need not have done so: Mrs. Marx had not merely inspected and reported on a number of possible places long before but in July she had indeed found a house near Primrose Hill for £60 a year which she heartily recommended. Eleanor and Jenny gave it the stamp of their approval and Marx advised him to take it: London was beginning to swarm with French refugees, bringing their money to safety, and "gentlemen's residences" would be in great demand—the price of house property was already rising—so that, despite the risks of taking and furnishing a place on a three-and-a-half years' lease at this time of uncertainty, Engels would always be able to dispose of it.

Thereupon Mrs. Marx and Lenchen with a keen eye to economy set about supervising the alterations, renovations and decorations of the house, which they lauded for its pleasing and attractive situation: near enough to the shops for Lizzie's convenience yet, at the very front door, an open space and the sight of thousands of Londoners taking the air. It was a four-storeyed house* with a basement, though modest in comparison with the Marxes' place. As the time for Engels' arrival drew near Mrs. Marx was suddenly abashed by this fact and wrote imploring him to stay at Maitland Park for a few nights until all was in order. There was plenty of room for his entire household: "After all, we live in a veritable palace and, to my mind, far too large and expensive a house."

Engels moved on 20 September 1870 and lived at 122 Regent's Park Road for the next 24 years.

This was not the only move that preoccupied the Marxes

---

* Still extant, still near to small shops and still with an unimpeded view of Primrose Hill.

at that period. Laura's second baby, a daughter, had been
born on the anniversary of the first but had survived only two
months, dying at the end of February. She was pregnant again
and now she, Paul and their little son were living at 7 Place de
la Reine Hortense,* Levallois-Perret, one of the most vulnerable
areas close to the fortifications and liable to be "among the
first casualties of the war" as their small house was threatened
with demolition should things take a turn for the worse. "They
will not listen; let us hope that they will not feel", and, on the
day Sedan was fought: "Those idiotic Lafargues' delay in
beating a retreat to Bordeaux is inexcusable", Marx wrote in a
passion. But in fact, as the family soon learnt, the idiotic
Lafargues had left Paris just before and in mid-September it
was known that Paul had brought out a journal, *La Défense
nationale*, in an attempt "to stir up the drowsy inhabitants of
Bordeaux".[40] His efforts were vain, however, and within a
couple of months the paper expired.

At the same moment of time Paris was completely invested,
Wilhelm I making his headquarters at the Rothschild's *château*
near Lagny, 18 miles outside the city. Versailles surrendered
and on 11 October the first three shells were fired on Paris.
From 7 November no one was permitted to enter or leave and,
after a siege lasting 135 days, starving Paris capitulated. The
armistice was signed at midnight on 27 January 1871.

* On 5 January 1872 this was renamed Place Cormeille until the liberation of 1945
when it became Place Anatole France under a communist municipality. The
succeeding social democratic local authority gave it its present name of Place
du Général Leclerc in the 1950s.

122 REGENT'S PARK ROAD, ENGELS' LONDON HOUSE FROM 1870 TO 1894

GUSTAVE FLOURENS

§ 5

The short-lived Paris Commune which lasted from 18 March to 28 May 1871 was to have far-reaching consequences, both public and private, for the entire Marx family and not least for Eleanor herself.

At the beginning of March, even before the Peace Treaty was signed, the Prussians staged a 48-hour token occupation of Paris, whereupon the National Guard—the proletarians trained in the use of weapons—seized and removed the cannon, bought with its own subscriptions, to the heights and outlying quarters of the city. An overwhelmingly reactionary National Assembly had been brought to power by an election rushed through on 8 February, before the war-weary and famished population had had time to rally. Headed by Thiers and installed at Versailles by grace of the Prussians on 18 March, the government sent troops to recapture the 400 guns now fortifying Montmartre. These were the opening moves in a Civil War and a second siege of Paris that was to claim 50,000 victims at the hands of their compatriots among the defenders of the Commune, who died in street fighting, indiscriminate slaughter, in cellar prisons, on transportation in coffin ships, in New Caledonia, in exile, on long terms of imprisonment and deportation.*

By the end of April "the shells, the bombs, battered the casemates, the grapeshot paved the trenches with iron"[43] and the defenders of Paris, with the connivance of the Prussians but no foreign intervention, were being mowed down, prisoners shot out of hand, and civilians massacred in greater numbers and with more appalling savagery than in any fratricidal conflict then known to modern times.

The Marxes were deeply affected: their oldest and best friends were involved in the carnage and they learnt with

* 70,000 others, the dependants of the killed and proscribed, who were deprived of their means of livelihood, fled the city, thus Paris lost 120,000 of its working population.[42]

horror of the hideous death of Gustave Flourens, "the bravest of the brave", as Mrs. Marx called him.[44] He had not fallen in battle, as was first reported, but had been murdered on the night of 3 April when, fighting under the command of the ineffectual Bergeret,* Flourens had continued the advance towards St. Germain while the two other columns had been surprised by artillery fire and forced to retreat. At the end of a gruelling day, unarmed and resting near the bridge at Chatou, he was denounced and surrounded by mounted gendarmes, of whom one, named Desmarets, dragged him to the river bank and, rising in his stirrups, cleft his head with a sabre stroke.

Flourens, the son of a Professor of Physiology, and himself a widely travelled ethnographer and scientist who, for a time, deputised for his father at the Collège de France, was a combination of scholar and man of action. A fervent revolutionary who "knew no division of mankind but of the oppressor and the oppressed",[45] he had fled to England in the spring of 1870, implicated in the alleged plot to assassinate Napoleon III. The French government demanded his extradition, which Gladstone refused. While in London he frequented the Marxes, beloved by them all and a particular favourite with Jenny.

Back in Paris when the Republic was proclaimed, Flourens stood as a candidate in the local government elections of 5 November 1870 and became vice mayor of the 20th *arrondissement* (Ménilmontant), which district again returned him as a deputy to the Commune on 26 March 1871.† On 30 March he

---

* Jules Bergeret (1820–1905) was on the General Staff of the National Guard and in charge of military operations in Paris. Having failed to reconnoitre before leading his troops to disaster in the direct line of the enemy's batteries, he was relieved of his functions and imprisoned from 8 to 12 April.

† The Central Committee of the Federation of the National Guard had taken control on 18 March. A week later it stood down to make way for an elected body of local deputies: the Commune. The election was held on 26 March and the results were published in the *Journal Officiel* of 27 March (though not officially announced until the next day). They showed the following returns for the 20th *arrondissement*:

Ranvier	14,127
Bergeret	14,003
Flourens	13,498
Blanqui (who was in gaol and elected *in absentia*)	13,338

The first three were appointed to the Military Committee and Ranvier (1828–1879), who was also a member of the Executive Committee of the Commune, became the heroic defender of Buttes-Chaumont (the 19th *arrondissement*) in the final assault. He was condemned to 20 years hard labour *in absentia* in 1871 and sentenced to death in 1873 for setting fire to public buildings. Returning from exile in 1879, he died a month later.

was appointed to the Military Committee with the rank of colonel. He was aged 33 when he was killed.

At this juncture and weighed down by such tragic events, Eleanor went to France with Jenny, arriving in Bordeaux on 1 May. Why she went is not altogether clear, though the circumstances provide grounds for reasonable conjecture. Certainly Laura was in need of help. Her third baby, a boy, had been born early in February and, like the little daughter who had died, was far from strong. Paul had gone to Paris in April "to obtain from the Commune *des pleins pouvoirs* to organise the revolutionary army in Bordeaux"[46] and had written to say that he was on his way home, but he did not arrive and nothing further was heard from him. This was hardly surprising since, though postal communications within the capital and the telegraph service had been restored by the middle of April,[47] the Versailles government was determined to isolate Paris from the provinces, to which end not only had railways been cut off but newspapers and letters were regularly intercepted and confiscated.*[48] Despite these good reasons for Paul's silence and failure to return, Laura was apprehensive, lonely and also alarmed when the baby now fell dangerously ill. Jenny's impulse, on learning the news, was to join her sister at once and "I do not mind confessing that in case of opposition on the part of my parents, I resolved to go off on the sly", she wrote.[46] She was dissuaded, however, by the fact that she would not be able to enter France without a passport and accepted the advice of her father and "Staff", as she now called Engels, to wait for the slow route by steamer. Probably, though Eleanor at the age of 16 could not offer much protection, it was thought wiser that Jenny should not make the journey alone at such a time.

On their arrival they found Paul back in Bordeaux, but as May advanced, and the Commune entered the Bloody Week of its final defeat on 25 May, making its last stand in the Père Lachaise cemetery,† it became imperative for the Lafargues

---

* All stamps were removed to Versailles from the Paris post offices, so that letters were franked, as they had been a century earlier, with a stroke of the pen.

† It will be noted that the final and fiercest resistance to the government troops, who had entered Paris on 5 May, took place in precisely those eastern districts of the city which had become working class strongholds as a result of Haussmann's enterprise. The National Guard, composed of male—and female—civilians in

to move. Paul was a marked man and no active supporter of the Commune was safe from the "legal" executions, wholesale denunciations and indiscriminate arrests now in full swing. Accordingly the four of them, with Schnappy and the sick baby, went to Bagnères-de-Luchon in the Haute-Garonne, a small town of some 4,000 inhabitants, close to the central Pyrenean range at the confluence of the rivers Ône and Pique, developed in the 18th century, with hotels, lodging-houses and a small casino, as "a place of fashionable resort".

Here they lived in complete retirement, seeing no one except the doctor whose services were in daily demand for the infant. On 13 June Marx who was, as he emphasised, *"in possession of full information"*—being in close touch with the progress of events through a German businessman, probably N. Eilau, who travelled constantly between Paris and London—wrote a carefully worded letter to his children recommending them to move to a better climate on the Spanish side of the Pyrenees. Paul's health in particular "will deteriorate and may even incur great danger if he any longer hesitates to follow the advice of medical men who know everything about his constitution and have besides consulted his doctors at Bordeaux, etc." He added that in London "the cousins from the country", meaning the Communard refugees, "are thronging its streets. You recognise them at once by their bewildered air. . . ."[49] Despite this very clear warning, Paul remained at Luchon for another six weeks. The reason is not far to seek: on 26 July, at six months old, the baby died. Within a few days, having been informed that his arrest was imminent, Paul crossed the frontier into Spain by mule path from Luchon by the Port de Portillon to Bosost, an ancient and rather derelict town 25 miles away. On 6 August the three sisters and Laura's little son went to visit him there. They had intended to go only for the day, but Schnappy was now ill with dysentery and Laura had to stay behind. Jenny and Eleanor, however, went back to Luchon that same evening.

Eleanor now takes up the story: "Jenny and I on returning from Bosost . . . were arrested on the French frontier and conducted by 24 gendarmes right across the Pyrenees from

arms, was locally based and assigned to the defence of the *arrondissements* from which its units were drawn.

Fos to Luchon, where we were staying. Arrived there we were driven to the door of M. de Kératry's house,* kept waiting in front of it in an open carriage with two gendarmes opposite us, and goodness knows how many around us, for three quarters of an hour, and then taken to our own house. At our house we found the police who had in the morning searched the house from top to bottom, and had treated our poor landlady and our servant who were alone in the house very badly. Kératry had already cross-examined them, and we were informed that he would presently arrive to do the same for us. At last he came, for he wouldn't leave the *parc* till the band stopped playing. Our room was already full of gendarmes, *mouchards*, and agents of every description when the *Préfet* Kératry arrived accompanied by Delpech, *procureur général*, a *juge de paix*, a *juge d'instruction*, the *procureur de la République*, etc. I was sent with the Commissaire de Toulouse, and a Gendarme, into a side room and Jenny's examination began, it being then about 10 o'clock. They examined her over two hours but to no use for they heard nothing from her. Then came my turn. Kératry told me most shameful lies. He got one or two answers from me by pointing to Jenny's declaration, and telling me she had said such and such a thing. Fearing to contradict her I said 'Yes, it is so'. It was a dirty trick wasn't it. However he heard precious little with all that. The next day when they came again we refused to take the oath. Two days after Kératry came and said he should in the evening send orders for our liberation (we were guarded by the police). Instead of that we were taken off to a 'gendarmerie', and there we passed the night. The next day we were, however, let off. Though we could not really move a step without being watched, besides we couldn't get back our English passports. At last we got everything, and arrived at last in London. Laura went through much the same adventures at Bosost, though not quite as bad as we, for she was in Spain. It appears that Kératry after the first evening did everything he could to get us free but Thiers wished us to be imprisoned. What was very amusing were the blunders Kératry and the police made—

---

* Emile, Comte de Kératry (1832–1905) was the first Police President of Paris under the Third Republic from 4 September 1870 till 12 October 1870, and Prefect of the Department of the Haute-Garonne in 1871.

E

for instance they looked in the mattresses for bombs, and thought that the lamp in which we had warmed the milk for the poor little baby who died, was full of '*pétrole*'! And all that because Lafargue is Mohr's son-in-law . . .".[50]

Marx, as he himself declared, had "the honour at this moment to be the best calumniated and most menaced man of London",[51] being accused of having instigated and controlled the Commune.

Jenny gave an even fuller account of the Luchon incident in a letter to the editor of *Woodhull and Claflin's Weekly*, written in September and published on 21 October 1871. From this it appears that the same "dirty trick" as had been played on Eleanor—the very use of this term betrayed her ignorance of police methods, pardonable in one so young—was first tried on Jenny who had been informed that the Lafargues were under arrest. It also emerges that Eleanor's interrogation lasted until two in the morning: something of an ordeal, as Jenny commented, for "a young girl of 16, who had been up since five a.m., had travelled nine hours on an intensely hot day in August, and only taken food quite early in Bosost". They were refused permission to write to their parents and Kératry was reported as having said to Jenny: "As for your sister and yourself, there is much more against you than against M. Lafargue and in all likelihood you will be expelled from France." The two girls were taken into custody on the following day at 11 p.m. and remained in the gendarmerie barracks, locked in, until five the next afternoon when Jenny demanded to see Kératry who explained that he had done them a kindness by confining them in the police station as "the government would have sent you to the prison of St. Godins, near Toulouse". Their passports were not returned to them for ten days after this, though they had received a *laisser-passer* to cross into Spain on 10 August. They were accused in the Toulouse press of being "emissaries of the International on the French and Spanish frontiers, 'But . . . the Prefect is taking energetic measures in order to reassure the inhabitants of the Haute Garonne'."

Laura remained tied at Bosost by her ailing child, and when the police broke into her bedroom at three in the morning Paul escaped by the back door, was guided by peasants over mountain routes and gained the Spanish interior, only to be arrested in Huesca. On the day they learnt this news their passports were returned to the girls who decided to go to Huesca to allay Laura's fearful anxiety. They reached St. Sebastian where they heard that Paul had been released on 21 August. They immediately set off for London.

Writing to Kugelmann on 31 October Jenny added several other details concerning the episode, including the fact that Laura's little boy had been so ill at the time that they had thought he was dying, and that a letter found on her by the police had been written to O'Donovan Rossa,* and was "an answer to his *shameful* condemnation in *The Irishman* of the Communal movement. I expressed my surprise that *he, of all men,* should believe the infamous calumnies against the Communists, invented by the wretched police organs. . . ."[52]

One point emerged only after Jenny's death. In an obituary article by Engels published on 18 January 1883 in *l'Egalité* he stated that, when arrested, Jenny was carrying in her pocket a letter from Gustave Flourens. Had it been found it would have been a sure passport to New Caledonia for both girls. Left alone in the police station for a moment, Jenny had swiftly inserted the letter between the leaves of a dusty old ledger left lying about. "Possibly it is still there", he added.

It is of some interest that, when arrested, Jenny should have been carrying these two letters—one to the exiled Fenian, the other from the murdered Communard—for she herself was the link between them. Rossa recalled that "while in prison in England I was treated pretty harshly and publicity of my treatment was the only protection I had for my life. There was a French exile in London named Gustave Flourens. He became interested in my case—more interested than many Irishmen."[53] Jenny had interested Flourens, "who would have died for the cause of Fenianism", in this particular case and he translated the *Irishman*'s account of Rossa's treatment for the *Marseillaise*,† to which paper Jenny contributed articles on Ireland under the pseudonym "J. Williams". "I do not know Rossa,"

---

* O'Donovan Rossa had been released from prison on 5 January 1871 together with other Fenians but, forbidden to return to his own country, went to America where he edited the *Irish World* and *United Ireland*.
† A daily paper, the organ of the Left Republicans, published in Paris from December 1869 to September 1870. It was suppressed by the Government between 18 May and 20 July 1870.

wrote Flourens in the *Marseillaise*, "but I love him for his simplicity, the calmness and firmness with which he relates his frightful tortures." It is small wonder that the Irishman's attacks on the Frenchman's cause should have angered Jenny, the more so since the one was safely on the other side of the Atlantic where, according to his own account, he had been received with "deputations, invitations, addresses and congratulations",[53] while the other's mutilated corpse had been thrown into a dustcart and gloatingly paraded through the streets to Versailles.

6

If the outer eddies of the defeated Commune had caught up with Eleanor in the Pyrenees, she found herself on her return to Maitland Park Road at the centre of its vortex. She had now read her father's *Civil War in France*, drafted during Bloody Week and presented to the General Council of the IWMA on 30 May: two days after the dislodgment of the last defenders of the Commune on the slopes of Belleville. This *Address* became at once both the target for the most vicious attacks upon its author and the magnet which drew the Communard refugees to his house. Marx's admiration for the first proletarians to seize power had been expressed much earlier in a letter to Kugelmann. "What flexibility, what historic initiative, what capacity for sacrifice", he exclaimed. "After six months of being starved into submission and brought to ruin by internal treachery rather than by the external enemy, they rise. . . . History has no like example of a like greatness." These people were "storming heaven" and it was "the most glorious deed of our Party",[54] even if it were to be crushed.

Crushed it was and, from the end of May, larger and ever larger numbers of those who had escaped massacre and deportation flocked to London, "without clothes on their back or a farthing in their hands".[52] Their needs were imperative and Marx and Engels turned themselves into an *ad hoc* relief committee, raising funds, writing to potential employers, pacifying landladies whose refugee tenants could not pay the rent and appealing to foreign sections of the International for help. "You have no idea what we have been through here in London since the downfall of the Commune", wrote Mrs. Marx. "All the nameless misery, the unending distress."[55]

"There are a great many members of the Commune here and the poor refugees suffer frightfully", wrote Eleanor to Liebknecht, "they have none of them any money and you can't think how difficult it is for them to get work. I wish they'd

taken some of the millions they're accused of having stolen."[56]
The fact was that, although on 16 April there had been a
Hyde Park demonstration in support of the Commune, British
public opinion had veered with the gales of atrocity stories
blown up by the press* and the defenders of Paris were looked
upon with "unmitigated horror". It came to Marx's ears that
the Home Office had been asked by the French government to
arrest and extradite the refugees so that they could be prosecuted for civil crimes; if they took work in England under
assumed names they were dismissed as soon as their identity
was known; their sufferings were "beyond description . . . they
are literally starving in the streets of this great city" and, while
they congregated in idleness and poverty in a bare club room
at No. 40 Rupert Street in Soho, "for more than five months
the International . . . supported, that is to say, held between
life and death the great mass of exiles".[57] Such was the prejudice
against them nourished by the hostile newspapers that when the
first anniversary of the Commune came round, they were
refused the use of a meeting place and "not *allowed* to meet in
any hall in London".[58]

Eleanor has left a graphic description of that occasion, written
twenty-one years later:

"No doubt few of you remember . . . the condition of perfectly frantic fury of the whole middle class against the Commune. To many of you it will seem strange when I remind you
that it was proposed—quite seriously—that the Communards
who had taken refuge in England should be handed over to
the doctors and the hospitals for purposes of vivisection. Perhaps exceptionally brutal in form, this proposition nevertheless
largely expressed the feelings of the whole of respectable society.
Saddest of all is the fact that in England the workers also, with
rare exceptions (just as there were some middle-class exceptions
among the Comtists) were as bitterly hostile to the Commune
as their exploiters. And so it was but a small knot of English
men and women who on that first anniversary came to meet

---

* "Up till now it has been thought that the growth of the Christian myths during
the Roman Empire was possible only because printing was not yet invented.
Precisely the contrary. The daily press and the telegraph, which in a moment
spread inventions over the whole earth, fabricate more myths . . . in one day than
could have formerly been done in a century", wrote Marx to Kugelmann on 27
July 1871.

the 'foreigners'—most of them persons escaped from Paris—
and to celebrate the memory of the Commune.* But that
meeting never came off at all. When we got to the Hall we
found it closed against us.† The landlord preferred to return
the deposit and to pay a penalty for breach of contract to
allowing such a set of 'ruffians' in his highly respectable Hall.
Then the said ruffians . . . adjourned to a modest inn,‡ and
sat down together to an improvised—and not luxurious—
supper. And . . . despite the tragic horrors of that terrible year;
despite the fact that most of these men and women had passed
through deadly peril, that they were miserably poor, exiled,
not a few suffering from still unhealed wounds; that there was
hardly one among us who had not lost some near and dear to
us, or—worse still—who had not some dear friend, who had
not father or mother, sister or brother or child rotting in the
horrible pontoons or on the awful plain of Satory; despite all
this we were a merry party. In the midst of so much suffering,
immediately after this overwhelming defeat, these men and
women were gay with the gaiety of perfect faith. . . . Alas!
to many the hour of triumph was never to come, never even
some small sign that it was approaching. Of all that goodly
company few are left now. Yet through the long years of waiting
and of exile they did not lose heart. . . . While all the world—
in England even the working class world—was thus against the
Commune, one great organisation stood by the revolutionists,
holding aloft the red flag. That organisation was the International Working Men's Association. In Spain, in Italy, in
Belgium, in Switzerland its members went to prison for expressing their sympathy with the Commune; in Germany not only
were they sent to prison, but when Moltke made a triumphal
entry in Berlin, the workers received him with cries of 'Long
Live the Commune' and were charged and dispersed by cavalry.
In England certainly many members withdrew from the
Association, but some remained faithful, even after the General
Council had issued its now world-famous pamphlet *The Civil*

---

* Those present included Marx, Eleanor, John Hales, George Milner, Martin
Boon and the Communards Vaillant, Frankel, Theisz, Serraillier, Longuet,
Lissagaray, Vallès, Ranvier.
† This was St. George's Hall, Upper Regent Street, famous from 1905 as housing
Maskelyne's Mysteries or "Home of Magic".
‡ The Cercle d'Etudes, Francis Street, off Tottenham Court Road.

War in France. This pamphlet, like nearly all the publications of the International, was written by my father, and is unquestionably the most valuable contribution to the literature of the Commune. To the brilliancy of its style even the reactionary press bore witness, although they did call its author 'infamous' and many demanded a State prosecution. It was then that my father publicly acknowledged himself as the author, though it was, of course, signed by the 'Council'. If the reactionary press admitted the literary excellence of the work, the Communards declared it to be a clear expression of what the Commune really meant, and had put clearly even to themselves, what they had only felt vaguely. . . . But while this pamphlet will tell you the true meaning of the revolution of 18th March, and will remind you of the unparalleled heroism of its defenders, there is one thing this pamphlet cannot tell you—for it was written in 1871. And that is the way these men and women lived —that, almost without exception, the after lives of these Communards were worthy of their cause. To fight heroically is much . . . But how many are there who can be heroic not for a day, an hour, but every hour, of every day, in the long weary years? Yet these people bore hunger and privation, disappointment and the agony of hope deferred without faltering or falling. All honour to their memory! . . ."[59]

Those who have mingled with the political refugees produced by the scourges of the present century will understand that there is no real contradiction between Eleanor's tribute to the spirit of the Communards, written in the light of memory, and Engels' words, penned in September 1874: "All these people want to live without any real work, their heads full of alleged inventions that are supposed to make millions if someone will put them in a way to promote these inventions, for which only a few pounds are needed. But should anyone be obliging enough to comply, he is not merely done out of his money but decried as a bourgeois into the bargain. . . . The disordered life during the war, the Commune and exile have hideously demoralised these people and only sheer hard necessity can bring a disorganised Frenchman to his senses. The great mass of anonymous French workers on the other hand has abandoned politics for the time being and found work here."

To the time-consuming activities on behalf of the refugees which left him no peace, day or night, Marx added a tremendous burden of work on the General Council, often attending its sittings till one in the morning, and was further distracted by the need to answer personal calumnies and defeat attempts to suppress the IWMA, accused of having instigated the murder of the Archbishop of Paris and setting fire to the French capital. While Engels had been forced to lay aside his researches into Irish history, Marx, far from continuing to write the next volume of *Capital*, was not even able to revise the first volume for its second German edition, now urgently demanded by Meissner. Eventually, in July, a sub-committee of the General Council was set up to issue appeals and collecting sheets and to give aid to the refugees, drawing in such middle-class Comtists, to whom Eleanor refers, as Edward Beesly, Frederic Harrison and Thomas Allsop. Marx and Engels served on the committee until early September when, coincident with Eleanor's homecoming, foreign delegates began to arrive for the London Conference of the International,* some of whom were given hospitality by Marx and by Engels.

Eight of the leading members of the Commune had been elected to the General Council of the International in August, including Charles Longuet,† Albert Theisz,‡ August Serraillier§ and Edouard Vaillant,‖ who became close friends of the family, while a new London-based section, *Section française de 1871*, was formed in the autumn, to be almost at once torn by internal strife, its 24 members indulging in bitter recriminations and the mutual denunciation of agents and police spies, not altogether without foundation, but nonetheless suicidal. Thus Eleanor's return from abroad in September 1871 was a time of turbulence both within the home and outside.

In all these years there have been but few glimpses of Eleanor's personal friends. She played in the street with the neighbours' children, she gave a small party, she romped with the young Freiligraths and caught infections from her schoolfellows but, since there was no occasion for correspondence

* Held from 17 to 23 September 1871.
† Had previously served on the General Council from 1866 to 1867 and now remained a member from 1871 to 72.
‡ A member and the Treasurer from 1871 to 1872.
§ A member from 1869 to 1872.   ‖ A member from 1871 to 1872.

with any but the little Alice Liebknecht of long ago, almost
nothing can be known now of her relations with people of her
own age. Was she as popular with them as with the grown-ups
who visited her father? Several of these went out of their way
to send her their greetings when they wrote. Henri Perret, a
Swiss engraver and member of the IWMA in Geneva, spoke of
Marx's two charming daughters—Jenny and Eleanor—as
"true international women who could serve as a model for
many of our women".[60] This was written when Eleanor was not
yet 16. Anselmo Lorenzo, the founder of the Spanish section
of the IWMA, wrote that he retained "the most pleasant
memory" of Tussy and laughed when he talked of "the conversation he had with her on the way to the post".[61] In his book
El Proletariado Militante[62] Lorenzo described this occasion:
"When I expressed my wish to send a telegram to Valencia to
report my safe arrival in London, Marx's youngest daughter
was sent with me to show me the way. I was most surprised
by the alacrity with which the young lady helped a foreigner
whom she did not know, this being contrary to the customs of
the Spanish bourgeoisie. This young lady, or rather girl, as
beautiful, merry and smiling as the very personification of
youth and happiness, did not know Spanish. She could speak
German and English well but was not very proficient in French,
in which language I could make myself understood. Every time
one of us made a blunder we both laughed as heartily as if we
had been friends all our life."

It is thus enlightening to find a letter, undated, but from
internal evidence written sometime in the summer or autumn
of 1871, to "My dearest Eleanor" from a certain "Aggie", then
aged 19.[63] The letter reveals a long-standing friendship and
one intimate enough to allow of confiding family troubles.
The writer, it emerges, is a Miss Agnes Frances C. The surname
is not given, but it is just conceivable that she was a Cunningham: a younger member of that family which, eight years
before, had offered to find posts for Jenny and Laura as
governesses and, in 1866, had asked them to be bridesmaids at
their daughter's wedding.* Miss C. has a bullying father, most

---

* The father in that case was quite possibly Dr. Cunningham, Sanitary Commissioner to the Government of India, who is known to have been home on leave in
1870. (See *Florence Nightingale* by Cecil Woodham-Smith.)

of the time in India, a spying mother, almost always at home, and innumerable "Reverend uncles" including "old Bishop T.". From this unpromising background the daring girl hopes to escape. She is dying to fight on the barricades; both she and Annie, her sister aged 15 who writes a postscript to this letter, are passionate revolutionaries and have read with attention the International's statement on the Civil War[64] which, by virtue of its force and clarity, Aggie attributes to Eleanor's father. She is, however, critical of the Geneva Programme of the International,[65] which she does not believe he can have written—as, indeed, he had not—arguing that it was foolish to propose abolishing God if He did not exist and that the equality of women could not be achieved by decree but must depend upon their being entitled to work like men. With such ideas and interests it is small wonder that Miss C. finds the "abominable home tyranny" irksome; this very letter has had to be smuggled out by a housemaid, given a diamond as a bribe, and she is under the necessity of "contriving means" by which she can continue to correspond with Eleanor. Her plans to run away, for which she steals £10 from her mother's desk, are foiled by a treacherous brother, Willy, who turns up from Brighton at the very moment of the theft of which, naturally, a servant is accused so that Aggie has to confess, whereafter an even closer watch is kept upon her. Horrid schemes are afoot to marry her off, but what she really cares about is the political situation—particularly that in France— and both sisters are authors, the elder having completed a work called *Rich and Poor* and being now engaged for the past year upon a long story, while Annie has written an excellent tale called *Home Rule* ("not Mr. Butt's!" Aggie exclaims).

The interest of this communication, which is signed "Yours for ever", lies not so much in the fact that Eleanor should be on close terms with young people of so totally different a social environment as that, leaving aside the farces and melodramas of that *milieu*, revolutionary politics should be the basis of this friendship in which Eleanor was clearly the dominant partner. While at this age she still, in letters to and from her adult correspondents—whether Marx, Engels, Liebknecht or others —seems young for her years, "Aggie" redresses the balance and shows that, among her equals and those slightly older,

Eleanor was regarded as a fount and source of political wisdom.

Returning to the letter written on the 22nd anniversary of the Commune, when Eleanor used the phrase "many members withdrew from the Association" she was indicating the seeds of dissolution within the First International which, following the Hague Congress of 1872, was transferred to New York where it suffered a lingering death, to be formally buried in 1876. "The fall of the Commune placed the International in an impossible position", wrote Eleanor in an obituary article on her father.[66] Much later she spelt this out in a letter to Kautsky saying that, to put it shortly, "there had been internal disintegration going on . . . almost from the end of the Commune"; that the quarrels among the French refugees had created difficulties enough, but that the defection of such people as Howell, Odger and Lucraft—the last two refusing to sign the General Council Address on *The Civil War in France* and resigning over this issue—had rendered the situation untenable. In face of opposition, Marx, she said, had remained firm on the matter of transferring the International to New York. "He said [its] *real* work is *done*, we must not outlive ourselves and fall ignobly to pieces; the end must be voluntary and decent." Though he had admitted it only to his intimates, Marx had known full well that it was the finish. Eleanor went on to say that she had been aware of all that was going on at the time and that for some two or three years her father had kept the "discordant elements" together by sheer strength of will. "He was far too keen-sighted not to know that such a keeping together was no longer possible."[67]

Eleanor's perfectly truthful account is not, of course, nor did she claim that it was the whole story. In particular it omits the role of the anarchists who, under Bakunin, had from as early as 1867 tried by every means to "conquer the leadership of the International"[68] and in 1871 captured the demoralised sections of the French political exiles in both London and Geneva. Engels put the matter in clear perspective when, with the demise of the International in New York in 1874, he wrote to Sorge to say that it was well that it should be at an end: "It belonged to the period of the Second Empire . . . It was the moment when the common, cosmopolitan interests of the proletariat could be put in the foreground. . . . Actually in 1864* the theoretical character of the movement was still very confused everywhere in Europe, that is among the masses. German Communism did not yet exist as a workers' party, Proudhonism was too weak to be able to insist upon its special fads,† Bakunin's new stuff-and-nonsense had not so much as entered his own head yet, even the leaders of the English trade unions believed that the programme . . . gave them a basis for coming into the movement. The first great success was bound to burst asunder this naive combination of all fractions. This success was the Commune, unquestionably the intellectual child of the International, although the International did not lift a finger to bring it about. . . . For ten years the International dominated one side of European history—the side on which the future lies—and can look back on its work with pride . . .".[69]

Combined with the wider issues at stake was also the fact that Marx's own position was fast becoming "untenable". "As long as he remains on the General Council", wrote Jenny to Kugelmann, "it will be impossible for him to write the second volume of *Das Kapital*",[70] adding that he had made up his mind to give up the secretaryship after the Hague Congress. His involvement with the refugees had been deep and personal, for he never forgot what it was to be a political exile, and when their disruptive activities bedevilled the General Council it was with bitterness that he wrote to Sorge: "This is my thanks for losing almost five months in work for the refugees and for saving their honour by the Address on the Civil War!"[71] On the same day, in a letter to Nikolai Danielson in St. Petersburg, he said: "Certainly, I shall one fine morning put a stop to all this, but there are circumstances where you are in duty bound to occupy yourselves with things much less attractive than theoretical study and research."‡

* The year when the IWMA was founded.
† Although the Proudhonists had formed the majority, the Blanquists the minority, on the Central Committee of the Commune.
‡ One of these much less attractive things was a vituperative exchange of letters with Charles Bradlaugh who had given a lecture for the benefit of the French refugees and used the occasion to misrepresent passages of the *Civil War in France* and to attack "the Communists". Over £7 was collected at the meeting, but the refugees returned it as dishonourable to accept aid from "a man who had traduced and insulted them". While Marx told Bradlaugh that he had nothing to do with this incident and, on the contrary, thought the money should have been accepted in order not to offend the English workers who had given it, he was angry about the attacks which were "either stupid or malicious" and he had decided they were the latter.[72]

Marx bowed to circumstances until the situation within the International and external political events combined to justify calling a halt. "How much better and happier it would have been for him had he quietly gone on with his work", wrote Mrs. Marx to Liebknecht. "And as for our private life, what ruin, what torture! Just at a time when our girls needed help."[73]

7

The reason why the girls needed help, or at least that some notice should be taken of them at this juncture, was that in March 1872 Jenny became engaged to Charles Félix César Longuet, Lafargue's former fellow-student, born at Caen, Calvados, in 1839. Under the Commune he had been a member of its Labour Committee and the editor of its official *Journal* until he applied for his release to take up military service.* At the same time Leo Frankel—a Hungarian socialist whose election to the Central Committee of the Commune as deputy for the 13th *arrondissement* (Gobelins), the head of the Labour and Trade Committee and a member of the Finance Committee, had demonstrated that there was no narrow nationalism among the defenders of Paris—was much drawn to Eleanor.†

"There is great rejoicing now in your family over the Longuet business", wrote Engels to Laura who was in Madrid where she and Schnappy had rejoined Paul in February. "Tussy, too, is very pleased about it and looks as if she should not mind to follow suit."[74] She did not merely look, she acted; but not in response to Frankel's marked attentions. Instead she became engaged to Lissagaray, a dashing character and one of the Commune's boldest fighters who was not, however, favoured by the Marxes as a son-in-law.

Jenny's engagement on the other hand elicited not only general approval but also Mrs. Marx's particular brand of eulogy and optimism. Longuet was "a very gifted and a very good, fine, proper man", she wrote to Liebknecht and, since the young people held the same views and convictions, "their future happiness is guaranteed". In the same letter she reported,

* In July 1866 he had been arrested in France while staying in Bagnères-de-Bigorre in the Pyrenees and imprisoned for eight months. He translated into French Marx's *Inaugural Address* to the IWMA and his *Civil War in France*.
† Frankel (1844–1896) shortly transferred his attentions elsewhere: to the Russian exile Elisaveta Tomanovskaya, known as Dmitriyeva, who had taken an active part in the Commune, and whose marriage to Ivan Davidovsky—either before or after the birth of her child—in 1874 came as a blow to Frankel.

with emphasis, that Tussy was *"lively and well* and a politician from top to bottom".[75] There was not a word of her attachment to Lissagaray. It was simply ignored. Indeed, although her engagement, entered upon secretly at first, lasted for nine years, there is only one recorded instance of her mother openly announcing it,[76] while her father refused to recognise it altogether. Possibly Lissagaray's nationality was against him, for Mrs. Marx, despite her bliss, expressed some anxiety about the Longuet alliance on that score: "I had sincerely hoped that Jenny's choice (for a change) would have fallen on an Englishman, or a German, rather than a Frenchman, who, combined with the national qualities of charm, is naturally not without their weakness and irresponsibility."[75] She also complained bitterly to Becker about French chauvinism: "if one does not choose to believe their pack of lies and French fiddlededee, which I find impossible to do, one is considered a 'Prussian' ."[77] Also, it must be borne in mind, Frenchmen—quite apart from carrying off two of his girls—had been a terrible nuisance to Marx in the recent past. Again, Lissagaray was seventeen years older than Eleanor: exactly twice her age at that point of time. But, above all, it was his flamboyance—the very quality that attracted Eleanor—which made him ineligible. Marx did not trust him. "I ask nothing of L.", he wrote to Engels, "but proof, not phrases, that he is better than his reputation and that one has some justification for relying upon him."

While preparations were in train for the Hague Congress, which Marx regarded as "a matter of life and death" for the International, another matter of life and death touched the family even more nearly as Laura's little son, her only surviving child, lay slowly dying in Spain. For a time Schnaps rallied, but by June all hope was relinquished and the end came early in July. Jenny's wedding, planned for that month, was postponed and the Lafargues travelled *via* Portugal to Holland where Marx and his wife met them on 1 September.* The Hague hotel registered and the police recorded the presence of "Karl Marx and wife with their daughter Laura and her husband Paul Lafargue".[78]

---

* The Hague Congress was held from 2 to 8 September 1872. Paul Lafargue was the official delegate for Spain and Portugal.

PAUL LAFARGUE IN LATER LIFE

CHARLES LONGUET

ELEANOR AT ABOUT 18

While her parents—and Engels—were abroad, Eleanor at home received a long scrawl from "yours lovingly, Maggie"[79] which throws out many dark hints concerning Eleanor's apparently tangled love life and sheds little light. "You may be sure he is under some restraint, perhaps some promise", wrote Maggie. This would account for "a change of tactic" that was admittedly puzzling but might be all for the best in the long run, though presently making Eleanor miserable. If she saw "*him*" she would do all Eleanor asked and lose no opportunity to put in a good word. "I hear Frankel is very attentive to you", she went on, "well after all he has always been so, if he did not show it always because he was afraid of being strangled by J.J."* The letter makes it clear that the families of the two girls were on terms of friendship and that the purport of this correspondence must be kept secret from the parents on both sides, though it is a little hard to say what they could have made of it. It does, however, suggest that Maggie was keen to smooth the course of true love for some contestant who had been warned off the field, and that can have been no one but Lissagaray.

Jenny was married at the St. Pancras Register Office on 9 October 1872 in the presence of Engels and Albert Theisz, she being then 28. Longuet, though not more than 33 or 34, appears on the marriage certificate as 38 years of age. More reliably this document states that he was a journalist residing at 132 Malden Road and that his father was a deceased hosier. The wedded pair then moved to "orthodox, snobbish Oxford", where Longuet hoped to establish a connection as a teacher of French but gave up after six fruitless weeks which had not produced a single pupil.[80] It was to Jenny in Oxford that Eleanor wrote early in November complaining of the offensive manner in which the Lafargues—recently arrived in London— behaved towards Lissagaray. They had "treated him to a very cold bow" when introduced at her parents' house, but Eleanor had attributed this to "a certain *gêne* at a first meeting". On

---

* The unknown strangler, evidently another of Eleanor's admirers, cannot be identified but may have been Jules Johannard (1842–1888), a Communard member of the General Council of the IWMA, who had reached London in November 1871. Another possible candidate is Jules Joffrin (1846–1890), a metalworker who was also a Communard refugee in London at the time, but he nowhere figures in the Marx circle.

taking their leave, however, they were equally distant while, on a second occasion, they shook hands with everyone else present and pointedly omitted Lissagaray. Eleanor was nettled: "Either Lissagaray is the perfect gentleman Paul's letter and his own behaviour proclaim him to be and then he should be treated as such, or else he is no gentleman, and then ought not to be received by us—one or the other—but this really unladylike behaviour on Laura's part is very disagreeable. I only wonder Lissa comes at all. He told me, too, that he would come one day this, or early next week to read me some extracts from the second edition of his book which is shortly to appear."[81]

By the spring of 1873 the whole situation had become "very disagreeable" indeed and reached a climax. Towards the third week of March Eleanor went to Brighton with her father. In reply to a cheerful letter, Mrs. Marx wrote to her there on the 25th, giving news of Jenny, then three months pregnant, and an account of various meetings at one of which, badly chaired by Maltman Barry, Alfred Milner had spoken, a number of difficult Frenchmen had threatened to walk out because the documents under discussion and the resolution proposed were not translated, while Lissagaray had insulted Ranvier, and Roullier* had made an uncouth joke at Marx's expense.[82] The tone and content of this letter assume that Eleanor would wish to be kept in touch with all that went on during a brief absence and, indeed, it expresses the hope that this " 'dead' fortnight" will do her good.

But on 1 April Marx came home alone leaving Eleanor in Brighton where she was determined to stay and earn her own living. That this decision was neither premeditated nor planned is clear.

Two days after Marx's return to London her mother is writing to Eleanor to say that she will send on "a little outfit" as soon as possible, that for the first week—the length of time it might take her to find a post—she had enough to wear and could always buy herself a few pairs of stockings in Brighton. "Be brave, be courageous", wrote Mrs. Marx. "Do not let this fearful crisis overwhelm you. Believe me, despite appearances to the contrary, nobody understands your position, your conflict,

* A Proudhonist Communard who was said never to have read Proudhon.

your embitterment better than I do. Let your young heart triumph and remember that where the *guilt* lies there also lies the heaviest suffering. . . . Forgive me if at times you have felt that I hurt you. . . ." There is much in this letter to suggest that Laura had played some part in the "fearful crisis", for the mother emphasises that whereas a sister may "cease to be and to feel as a sister", the child always remains the child, even if at fault and in the wrong. "The more at fault, the greater the compassion and sympathy", said Mrs. Marx and Eleanor's burden was the lighter in that she had nothing, or barely anything, with which to reproach herself.[83] But where the guilt lay, who was to blame, and for what, are not disclosed.

Eleanor had friends in Brighton—in particular a French socialist pastor and his wife named Pascal—through whom she hoped to get pupils. She also applied to an agency. "You see, I'm 'going in' for it with a vengeance", she wrote to Marx.[84]

Neither of her parents opposed this step, unforeseen though it was and taken at an age when her sisters had been looked upon as children whose smallest attempt to stand on their own feet had been frowned upon. Mrs. Marx, though now approaching 60, had greatly modified her views on this subject, writing to Tussy that "I alone understand how dearly you long for work and independence, the only two things that can help one over the sorrows and cares of present-day society".[85] She sent off Eleanor's wardrobe without delay, hoping she would "recognise her old friends again" and promising other things to follow. There was a great deal more about clothing which, her mother was sure, would bore Eleanor to tears because: "I know how little store you set by such things and how lacking in vanity and a love of finery you are."*[86]

Eleanor quickly found private pupils, who paid her 10s. a week, and throughout April she took all that came her way. She was also busy reading Polybius and asked her father for "some other of the old histories you promised me".[84]

But it was not until 5 May,† having turned down an offer

---

* In this connection it is interesting to note that, although Eleanor is shown as rather "dressy" on posed photographs—no casual snapshots, these—later evidence is that "she didn't go in for floating things . . . she wore severe, plain, simple clothes . . . always very neat and tidy . . . She wouldn't have looked good in frilly things".[87]
† i.e. The start of the summer term.

from another school, that she started in regular employment with the Misses Hall who ran one of the 14 seminaries for young ladies (there were also three for young gentlemen) in Sussex Square. She was not, of course, engaged to give instruction on the fundamentals of socialism or current revolutionary affairs, though she had the good fortune to find at least one pupil who took "an immense interest" in these subjects and for whom she begged a copy of *The Civil War in France* from her mother.[88]

Eleanor did not live at the school, but in lodgings, first at 2 Manchester Street* and then at 6 Vernon Terrace.† Mrs. Marx strongly approved her decision to stay with strangers rather than with friends who, like the Pascals, were involved in finding jobs for her, since if "business questions take on a sociable form . . . independence and freedom are lost".[85] In any case, although Eleanor liked Pascal, she did not much care for his wife of whom he seemed "to stand rather in awe".[84] Her attendance at the school was part-time and she continued with her extra-mural teaching, for she found that prices in Brighton were almost double those in London.

Throughout this period Mrs. Marx wrote constantly to "Tussychen" and, indeed, at no other period of their lives was the correspondence between mother and daughter so frequent or more loving. At the outset Mrs. Marx had doubted the wisdom of Eleanor taking the post with the Misses Hall. "The one thing that troubles me is the thought that your health is not strong enough to recuperate on the treadmill of a boarding school with its strict routine and drudgery of business. Mohr and the others are very glad about your success and earnestly beg you not to overwork."[86] She also feared that the food would be too stodgy and too coarse for Eleanor's ticklish appetite and kept on sending potted meat, chocolates and bottles of mineral water with the incessant plea: "Tell me what you would fancy"; "Let me know exactly what I should send you in the way of nourishment". The letters are equally concerned about clothes: "Next week I shall send you a light modern costume for church and promenade", also a new

* Now a motor tour office. Near the old Chain Pier, swept away by a storm in 1896, and replaced by the present Palace Pier.
† Now flats. Near the station.

canary-yellow cotton frock, her old summer dresses being too
shabby and washed out—"Shall I send you your black grena-
dine?"—"Shall I send you your black suit? As it is rather cheap
and common, you could wear it out for everyday. The skirt is
very trim"—while again and again she advises Tussy not to
stay too long in the water, to worry her head about funds or to
tire herself out by taking on more private pupils. Though there
are few references to Marx or the Lafargues in these letters,
there is much about Jenny whose late employer, Mrs. Monroe,
had died in April and who, despite a difficult pregnancy, had
become governess to the Manning family* and had placarded
every window in Chalk Farm advertising lessons in singing,
elocution "and the Lord knows what besides"[85] until, owing
to her "dimensions"—so embarrassing to her that she would
not go out until her mother had fashioned a polonaise† for
her—she finally gave up in June and turned to making baby's
clothes, as the "great catastrophe"‡ was expected—quite
erroneously—at the end of July.[89] Mrs. Marx also reported on
the little outings of the day: Lenchen was going to Astley's
Circus; she herself had been to the theatre and once or twice
to the "bonnefemme Redcap" for a drink with Lina Schoeler.

All these letters—homely, gossipy and solicitous though
barely legible§—show Mrs. Marx in a most kindly light, but
also that she regarded the whole Brighton episode as a prolonged if misguided form of convalescence. There is a hovering
anxiety about Eleanor's health: her chest is weak, her back
aches, her appetite is wretched, she is sleeping badly but,

---

* That of Laura's former suitor.
† *Shorter OED:* "A dress or over-dress consisting of a bodice, with a skirt open
from the waist downwards." Mrs. Marx had earlier proposed making such a gar-
ment for Eleanor too.[86]
‡ It is now clear that "catastrophe", in its sense of dénouement rather than disaster,
was used as an accepted euphemism for parturition, since it was applied not
only to the forthcoming birth of children like Eleanor (see p. 21) who, by reason
of hardships, might be seen as something of a calamity, but also to those joyfully
awaited.
§ "I fear you will have trouble deciphering my letter", wrote Mrs. Marx at one
point, "but at all events nothing is lost and it is good practice for you as a 'German
teacher'."[86] The truth is that Mrs. Marx's old German script is legible only to
people of high endowments. Although many of the originals were kindly put at
my disposal by the archivists of Moscow, Amsterdam and Berlin, the extracts
quoted here are taken from letters written in Latin script, in a mixture of German
and English, decoded (i.e. transcribed in typescript) or else the result of the most
arduous labour. I am still dumbfounded by the thought that Mrs. Marx was her
husband's calligrapher.

though recommended to take chloral, is warned in the next letter not to do so without medical advice and, in general, she is addressed as a semi-invalid. None of this emerges from any of Eleanor's traceable letters. While she promises not to overwork, she does not complain of her health nor appear to care about the advice and admonitions—or the garments—proffered. She enters little into her mother's chat concerning people and events in London, but reports on the weather in Brighton, her pupils and acquaintances in a cheerful yet colourless tone.

On 22 May Marx went for twelve days to Manchester to consult Dr. Gumpert. No sooner had he left than Mrs. Marx visited Eleanor in Brighton.* There she learnt from one of the Misses Hall that Lissagaray had been calling on Tussy at the school, which was allowed "since she was engaged". This put Mrs. Marx in a dilemma but she extricated herself by voicing neither objection nor denial, merely saying that the "position" ruled out anything definite for the time being. "The question of 'position' is understood by every English person", she commented, adding that Marx would not be told of this but would be writing to Tussy who, she hoped, would have her mind set at rest by his letter and was not to worry until she had heard from him.[90]

The parents were not wholly frank with each other about the situation. While Mrs. Marx could connive at Lissagaray's visits to Brighton, Marx was confiding only in Engels. He had been corresponding during these weeks with both Tussy and Lissagaray and, though neither his letters to them nor their replies have come to light, their content is indicated thanks to his absence from London and Engels' presence there at a critical moment.

The promised letter to Tussy was written from Manchester on 23 May, as he reported to Engels on the same day, concluding with the words: "for the moment Mr. L. will have to make the best of a bad job".† Unwisely Engels showed the

---

* Mrs. Marx rarely, if ever, dated her letters. Where dates are assigned to them these are based upon the internal evidence of known events referred to as having occurred "yesterday", "last Monday" etc. and worked out on a Perpetual Calendar. This method, whose accuracy is infallible, sometimes produces results that conflict with the dates given for these and other letters from Mrs. Marx in the various archives by whose courtesy they were read.

† Marx used the French phrase "*bonne mine à mauvais jeu*".

letter to Mrs. Marx who pondered over this last sentence for a long time but said nothing. Engels hastened to tell Marx that no harm was done since she could have made little or nothing of it "and, should she ask me, I shall simply tell her that you expressed the assumption that L. was not to be relied upon implicitly and therefore, even before you went away, you had spoken of writing to Tussy to try to influence her".

A week later Marx received a reassuring letter from Tussy, which he enclosed—together with one from Lissagaray—for Engels to read. He had told her there were no grounds for her accusation that he had been unjust to Lissagaray. "The damnable thing", he wrote on 31 May, "is that for the child's sake I have to tread very considerately and cautiously. I shall not reply until I have consulted you on my return. Keep the letter to yourself." With that return, on 3 June, the confidences are again verbal and the curtain comes down.

But while Eleanor and her father might try to sort things out by correspondence and otherwise conduct themselves as though nothing untoward—no "crisis"—had occurred; though she had written him a lively birthday letter for 5 May, quite as if their relations were not strained for the first time in their lives, the truth is that it made them both ill.

Since Eleanor was an 18-year-old, wildly in love and thwarted, it would be no overstatement to say that she was the greater sufferer. But it was Marx's illness that made news and, to his fury, Maltman Barry published in *The Standard* alarming reports on the state of his health which drew enquiries from all over Europe and made severe demands on Engels' powers of discretion, great strategist though he was. He assured Kugelmann that the rumours were grossly exaggerated, that Marx was merely suffering from the effects of overwork "attended by other unpleasantnesses". When Marx had decided to go to Manchester Engels had written a letter for him to take to Gumpert which, while giving every particular of his physical condition, deliberately left out any reference to the domestic upheaval that lay behind it. The Marxes were "very particular about family matters", as Engels wrote to Sorge when bidding him not to betray the great secret that Jenny was about to give birth.*

* This was written on 26 July 1873 at the end of which month, as is known, the child was confidently expected.

Despite her lack of formal qualifications as a teacher Eleanor was not only popular with the girls, as Mrs. Marx had observed on her visit, saying she had seldom met nicer children,[90] she also gave satisfaction to the Misses Hall who were outraged when, after scarcely a month, Mrs. Marx proposed that Eleanor should go abroad. Lenchen had received news that her sister was dying and she planned to leave at once for her native village. To Mrs. Marx, with her disdain for such paltry matters as the school term, nothing appeared more fitting than that Eleanor should accompany Lenchen, to benefit by the steamer journey down the Rhine and the simple country fare of St. Wendel. The Misses Hall argued that unless she could find someone to replace her, Miss Marx must carry on the duties she had undertaken. This struck Miss Marx's mother as thoroughly unreasonable. She proposed coming to Brighton again "to talk to the old maids" but was dissuaded and a tart exchange between one of the "old maids" and the mother ensued.

"Dear Madam", wrote Miss Hall, "I am much surprised and annoyed at your daughter requesting to leave me . . . without any notice whatever to enable me to supply her place. She tells me it is your wish that she should do so, at which I must confess I am *much astonished*. . . . With compliments, etc." To this Mrs. Marx retorted, at Jenny's dictation: "Dear Madam, I am much annoyed to hear you cannot spare my daughter . . . It is the opinion of our medical adviser, Dr. Matheson, that she requires a change of air and scene. I greatly fear that in her delicate state of health her school duties will be too trying for her especially during the very warm weather. I know my daughter has made no arrangement with you or contract to stay a certain time; however she nevertheless considers it would not be right to leave without having given due notice, etc., etc."[91]

While everyone was annoyed with everyone else Eleanor herself had no intention of falling in with the plan. "Under present circumstances", she wrote to Mrs. Marx, "I do not think of going home. Of course", she went on, "I shall be only too glad to see some of you, but I think you had better come some other Saturday or Sunday."[88] In the event, Lenchen was seen off alone by Marx some time in mid-June, having had to postpone her departure owing to her own ill health, and

Eleanor remained at Brighton until the end of the school term. She was at 1 Maitland Park Road again when Charles Félicien Marx Longuet was born there on 2 September 1873.

Back in the family circle there was no dodging the issue over Lissagaray whom Eleanor was now forbidden to see. Precisely when and why this interdict was laid upon her is not known. That it caused no serious breach between her and Marx is told by the fact that, both being far from well, they set off together on 24 November to stay for three weeks in what Mrs. Marx called "aristocratic German Harrogate".[92] As a health resort this was a great improvement upon Brighton, for here, under Dr. Andrew Myrtle—a Scot, a Jacobite and the author of a work entitled "On Jaded Brains"—Eleanor took Kissingen waters, baths and was prescribed complete rest and early nights. Marx's cure differed from hers only in that it included much vigorous exercise. Of an evening they "took refuge" in chess.

There is much that remains obscure about this passage in Eleanor's life; and not surprisingly, for not only did it take place in the bosom of the family, but on two separate occasions— once after Marx's death and again after that of Engels—letters of a private nature are known to have been destroyed, while the long Odyssey of the Marx and Engels literary remains has still not been told in full.[93] But some things are abundantly clear: this family row, this break, this bid for independence on Eleanor's part when she stayed in Brighton—her first experience of self-reliance—was in no way a "rebellion". As for running away with Lissagaray, the thought seems never to have entered her head; and, though Franziska Kugelmann claimed in her reminiscences[94] that he addressed Eleanor in letters as "*ma chère petite femme*", there is no evidence to suggest that she had or was prepared to set the conventions—or her parents—at defiance. On the contrary, the only direct evidence of her attitude points quite the other way and is contained in a troubled, sweet letter written to her father on 23 March 1874. Letters from girls in love to unrelenting fathers are not rare; they seldom plead their cause with a spirit so touching in its candour and affectionate obedience.

"My dearest Mohr,
I am going to ask you something, but first I want you to

promise me that you will not be very angry. I want to know, dear Mohr, when I may see L. again. It is so *very* hard *never* to see him. I have been doing my best to be patient, but it is so difficult and I don't feel as if I could be much longer. I do not expect you to say that he can come here. I should not even wish it, but could I not, now and then, go for a little walk with him? You let me go out with Outine,* with Frankel, why not with him? No one moreover will be astonished to see us together, as everybody knows we are engaged. . . .

When I was so very ill at Brighton (during a week I fainted two or three times a day), L. came to see me, and each time left me stronger and happier; and more able to bear the rather heavy load laid on my shoulders. It is *so* long since I saw him and I am beginning to feel so very miserable notwithstanding all my efforts to keep up, for I have tried hard to be merry and cheerful. I cannot much longer. Believe me, dear Mohr, if I could see him now and then, it would do me more good than all Mrs. Anderson's prescriptions put together†—I know that by experience.

At any rate, dearest Mohr, if I may not see him now, could you not say *when* I may. It would be something to look forward to, and if the time were not so indefinite it would be less wearisome to wait.

My dearest Mohr, please don't be angry with me for writing this, but forgive me for being selfish enough to worry you again.

Your
Tussy

This is quite 'entre nous'."[95]

* Nikolai Isaakovich Outine (or Utin) (1845–1883), a Russian revolutionary who had been a member of the student movement and of the underground organisation *Zemlya i Volya* (Land and Freedom). Emigrating at the age of 18 he remained in exile until the late '70s, when he returned to Russia. Marx referred to him as "one of my dearest friends". He married a fellow exile at the age of 35 when he was already suffering from the heart condition from which he died three years later.

† Elizabeth Garrett (1836–1917). Overcoming great difficulties she became the first woman to qualify as a doctor in England, her name appearing on the Medical Register in 1866. (Elizabeth Blackwell had been put on the Register in 1858, but, though English, she had qualified in America.) In 1869 Dr. Garrett was appointed to the staff of the North Eastern (Shadwell) Hospital for Children (later known as the Princess Elizabeth of York's Hospital, closed in 1963 and now demolished). Dickens visited and described the Hackney Road branch of this institution, "A Small Star in the East" (*The Uncommercial Traveller*) in 1868, the year it was opened. Dr. Garrett married James Anderson in 1871 and was admitted to the B.M.A. in 1873 where, for the next 19 years, she was the only woman. She became Eleanor's doctor some time in the early '70s.

8

Hyppolite-Prosper-Olivier Lissagaray, who never called himself nor was ever known by any but his surname, was born into
an old Basque family on 24 November 1838 in Auch, the chief
town of the department of Gers.[96] Nothing is known of his
childhood, but as a student he read classics and graduated
before he was 22 when he went briefly to America. On his return
to France at the end of 1860 he organised a series of lectures,
a kind of "popular university", which became celebrated as
the *Lectures de la Rue de la Paix*,* where progressive writers,
journalists and also professors who had been deprived of their
Chairs attracted large numbers of young people. Lissagaray
was bent upon reviving freedom of thought and speech in the
repressive first decade of the Empire. "Youth", he declared,
"must be earnest and austere rather than light-hearted, for
we have no time left to be young." He also launched the first
of his many ephemeral journals, *La Revue des cours littéraire* and,
in August 1868, founded *L'Avenir* in Auch, where in December
he was sentenced to a month's imprisonment for incitement
against the government and violation of the new press laws,
passed in March of that year as one of the pre-election measures
to silence the anti-Bonapartists. This was merely the first of
a series of arrests, imprisonments and penalties—amounting in
all to over two years in gaol and fines of some £150 before,
during and after the 1869 elections—on charges of "provocation, outrage and violence", "misdemeanour" and violations
of the laws on public assembly. While retaining the editorship
of *L'Avenir* in Auch he started *La Réforme* in Paris where he
held public meetings attacking the régime which earned him
a year's sentence for "offences against the Emperor". During
the first term of this captivity in Ste. Pélagie prison he wrote a
book called *Jacques Bonhomme: Entretiens de politique primaire*,
dedicated to the Democratic and Social Republic, which traces

* Later renamed the rue Cadet in the 9th *arrondissement* (Opéra).

the history, stage by stage, of Bonhomme, the eternally defeated common man who makes revolutions—for others. On his release Lissagaray compounded his political offences by championing the killer of a policeman, then issued a seditious appeal to soldiers to mutiny and, this time, to escape inevitable arrest, fled the country, remaining in Brussels until after the outbreak of the Franco-Prussian war and the first French defeats. He then returned to Paris and was among the crowd storming the gates of the Palais Bourbon* on 9 August 1870. Lissagaray now joined the army at Tours and saw fighting under Gambetta to whom he proposed a scheme of training camps for *francs-tireurs* at Toulouse where, in November, he was appointed Quartermaster to the army of the south-west, and, as such, was Gambetta's personal representative. His main self-imposed function as *commissaire de guerre* was to inspire the men, whom he proposed to accompany into battle, with patriotic fervour and a spirit of sacrifice. Impatient of his responsibilities for the clothing, equipping and provisioning of the troops, he remained at his post only until early January 1871 when he went off to fight with the 2nd army of the Loire under General Chanzy. There the armistice caught him unawares. He was demobilised before the rising of 18 March which found him back in Paris where in April he brought out a daily paper under the title *L'Action*, of which only six numbers appeared. This was followed in May by another of his short-lived journals, *Le Tribun du peuple*, which again lasted but a week. Then, abandoning these journalistic efforts, he joined in the street fighting, first in the 11th *arrondissement* (Popincourt) and later on the heights of Belleville where on Whit Sunday, 28 May, he defended single-handed for a quarter of an hour the last barricade to be manned (at the intersection of the rue de la Tourtille and the rue Ramponeau)†. When his ammunition

---

* The Chamber of Deputies, originally built in 1722 for the Dowager Duchess of Bourbon, was later enlarged at great expense for the Prince of Condé and declared national property in 1790. In 1814 it was restored to the Prince, but the Legislative Assembly, which had sat there, continued to use it, paying rent until the Government decided that it would be cheaper to buy it outright.

† "The last barricade of the days of May was in the Rue Ramponeau. For a quarter of an hour a single Federal defended it. Thrice he broke the staff of the Versaillese flag hoisted on the barricade of the Rue de Paris. As a reward for his courage, this last soldier of the Commune succeeded in escaping," wrote Lissagaray.[43] This anonymous marksman is always thought to have been Lissagaray himself since no other witness was present.

was spent he walked away and disappeared. It is not known how he escaped from Paris, but when he reached London—as he thought, undetected—he found himself among those whose arrest and extradition was immediately demanded by the French ambassador. Two years later, a military court sentenced him *in absentia* to deportation and confinement in a fortress.

From 1871 to 1880 he lived in exile. Thanks to letters intercepted, private papers searched and dossiers compiled by the Paris police,[97] it is known that Lissagaray's London address was 35 Fitzroy Street and that he was in regular correspondence with his former associates in France.

Aware that his letters were being tampered with, he thought to outwit the spies by having the envelopes addressed to "Evelyn Herbert". Naturally this failed of its aim, but the police, ever alert if a trifle confused, were now under the impression that Lissagaray was in correspondence with someone of that name, while Carl Hirsch* was reported to be in touch with a certain Herbert Velyan and also Herbert Evelin, residing in Fitzson Street, when not in Fitzroy Square. (Meanwhile Engels was thought to be living at 112 Regent's Park Road whose occupants must have been entranced to receive his well-thumbed mail.†)

But for all their insouciant ways with names and addresses, the police recorded most exactly the restaurants where their suspects lunched and the cafés they frequented (which proves that, given a congenial field of operations, police intelligence is of a high order and not to be misprized). Thus we know that on 29 May 1877 Monsieur N. Azane ("lunches every day at the Café de Madrid"‡) undertook to place Lissagaray's book

* Carl Hirsch (1841–1900) had taken over the editorship of the *Volksstaat* on Liebknecht's imprisonment in the spring of 1873 until his own arrest. Released in 1874 he went to Paris, where he remained for four years, going to Brussels in 1878 to edit *La Lanterne* which was smuggled into Germany. In 1875, in 1879 and on various other occasions he was in London.
† Oddly enough Engels himself made precisely the same mistake in writing to a Russian emigrée in Paris (Minna Gorbunova) in August 1880.
‡ This café in the boulevard Montmartre had long been regarded by the authorities as a meeting place for undesirable if not dangerous characters. In an illustrated volume on the Commune, with text written "By an Englishman, Eye Witness of the Scenes and Events of that Year", the Madrid is described as "the resort of a certain class of Parisian Journalists, more famed for the manufacture and circulation among themselves of current *bons mots* and passing flights of fancy involving delicate (and indelicate) innuendos than for the more solid parts of their pro-

in France and also that Herman Lopatin, one of the Russian translators of *Capital*, was an *habitué* of the Café Copenhagen in the rue d'Argenteuil where he made appointments to discuss subversive matters.

The postal department was splendid, too, if less constant in its vigilance than the café squad, so that there are some gaps in otherwise fascinating correspondence. Eleanor's letters, written in French, were faithfully transcribed[99] and on 12 May 1876 she expressed on Lissagaray's behalf the hope that both Hirsch and Naquet—who was planning to start a paper, *La Revolution française*, which finally appeared in October of that year—would come to London to discuss it: "Lissagaray writes to him of course but that is not the same thing as talking". In July Eleanor wrote two letters asking Hirsch to trace material needed for Lissagaray's book* and on 20 October she announced that the *History* was due to come out at the end of November, in which month† she told him to expect a visit from its publisher, Kistemaecker, to arrange for the book's distribution in Paris.‡

In 1877 Lissagaray wrote a whole series of letters to Hirsch about unspecified "socialist journals", which may well have included *L'Egalité*, since this weekly, edited by Guesde, appeared for the first time at the end of the year (November), and continued until the following July.§

Lissagaray's correspondents also included Henri Oriol, an employee of Lachâtre‖ and, in 1878, one of Marx's letters acquainted the police with the fact that Lissagaray was keeping him informed of events in France and of the attempts by Pyat's followers to rehabilitate posthumously "that buffoon" Thiers.¶

fession. It is the 'Exchange' of tales of the hour and the birthplace of much 'News' derived from 'authentic sources'. From the depths of 'bocks' consumed within its precincts, many a wild rumour startling Paris and echoing throughout Europe has been evolved".[98]

* Lissagaray required the full deposition made by Commandant Papillon and details concerning Bayard's part in the surrender of the fort of Vincennes which were to be found in the June 1872 files of *Le Radical* and in *Le Droit*.

† On 25 November 1876.

‡ She adds, unconscious of absurdity: "This visit should not be talked about in case the police get wind of it."

§ 31 issues appeared. The paper was restarted in January 1880 as the organ of the French Workers' Party.

‖ The publisher of the first French edition of Volume I of *Capital*.

¶ Died of apoplexy at St. Germain-en-Laye on 3 September 1877.

As early as the end of 1871 the *Petit Journal* offices in Brussels
had published a small volume by Lissagaray under the title
Les huit journées de mai derrière les barricades—the work from
which he read extracts to Eleanor—in effect a preliminary
sketch for his classic *Histoire de la Commune de 1871*. In 1873 he
also brought out a pamphlet, *La Vision de Versailles*, which has
never been translated into English but has been described as
"a literary evocation of the nightmare of the Versailles judges
present at the resurrection of their victims".[1] His great work,
the *History*, which has made his name known and remembered,
was first published in Brussels by Henri Kistemaecker in 1876
at a moment when a Paris Congress, from which the first rudi-
mentary organisation of a French Workers' Party was to
emerge, disgraced itself by condemning the Commune.
Lissagaray's *History* came out in a German translation in 1878
and again in 1891 and 1894, while the English version, translated by Eleanor, appeared in 1886 and, in Lissagaray's defini-
tive edition, in 1898. He is said to have worked on this book for
25 years, constantly making fresh researches, assembling new
material and rewriting.

In the meantime, while taking part in the first London
anniversary meeting of the Commune in 1872, described by
Eleanor, Lissagaray was active in the campaign for the proscribed Communards to return to France. In July 1876 and
again in June 1878 he visited Jersey and, as soon as an amnesty was granted in July 1880, he finally went back to
Paris, where, in May 1882, he started a daily paper, *La Bataille
politique et sociale*. This paper had a longer life than its pre-
decessors, lasting full five months, but by no means a tranquil
one. At daggers drawn with Paul Lafargue—with whom he
had quarrelled violently in the early days of his exile in London,
thereby contributing to the crisis in Eleanor's affairs—and not
in sympathy with the French Workers' Party (*Parti ouvrier
français*) formed by Jules Guesde* and Lafargue in 1880,
Lissagaray allowed his paper to be used by their opponents

---

* Mathieu Basile, known as Jules Guesde (1845–1922), had been imprisoned under
the Second Empire and defended the Commune in his journal *Les Droits de l'Homme*,
published in Montpellier and suppressed in June 1871. He took refuge in Switzerland
and in 1877 founded *L'Egalité*. The programme of the French Workers' Party was
jointly drafted by Guesde and Lafargue with the help of Marx and Engels. (See
fn. p. 195.)

to foster private feuds. In October, with the connivance of the proprietor, Adigé, Lissagaray absorbed the Guesdist paper, *Le Citoyen,* of which he claimed sole editorship, having first turned out Guesde, Lafargue and Deville. A monumental rumpus ensued and for several days each issue of the paper appeared under a new title. The differences were never composed and Lissagaray continued to edit this paper until the competition of Guesde's *Cri du peuple,* revived in October 1883, put *Le Citoyen* out of business, whereupon he re-started *La Bataille,* only to be manoeuvred out of its editorship: "The same trick has been played on M. Lissagaray as he played on us . . . they are but following the glorious example he once gave them", wrote Paul Lafargue to Engels.[100]

In 1885, before he had been ousted from the paper, he used it to set up an aid committee for the disabled Communards, many of whom had been mutilated in the fighting or were suffering the after effects of transportation. A great admirer of Victor Hugo, he organised a contingent of these veterans to attend the writer's funeral,* carrying a red flag.

Twice Lissagaray stood in the Paris municipal elections, but was not returned, though on the second occasion, as a candidate for Montmartre in 1890, he polled a higher vote than one of his opponents, Charles Longuet.

For the next many years he devoted himself to the revision of his *History of the Commune* for the 1898 French edition and is not known to have played an active part in politics. On 25 January 1901, too weak to undergo the tracheotomy which alone could have saved his life, he died at 43 rue Richer, within a stone's throw of the scene of his earliest exploits in the rue Cadet. He was 62 years of age. Two thousand people came to his burial in the Père Lachaise cemetery, including both Vaillant and Longuet.

A hot-headed and undisciplined individualist of superb physical courage, a dead shot and an enthusiastic duellist,† Lissagaray was a colourful figure, with a flair for leadership and a supreme contempt for authority, who is never known to have written for any paper which he did not himself edit. He

* On 1 June 1885.
† In one sword duel, fought with a kinsman, Paul de Cassagnac, in 1868, he was wounded in the chest. In another, fought with Rochefort in 1889, both duellists were severely injured.

was a man of few intimates, possessed of a gift almost amounting
to genius for quarrelling with those he had, his friendships and
love affairs—except in the case of Eleanor—generally ending
"in a row and blue fire".[101]

As a frequent guest at Maitland Park Road in the '70s and
under Marx's tutelage, his views on socialism—which had been
of the utopian variety—underwent a change, but he boggled
at the corollary: the need for organised workers' parties. Thus
when he returned to his native land at the age of 42, to find a
political climate very different from that engendered by the
conspiratorial sects of the past, he was rejected by the revolutionaries who had begun to learn the more up-to-date lessons
of discipline and organisation. Dedicated, fiery and self-willed
he remained, but a self-appointed leader without a following,
owing allegiance to none, his star had set by the '80s, though
in his famous *History of the Commune* it still shines brilliantly.

In the Preface to the first English edition, translated by
Eleanor, he wrote in November 1877: "No doubt it is an exile
who speaks, but an exile who has been neither member, nor
officer, nor functionary of the Commune; who for five years
has sifted the evidence; who has not ventured upon a single
assertion without accumulated proofs; who sees the victor
on the look-out for the slightest inaccuracy to deny all the
rest; who knows no better plea for the vanquished than the
simple and sincere recital of their history. This history, besides,
is due to their children, to all the working-men of the earth.
The child has the right to know the reason of the paternal
defeats, the Socialist party the campaign of its flag in all
countries. . . ."[43]

9

The cure in Harrogate had helped to restore Eleanor but it had done little for Marx who was advised—not for the first time—to take the waters in Carlsbad. Accordingly he wrote to Dr. Kugelmann to say he hoped they might meet there in the summer and, towards the end of June, asked him definitely to arrange lodgings for Tussy and himself from mid-August.

Before that time was reached, on 20 July 1874, Jenny's little boy died—as he had been born—at his grandparents' home, of gastro-enteritis* at the age of eleven months. Eleanor had nursed him devotedly, earning Jenny's "deepest love and gratitude",[102] but she collapsed under the strain. Her parents were in Ryde on the Isle of Wight and Marx at once hastened to London on learning of Eleanor's condition, to be followed by his wife who arrived on the day the baby died.[103] The loss of this, the fourth grandchild, hit Marx hard and he confessed that, being so much cut off from the outside world, he felt the more emotionally involved in the life of his family circle. For some three weeks Eleanor was dangerously ill and was attended daily by Dr. Garrett Anderson. Then she began to improve, her appetite growing "in geometric proportions", according to Marx who went on to say that one of the curious features of women's ailments "in which hysteria plays a part" was that you had to affect not to notice that the invalid lived on earthly sustenance, which also became unnecessary once recovery was complete. He regarded Eleanor's illness as a recurrence, in severe form, of her trouble in the previous year, as it certainly was; and, while attributing it to "hysteria"—what is now called stress—he was not so obtuse as to pooh-pooh it for that reason but, on the contrary, thought that she should be spared all exertion; the journey to Carlsbad to be made by easy stages, taking four days.

It was now that Marx, foreseeing trouble at the hands of the

* Summer or "European" cholera sporadic.

Austrian police, resolved, after exactly a quarter of a century's permanent residence in England, to apply for British nationality.

Though not of a naturally sanguine temperament where his personal affairs were concerned and deeply learned in the works and ways of the British governing class, Marx showed a quaint, an even deluded faith in its Civil Service. He assembled his sponsors before a Commissioner for Oaths who drew up his petition to the Home Office for naturalisation on 1 August— a Saturday, of all days—two weeks before he was due to leave for Carlsbad. Incorrectly submitted, it was returned for amendment. Nevertheless he was confident that he would be a full-fledged British citizen in time for his departure and was perplexed when, after ten days, his status was unchanged. He need not have worried: the application was quite expeditiously turned down within the month.

(In parenthesis it may be said that, while Marx was on his way to Austria with Eleanor, Detective-Sergeant W. Reimers begged to report in his own inimitable Scotland Yard style that this was "the notorious German agitator, the head of the International Society, and an advocate of Communistic principles. The man has not been loyal to his own King and Country." Sergeant Reimers forbore to mention that the man had twice been expelled by that King and Country; but then, so did Marx whose memorial tactfully stated that he, a "natural-born subject of the Emperor of Germany, having emigrated by permission of the Prussian Government in the year 1846 ceased to be a subject of Prussia and has not since been naturalized by any country". Marx's referees,* whose names the sergeant graced with inverted commas, as if he detected *aliases*, were passed as "respectable householders" and their claim to have known the petitioner for a stated period of time was endorsed, signifying that for long years Marx's most innocuous acquaintances had been kept under observation. The document was then passed in the approved manner from one official to another, each making a comment—"Report *not* satisfactory"—"Refuse certificate"—"I think so?"—with an appended squiggle; the last word:"Refused" being initialled

* R. W. Seton, who vouched for Marx's respectability and loyalty, was his agent and attorney; Farquhar Matheson of 11 Soho Square, his doctor; Julius Augustus Manning, Jenny's employer, a merchant, of 55 Fellows Road Hampstead; and William Frederick Adcock, gentleman, of 6 Southampton Road, Maitland Park.

by the top squiggler on 26 August 1874. A heavily polite letter was sent by Mr. Robert Willis, Commissioner for Oaths of 18 St. Martin's Court, Leicester Square, asking whether the refusal was "on account of any and if so what defect in the form of application" and, if not, "esteeming it a favour" if he could be informed on the grounds for refusal "in order to enable me to renew the application at a future period if so desired by my client". This was tentatively minuted "?Decline to give reasons", the query being eliminated on 2 September,[104] by which time Marx had been abroad for almost three weeks.)

Carlsbad, "The Queen of Bohemian Watering Places", as it was called by an English enthusiast,[105] had a long history of royal patronage. Named, according to legend, after the 14th-century King of Bohemia and subsequently Holy Roman Emperor, Charles IV, it was visited by Frederick I of Prussia, Peter the Great—who took the health-giving waters by the pitcher—the Emperor Charles VI and Napoleon's Empress Maria Louisa. A different category of distinguished visitors included Leibniz, Bach, Goethe—who came no less than a dozen times between 1785 and 1806 for his kidney trouble—Schiller, Beethoven and Paganini, while Mozart's son (Wolfgang Amadeus) lies buried in the churchyard and Turgenyev—Marx's exact contemporary (1818–1883)—had spent June 1874 there, a few weeks before Marx and Tussy came.

In earlier days the arrival of every guest was heralded by a fanfare from the castle turret and a serenade outside his place of residence. This pretty welcome fell into disuse when, in the early 1850s, a jarring note was sounded by the horn-blowers and serenaders who took to asking for tips. Indeed, a marked change came over Carlsbad at this time, making it less a pleasure-resort with therapeutic adjuncts than a serious, even earnest *Kurort*, though the number of visitors rose by leaps and bounds and ladies were still presented with nosegays on departing, for which, however, they surreptitiously paid. The whole place, with its population of 9,000 and its one unprofitable local industry of pin-making* was put on to a sound

* The population figure refers to 1873. For the *souvenirs* market of some 20,000 visitors in the season curious little objects of iron, steel, ceramic, tin and wood were produced. By the '90s, when the population had grown to 12,000 and the number of annual visitors to over 42,000, porcelain, stoneware and cutlery factories were established. Later it became one of the centres of the Czech glass-making industry.

economic footing: there were charges for *séjour*, for listening to the band, for swallowing the waters, for wallowing in them and for every other boon offered by a spa that boasted no fewer than ten mineral springs.

For 40 years, until his retirement in this year 1874, Dr. Hlawacek had been the reigning physician who had laid down the regimen followed by the innumerable flourishing doctors and by their patients. Another leading doctor of long standing who had published works on the Carlsbad cure was Dr. Leopold Fleckles who practised there from 1839 until his death in 1879. His son, Dr. Ferdinand Fleckles, had joined him from Vienna in 1864.

The tax Marx had to pay into the town funds was doubled both for himself and Eleanor because he had registered as Charles Marx, "private gentleman" in the hope of evading suspicion.* Dr. Kugelmann, his wife Gertrud and their 17-year old daughter Franziska were already installed, and had taken rooms for the Marxes, at the Germania in the Schlossburg: a narrow lane debouching into the wider more fashionable street misnamed the Schlossplatz. Though a guest-house† rather than an hotel, it was in an expensive quarter and, while acknowledging that "respectable appearances" had their advantage in putting the police off the scent, Marx wished he could have been accommodated more cheaply.

Eleanor found Carlsbad delightful and every prospect pleasing: "indeed one must be very *difficile* not to be enchanted with such admirable scenery", she wrote to Jenny on 5 September.[108] Marx, too, declared that he could never tire of the wooded mountain walks. These they took each day as part of a strict routine of which he gave an hour-by-hour account to Engels. "We are very exact indeed in all our duties", wrote Eleanor. "Papa being . . . at the Brunnen‡ by 6 o'clock, frequently still earlier."[108]

---

* Professional men paid a reduced tax and, Marx's hope proving vain on this first visit—for he was immediately identified and denounced in ugly terms by "the Vienna scandal-sheet *Sprudel*"—he registered the following year as Doctor of Philosophy and was let off more lightly. The denunciation had been written—and later regretted—by Dr. Ferdinand Fleckles.
† Run by Herr Friedrich Stadler and his wife Marie. During World War II the Nazis turned the place into a military hospital and the grand-daughter of Marx's landlord was pressed into service as a nurse.[106] It is now known as the Spa Hotel Karl Marx[107] in Karlovy Vary.
‡ The equivalent of the English pump-room in a watering place.

There was no lack of social life and Eleanor gave a lively description of their circle. There was Simon Deutsch, an Austrian bibliographer with whom Marx, a fellow exile, had quarrelled in the far-off Paris days, but who was now accepted as an old friend, "a most amusing fellow and has known and knows *everybody*". There was the painter Otto Knille, "a charming fellow", as well as "an awful Frenchman"—fortunately departed—"a perfect idiot . . . the most unbearable example of the bourgeois species that it is possible to imagine". There was also Count Platen, "good fellow enough in his way", who was "a regular aristo and catholic, but good Pole and Russia-hater. He was described in the local paper here as *chef* of the Nihilists (you may suppose how horrified the old fellow was) and was announced as being here with the *chef* of the International."[108] In addition "half the local medical faculty gathered round me and daughter", Marx reported, adding that they made rather a lot of noise but were congenial enough in an environment where much laughter and little thought were prescribed.

Yet this Carlsbad sojourn, for all the salutary waters, delightful surroundings and pleasant company, was not an unqualified success for it was marred by Kugelmann's behaviour which came near to wrecking Marx's cure.

Five years earlier Jenny and her father had stayed with the family in Hanover; Kugelmann had also met Mrs. Marx and Laura when he attended the Hague Congress in 1872.* This was Eleanor's first meeting with them, but it was also to be the last occasion for any intercourse between the families.†

This final rupture was dismissed in Franziska Kugelmann's reminiscences[94] as "a difference . . . which was never smoothed out" owing to her father's over-zealous convictions which "Marx could not countenance in a man so much younger". It was rather differently described by Eleanor at the time.

Kugelmann, nicknamed Wenzel by the Marxes, was "such an impossible person that it was inevitable that he and Papa *could* not help quarrelling", she wrote. And, indeed, Marx, whose nerves were frayed by the man's "incessant, deep-

* Where he had also met and was said by his daughter to have been unfavourably impressed by Lissagaray.[94]
† Apart from a few letters exchanged by Eleanor and Mrs. Kugelmann.

voiced, earnest trumpetings", called him "insufferable": "an arch-pedant and small-minded bourgeois Philistine", a bully and a bore. But the nub of the matter was that he browbeat his wife, "a charming little woman", according to Eleanor, and that the life he led her and their young daughter was abominable. "It's a hard thing", wrote Eleanor, "when a woman has no money of her own and her husband tells her every minute that she is ungrateful for his *Wohltaten** to her and the child. You cannot imagine how brutish Kugel. is and how shameless."[108] He made rows, he sulked, he took offence at the slightest provocation but, embarrassing as this was, he might yet have concealed his unattractive character had not Marx, in whose presence he tried to preserve a certain dignity, occupied an adjoining room at the Germania separated from the Kugelmanns only by a door. He thus became an unwilling listener to the most odious scenes. Eventually Marx removed himself to another room on an upper storey, but not before the distracted wife and daughter had poured out their hearts to him. Franziska had hoped for her mother and herself that Marx would restrain her father and procure "at least four weeks' peace" from the perpetual quarrels that had soured the girl's whole life. Marx and Eleanor sided with the unhappy creatures, causing further unpleasantness, and the parties ceased to be on speaking terms.

Thus ended the friendship of twelve years, begun by a correspondence that elicited from Marx some of his most illuminating letters on the political events and his own work in the period from 1862 to 1874.[109]

There was no question now of Marx and Eleanor accepting the invitation to stay with the Kugelmanns in Hanover on leaving Carlsbad. Instead—though they met, liked and remained on excellent terms with Mrs. Kugelmann's brother, Max Oppenheim of Prague, whom Eleanor characterised as "the kindest person"—they went to Dresden on 21 September and then to Leipzig to visit Liebknecht for three days. After a brief stay in Berlin they arrived in Hamburg on the 29th for Marx to discuss his affairs with Meissner. They embarked for England at the beginning of October.

* Benefactions.

10

Perhaps the most lasting result of Eleanor's travels in 1874 was
the renewal of her old friendship with Liebknecht and his
daughter Alice after twelve years and her meeting, for the first
time, with his second wife, Natalie, and their young family.*

"When I was in Leipzig", she wrote on 13 October, "I could
not find words to tell you how happy I was to see you all. It
has been one of my dearest wishes to see you again, for you
know, dear Library, I have grown up with the remembrance
of many a happy day spent with you. . . . The three days we
passed together . . . will always be a bright and joyous
souvenir."[110]

From that time forth she was never again wholly out of touch
with her "dear Library".† The start of this revived correspondence was for the most part concerned with arranging for
an exchange of reports on the socialist movements in France
and Germany,‡ for publication in Liebknecht's *Volksstaat* and
Lissagaray's newly launched *Rouge et Noir*.§ Eleanor also
gave the Liebknechts news of the situation in England, saying
that, during her stay in Germany she had "seen how much the
police do to help our Cause" and could not "but regret that
the Prussian regime is not possible in England. It would
do more than all the Trade Unions and Workingmen's
Societies put together to bring life into the movement here",[111]
which was at a standstill. "A kind of internal movement
(strikes etc.) never entirely ceases in England, but John Bull

* Gertrud, the daughter of the first Mrs. Liebknecht, was then seven years old;
Natalie's elder son, Theodor, was four and the younger, Karl, three. The third
boy, Otto, was not born until 1877.
† In April 1878 he came to London for a fortnight and again for the last three
weeks of September 1880.
‡ Though the French Workers' Party was not yet formed, the German Social-
Democratic Party had been founded, on Marxist principles, at Eisenach in 1869
by Liebknecht and August Bebel.
§ Only three issues appeared. Lissagaray, whose letters were still being intercepted,
advised Liebknecht to send his contributions addressed to Mr. A. Bourgoyne at
7 South Crescent, Bedford Square (i.e. Store Street).

has been accustomed for so long a while to behave himself that he goes the way he should go to an alarming extent. Who would think that in quiet respectable happy England millions of people are on the verge of starvation! Not a day passes in which 'death from want' of some 'pauper' is not recorded. It passes all understanding how the thousands of men and women starving in the East End of London—and starving by the side of the greatest wealth and luxury—do not break forth into some wild struggle. Surely nothing could make their lot worse than it is now. . . ."[112] She reported the opening of a Medical School for Women, with Professor Huxley and Dr. Garrett Anderson as "the chief promoters",* adding that this was of benefit only to middle-class women though, she conceded, this was "always something".† Her words suggest that the achievements of British bourgeois democracy were not much in her line. Any but the most draconic methods of enforcing reactionary legislation, any widening of opportunities for women, regardless of the human suffering caused by the one and the human advantages offered by the other, were to be deplored since neither of them directly incited the working class to "wild struggle". Eleanor was not, of course, speaking in terms of political realities. In these "Leftist" opinions, as we should call them now, she was merely expressing the pity and passion that social injustice aroused in her warm nature, conditioned as it was by the most impressive and the central experience of her time—the heroic Commune, a fight that had indeed been waged by a wretchedly poor and largely unorganised proletariat—and the sense of frustration felt by many ardent young people of her (and not only of her) day when faced with the apathy of the masses and the political nullity of the trade unions in her own country. Her reactions also reflected Lissagaray's influence and, indeed, the furtherance of his interests and activities was Eleanor's main preoccupation as she approached her 20th year. For his sake she undertook,

* The leading spirit was, in fact, Sophia Jex-Blake who founded the London School of Medicine for Women opened on 12 October 1874 at 30 Henrietta Street off Cavendish Square (now Henrietta Place).

† Eleanor sent Natalie an advertisement from *The Times* to illustrate the "horrible position of governesses" (presumably also middle-class women): "A young lady desires an engagement as governess. She can give good references and teaches German, French, music and drawing, learnt abroad. Terms six shillings a week."[111]

with some misgivings, the translation into French of the speech Liebknecht had made in the Reichstag on 21 November.*

By the end of 1874 the Lafargues had settled at 27 South Hill Park and the Longuets had moved to 58 Fleet Road, both in Hampstead.† Jenny's husband had been appointed as Assistant Master in French at King's College in the University of London at a salary of £182 a year,‡[113] while she herself began teaching German at St. Clement Danes Parochial School in Stanhope Street.§

The house occupied by the Marxes for the past eleven years was now too large for them. In March 1875 they moved to 41 Maitland Park Road,‖ a substantial terrace house, by present day standards more than adequate for four people but, rated at £44 a year, far cheaper than their former spacious dwelling.

It was from this address that Eleanor now began her correspondence, in French, with Carl Hirsch. It shows another aspect of Lissagaray's influence upon her, for not only was she extremely well-informed on the political situation in France, both that of the present and of the immediate past—the *History of the Commune* was now being written—but her facility in French had vastly improved, at the expense of her German which was so shaky that she "felt quite ashamed of herself", as she told the Liebknechts to whom she wrote in English.

One of her earliest letters to Hirsch, dated 25 October 1875,

---

* In which he demanded the suspension of the sentences on the Social Democratic Deputies who were in prison while condemning the conduct of their trial and the verdicts.
† From September 1875 to 1877 the Lafargues lived at 225 Camden Road. (Ellen Terry was two doors off at 221.) They then moved to 37 Tremlett Grove, Junction Road, Islington.
‡ He held the appointment officially from 1875 until 1881, but in fact resigned in November 1880. Fourteen years earlier Thomas Hardy, then aged 21, had attended the French lectures at King's College.
§ Founded in 1700, this was one of the oldest 'voluntary' (Church of England) schools in London. Stanhope Street itself was demolished for the building of Aldwych and Kingsway (1899–1905), though the school had been rehoused in 1881.
‖ Known until May 1868 as 9 Maitland Park Crescent. In 1935 the then LCC put up a plaque bearing the words "Heinrich Karl Marx (1818–1883) Socialist Philosopher Lived and Died Here". Early in 1936 this was destroyed by vandals, replaced and once more smashed on 1 May. The County Council was prepared to restore it yet again but the occupant of the house, unwilling to be the target of further violence, refused consent.[114] The house was demolished after severe bombing in the area during the Second World War, though it was still standing in 1958, completely derelict. (See fn., p. 57.)

LISSAGARAY

41 MAITLAND PARK ROAD, THE MARXES' HOUSE FROM 1875 TO 1883

shortly after he had spent a few days in London, concerned an
article on Henry Irving written by Mrs. Marx. Eleanor asked
Hirsch to use his many connections with the foreign press to
have this published in the *Frankfurter Zeitung*. She also hoped
that a review on the same subject by a Russian lady of her
acquaintance might be printed in *Le Journal des débats*, *Le
Temps* or *Le Siècle*. Marx himself, she said, would have written
something on Irving had he found the time. This fervent
propaganda for an actor who was not unknown nor yet in his
first youth—he was then 37—was occasioned by the production
in October 1874 of his *Hamlet* whose novelty had puzzled and
even shocked audiences—"why could not Mr. Irving be
original in old-world fashion?" asked *The Times* of 2 November
1874—followed by his *Macbeth* in September 1875. These were
Irving's initial Shakespearean ventures and both met with a
mixed reception, the "peculiarities" of his *Macbeth*, in particular, forming "the chief topic of discourse in theatrical circles",
according to *The Times* of 2 October 1875. The press as a
whole had been loud in its praises, but Irving had his detractors
and controversy raged. The Marxes did not know him personally but they were acquainted with the Batemans, under
whose management Irving had originally appeared at the
Lyceum. Their eldest daughter Kate had played opposite
him as Lady Macbeth, but it was certainly disinterested
enthusiasm for an artist of rare talent, allied to her lifelong
devotion to Shakespeare, that inspired Mrs. Marx's first
journalistic essay. She asked Eleanor to make clear to Hirsch
that her name was not to appear in the *Frankfurter Zeitung*
should the article be printed, though its authorship could be
revealed "among friends".

The article was published* and a few months later Mrs.
Marx herself sent a letter to Hirsch to say that as a result of
this initial success she had been seized by a writing mania and
had submitted a little report on the London Season which, to her
astonishment, had appeared on 4 April 1876.†[115]

---

* On 21 November 1875.
† Mrs. Marx was referring, of course, to the theatrical rather than the social
Season, of which she cannot but have held unprintable views. In her letter to
Hirsch she mentions that her article appeared below an obituary notice from Paris
on the Frankfurt-born Countess d'Agoult (1805–1876), who wrote under the
pen-name Daniel Stern and was chiefly famous for having been Liszt's mistress and

Eleanor's own interest in the theatre was probably stimulated by the founding in 1873 of Furnivall's New Shakespeare Society, which she joined.*

Mrs. Edward Compton, then Virginia Bateman who, like her sisters, Kate, Ellen and Isabel, was on the stage, using the name Virginia Francis, recalled that when "in her 'teens" she had visited the Marxes' "horrid little house"—more often than her parents because Eleanor was much attached to her—her young friend was always "most anxious to make me take Shakespeare seriously, indeed, she used to drag me to Furnivall's Shakespeare Society meetings".†[117] This interest in the theatre was to play an increasing part in Eleanor's life, was never entirely abandoned and, at one point, threatened to become her chosen career. But for the time being it played a secondary part to her concern for Lissagaray's work.

From 15 August to 11 September in 1875 Marx went to Carlsbad alone—missing Tussy sadly but thankful for the absence of Kugelmann—while Mrs. Marx took a holiday in Lausanne until 21 September. Though there is no indication of where the Longuets had been, nor yet whether Eleanor had gone away that summer at all, Jenny wrote to her sister on 1 September, announcing her return to London, and recalling

figuring as such in Balzac's *Béatrix*. She had been known to Mrs. Marx 33 years earlier in Paris, at which time she was "running after the young Herwegh and Heine was fleeing from her". The *Frankfurter Zeitung* published in all five articles by Mrs. Marx: "The London Theatre World", 21 November 1875; "The London Season", 4 April 1876; "Shakespearian Studies in England", 3 January 1877; "Shakespeare's *Richard III* at the Lyceum Theatre London", 8 February 1877 and "From the London Theatre", 25 May 1877.

* Frederick James Furnivall (1825–1910) was the secretary of the Philological Society in 1853 and responsible for organising the preliminary work on the *New* (Oxford) *English Dictionary*. In 1861 he became the editor but, realising the long years that must elapse before it could be completed, he conceived the notion of the *Concise* (Oxford) *Dictionary*. He founded the Early English Text Society in 1864, from which stemmed the Chaucer Society (1868), the New Shakespeare Society (1873), the Sunday Shakespeare Society (1874), the Browning Society (1881) and the Shelley Society (1886). An "agnostic"—he adopted Huxley's neologism—with strong socialist leanings, Furnivall's enthusiasms included boating—he formed a Ladies' Rowing Club for Harrods' shop girls—women's higher education and working men's colleges. For many years he held court every afternoon at an ABC teashop near the British Museum.[116] Marx described him as looking like a pilgrim on the way to the Holy Land to seek St. Anthony's beard.

† Mrs. Compton (1853–1940) wrote this account when she was over 80. Since she remembered that the Marxes' house was approached by a "high flight of steps to the front door", this must have been at 41 Maitland Park Road and, quite apart from her reference to the Shakespeare Society, it is evident that the period was not, as she thought, in the sixties, but after 1875 when—like Eleanor herself—she was no longer "in her 'teens".

that on the morrow her little son would have been two years old had he lived and that, on this sorrowful anniversary, she would be thinking, too, of Tussy's loving-kindness.[102]

No celebration to mark Eleanor's 21st birthday on 16 January 1876 has been recorded, unless the present of a packet of cigarettes, for which she thanked Hirsch on 30 December, may be counted as a salutation to her coming of age.* Jenny was pregnant again at the time and early that spring her husband suffered a fever. They had recently moved to 30 Leighton Grove in Kentish Town where, on 10 May 1876, Frédéric Jean Florent Longuet—always known as Jean or Johnny and sometimes Jack—was born: a weakly infant, according to Mrs. Marx, but one who developed into a sturdy little child.[118] Two days later Eleanor wrote a long letter to Hirsch without mentioning this event, entirely concerned with the moves afoot to get a Bill passed by the French Government to amnesty the proscribed Communards.† The impersonality of this political correspondence was modified when Hirsch sent her a pair of pince-nez which, although the lenses were no good, she found enchanting: they were so much lighter and more comfortable than those she habitually wore. Ten days later the police must have been relieved to learn that she had changed the lenses.

This was in July, when Lissagaray had gone to Jersey and she was preparing to accompany her father for the second time to Carlsbad. She sent Hirsch her address—the old Germania—before she and Marx set off.

Their journey was not favoured by fortune or planned with foresight. Reaching Cologne on Saturday, 13 August, their arrival in Nuremberg coincided with the opening of Wagner's Bayreuth *Festspielhaus* and the first performance of the Nibelungen Ring, attracting an audience from the ends of the earth.‡

---

* Only this sinister item of information in the letter was filed by the police.
† The Bill was defeated in the Chamber of Deputies.
‡ As Shaw wrote in *The Perfect Wagnerite*: "When the Bayreuth Festival Playhouse was at last completed and opened in 1876 for the first performance of The Ring . . . the precautions taken to keep the seats out of the hands of the frivolous public . . . had ended in their forestalling by ticket speculators and their sale to just the sort of idle globetrotting tourists against whom the temple was to have been strictly closed . . . The money . . . was begged . . . from people who must have had the most grotesque misconceptions of the composer's aims—among others the Khedive of Egypt and the Sultan of Turkey."[119]

In addition to this "Fools' Festival", as Marx called it, Nuremberg itself had chosen that weekend to stage a Bakers' and Millers' Congress which, if less renowned and well-attended, also had its *aficionados*. With these and the "Siegfrieds, Valkyries and Götterdämmerung heroes" streaming into the town[120] there was not a bed to be had. For a radius of 50 miles every lodging, from the most expensive hotel to the humblest inn and doss-house, was full and could have been filled twice over. Somehow the Marxes had not got wind of these revels but had allowed their trunks to be taken off the train and placed upon a barrow whose sweating owner lugged it round the town for hours only to trundle it back to the station. Here they took tickets for Weiden: the nearest junction for Carlsbad on a branch line from Neukirchen. But the guard was tipsy and incapable of telling them when they reached Neukirchen, so they were carried on to Irrelohe where they waited a couple of hours for a train back to Weiden, which little place with its one hotel also happened to be the junction for Bayreuth, thus offering not the smallest hope of accommodation. They had arrived at midnight and, until four in the morning, they had to make the best of the wooden benches at the railway station.

Small wonder that they were exhausted when they fetched up at the Germania. The tribulations of the journey were recounted to Mrs. Marx who, unmindful of her own past misadventures, pronounced them rather quixotic.[120] A few days later Eleanor wrote again to say that they were fast recovering but she wished to remind her mother "how proverbially stupid one gets at Carlsbad, so don't be surprised if I seem rather incoherent". At all events it was a relief to be without the "grumbling and quarrelling of Kugelmann" and the place was full. "There are as many Jews as ever, and more anxious than ever to get as much water as possible."* However,

---

* This little gibe is as nothing to the scurrilous comments on Jews that run through the private correspondence between Marx and Engels, entirely in accord with Marx's early assessment: "Let us not seek the secret of the Jew in his religion, but let us seek the secret of the religion of the real Jew. What is the profane basis of Judaism? *Practical* need, *self-interest*. What is the worldly cult of the Jew? *Huckstering*. What is his worldly god? *Money*." This was written in 1843.[121]

One should also, however, read Engels' letter to an unknown correspondent written in April 1890 and published in the Vienna *Arbeiterzeitung* of 9 May in which he analyses and denounces anti-Semitism as serving only reactionary ends.[122]

It should be said that not until news of the peculiarly bestial Russian pogroms of 1888 filtered through did the rabid and unthinking anti-Semitism prevalent in

they were outdone by an American who managed to swallow 24 glasses in one day: "It's a wonder he didn't die of it", she wrote.[123] In later life Eleanor was distinctly proud of her own Jewish antecedents, proclaimed herself a Jewess and, just as she revised her views on drunkenness—no longer regarding it as a joke once she had seen to what degradation and misery it could reduce whole working-class families—so she ceased to treat the Jews as a butt when she worked among the immigrants in Whitechapel.

Marx met and mixed with former Carlsbad acquaintances and made many new ones—a few Poles but for the most part German university professors and doctors—as did Eleanor, who took a great liking to the younger Dr. Fleckles—"really very witty and a very good fellow"[123]—and became friendly with Professor Heinrich Graetz of Breslau to whom she later sent a copy of Lissagaray's book, when it transpired that he had guessed she was engaged to the author.* The main subject of conversation, Marx reported, was Wagner's love life,† though no doubt he also found other matter for discussion in the company he kept. Nevertheless, his letters to Engels show a decided taste for the sort of gossip prevalent at watering places.

The cure was to come to an end on 10 September and Marx

Western Europe receive a momentary check, a fund for the relief of the surviving victims being publicly launched by the Lord Mayor of London in 1890. Very shortly before this, Miss Beatrice Potter had been making her study of the Jews in the East End, published in Volume I of Charles Booth's *Life and Labour of the People* in 1889. Here she described the attitudes and habits of mind induced by the appalling persecution of Polish and Russian Jews. The following is but a short extract from this magisterial passage: "The Russian Government deliberately encouraged mob-violence of a brutal and revolting character as a costless but efficient means of expulsion. Robbed, outraged, in fear of death and physical torture, the chosen people have swarmed across the Russian frontier, bearing with them, not borrowed 'jewels of silver, and jewels of gold, and raiment', but a capacity for the silent evasion of the law, a faculty for secretive and illicit dealing, and mingled feelings of contempt and fear for the Christians amongst whom they dwelt . . ."

* It will have been remarked that, in her letter pleading to be allowed to see Lissagaray, Eleanor had used the phrase "everyone knows we are engaged", by which she meant that certain indiscreet friends knew it and would have passed the word round. But there is no evidence that she herself ever concealed the betrothal, nor any that her father ever acknowledged it. Professor Graetz wrote: "I think you were already secretly engaged in Carlsbad. Hence your happy mood. In which case may I congratulate you on such a fiancé. Mr. Lissagaray's book is well-written, it has style and feeling. . . . please convey to your betrothed the greetings of an admirer."[124]

† Cosima (1837–1930)—the youngest of Liszt's three illegitimate daughters by Mrs. Marx's old Paris acquaintance, the Countess d'Agoult—married Wagner in 1870 after her divorce from the Munich court musician and pianist Hans von Bülow.

had accepted an invitation from Max Oppenheim—Mrs. Kugelmann's brother—to visit him in Prague,* but on the Wednesday before they were due to leave Eleanor suddenly developed a fever. Dr. Fleckles by taking swift action "saved her from a long and dangerous illness", Marx wrote to Oppenheim. Nevertheless, some days of convalescence were advised and the journey to Prague was not made until 15 September.

They stayed only a few days and on the 21st were writing to Fleckles in Carlsbad from Liège, having on the homeward journey paid a flying visit to Kreuznach where Marx had been in 1843, before his marriage, and where, in fact, the wedding had taken place on 19 June. For that occasion the Baroness von Westphalen with her daughter and her son Edgar had travelled from Trier,† preferring that reactions to this unpopular event should not be manifested in their home town. No other member of either the bride's or the groom's family was present, the witnesses being four Kreuznach citizens: a doctor, a law student, a Jewish gentleman of private means and an innkeeper.[126]

Back in England on 23 September, while Eleanor resumed her correspondence with Hirsch, Marx took on an unexpected role.

It must be admitted that he had reason to feel tepid towards his sons-in-law. Lafargue, having finally turned his back on a medical career, struggling with more optimism than success to establish himself as a commercial photo-engraver for which he had invented a new process, was writing every few days to Engels not so much begging letters as peremptory demands for sums of money that even in his days of direst need would have made Marx blush. Longuet, though he held to his modest teaching post at King's College, had not only introduced an odious mother into the family on the occasion of Jenny's confinements—"*la mère, la mère,*" moaned Mrs. Marx[115]—but had turned out to be of a nervous and irritable temper: "he fumes, shouts, and argues";[118] while Jenny, to make ends meet

---

* One branch of Oppenheim's chemical dye and mineral oil manufactory was in Dresden, the other in Prague, where he lived.[106]

† Arriving in time for the mother to witness the Marriage Contract between "Herr Karl Marx, Doctor of Philosophy, resident in Cologne, on the one hand, and Fraülein Johanna Bertha Julia Jenny von Westphalen, without occupation, resident in Kreuznach", signed on 12 June 1843.[125]

and despite her now persistent asthmatic cough, was burdened
with her morning duties at St. Clement Danes School to add to
the care of her house, a young baby and this choleric husband.

For neither Longuet nor Lafargue did Marx lift a finger.
But for Lissagaray—Lissagaray the unacceptable, the aspirant
son-in-law who was not to be trusted, relied upon or so much as
countenanced—Marx went into action, all guns blazing.

No one could have championed Lissagaray's interests with
greater force or more partisan zeal than Marx displayed in his
negotiations for a German translation of the *Histoire de la
Commune* to appear simultaneously, as he hoped, with the
French edition, now in the press.

The fact was that, despite reservations, he held the highest
opinion of this book. It was, he emphasised "the first *authentic*"
account and had, in his view, the unique quality of a work,
almost a personal memoir, by a man who had been an eye witness to and participant in the events described, drawing upon
all published sources as well as material available to no one
else. As such, it could not be matched by any other book on the
subject and its translation must be impeccable. Thus when a
certain Julius Grunzig in Berlin volunteered to bring out a
German edition, Marx wrote to Wilhelm Bracke, the socialist
publisher in Brunswick, demanding that the character and
credentials of this Grunzig be thoroughly investigated. Marx
was taking no chances: the translator of this book must be not
only a "professional" but also a party man. Grunzig could not
be considered as the publisher while his competence to translate
would have to be established before he could be accepted in any
capacity whatsoever. "I suggest that you take on the publication
of this interesting work, so important for our party and for the
whole German reading public", Marx wrote to Bracke. He
went much further, transacting the practical details to safeguard
Lissagaray's rights: the life of a Communard refugee in London
was a hard one and he must have his share of any profits from a
German edition. However, since Grunzig was the first applicant
to come forward Marx allowed that he might be sent a few
pages of the French proof sheets to translate and convince Marx
of his ability to undertake "this far from easy task".

These were but the first shots fired in the campaign waged on
Lissagaray's behalf. Throughout that autumn of 1876 and the

whole of the following year Marx took upon himself—even
though slightly against his will[127]—the entire burden of seeing
justice done to the *History of the Commune*. Until January 1876
he had laboured for months on the French edition of *Capital*,
but never had he taken more pains over any work other than
his own to ensure that a translation should be treated with so
much respect as he claimed for Lissagaray.* At the end of
September he learnt that another book of the same title was
being written by a German, Bernhard Becker. Marx went into
the question from every angle, discussed it with Engels—"as
we always exchange views on matters concerning party interests"—and came to the conclusion that this work, "at best
written from the standpoint of a *German critic*", could not be seen
as a rival to Lissagaray's, whose first French edition was due to
come out in a matter of weeks while Becker's book would not
be finished until the following May. The only conceivable link
between them was that the German author would be unable to
ignore so important a new source.†

Early in November Grunzig submitted his test piece and
Marx, after comparing it closely with the French original,
wrote to say that he must decline his services. With this the
hope of simultaneous publication was abandoned. Marx
wrote to Bracke that, while "revisions *here and there* would
doubtless be necessary in any translation", the improvements
to Grunzig's effort would "cost more time than if I did the
translation myself from start to finish".[128] He suggested another
possible candidate—Samuel Kokosky—but feared that he
lacked the polish and felicity of style required for this particular
book. He applied to others, too, while Engels proposed Wilhelm
Blos of Hamburg, who consented but did so just at the time—
only two days after—Marx had approved a specimen translation by a lady named Isolde Kurz who was then entrusted with
the work.

Lissagaray himself, on Marx's advice, made a number of
substantial changes between the first publication in November

---

* It is true he had also worked on J. J. Most's English edition of *Capital and Labour*
(published October 1877) but, as he later wrote to Sorge, the French version of
Capital had cost him so much time that he would never again co-operate personally
on any translation whatsoever.
† The book was published in Leipzig in 1879 under the title: *The History and Theory
of the Paris Revolutionary Commune of the year 1871.*

1876 and the following February. All these, Marx insisted, must be incorporated by Miss Kurz. In April he was complaining of her howlers—she was sending in her work piecemeal for his scrutiny—and also that she was "damned slow", while in the following month, by which time the harassed lady had spent almost half a year on the job, he delivered his final verdict: "The translation as a whole, where not downright incorrect, is often clumsy, pedestrian and stilted."* Possibly, Marx went on, this might suit certain German tastes, but not his, and he appended—as he had done several times before—a detailed list of her mistakes with scathing comments upon them: indubitable if insulting evidence that he had studied the text far more thoroughly than Miss Kurz. By August he was contemptuously remarking that she seemed to be better at pressing for money than translating.

At last, in October 1877, Wilhelm Blos was asked to re-work the translation as edited by Marx who wrote on 10 November to say that he had long tried to shake off and had roared in vain at the "abominable Isolde". He was far ruder about this misinterpreter of Lissagaray's book than ever he had been about its author.

By a coincidence quite fortuitous—for he was no longer speaking of anything connected with his painstaking and anonymous work on the *History*—Marx included in this same letter to Blos what could almost be called a declaration of integrity: neither Engels nor he gave a straw for popularity, he wrote: "A proof, for instance, is that, during the time of the International, in my aversion from any cult of the individual, I never allowed the numerous manoeuvres of recognition by which I was molested from various countries to receive publicity; I never even answered them, except now and again with a rebuke. When Engels and I first joined the clandestine Communist League we did so only on condition that anything tending to foster irrational beliefs in authority should be expunged from the Rules."

The German edition of the *History* appeared, published by Bracke, in 1878,† by which time Lissagaray had made further

---

* What would he have thought, one wonders, of some of the translations of his own work that have girdled the earth in the present century.
† It was banned in Germany.[129]

emendations, while he wrote nearly a hundred more pages especially for the English version which Eleanor was to produce. Her translation, though it did not appear until 1886, was done many years before. Indeed, Mrs. Marx told Sorge in January 1877 that Lissagaray's book was "being translated at the present time into English and German". As Eleanor explained in her Introduction, she had done the work "at the express wish of the author . . . from the *Histoire de la Commune* as prepared for a second French edition—an edition which the French Government would not allow to be published. This explanation is necessary", she went on, "in view of the differences between the translation and the first edition of Lissagaray's book." Though much had happened in the years between her original translation and its publication which made certain passages out of date, she was "loth to alter the work in any way. It had been entirely revised and corrected by my father. I want it to remain as he knew it."[43] This is perhaps the only public reference to Marx's stubborn toil in the interests of a man whom he disliked and rejected in the family circle but whose work he thought of importance.

§ 11

A conjugation of circumstances at this period of her life drove
Eleanor back upon her own resources. The demise of the
International in 1872, its final winding up in so far as it
affected her family in 1874, followed in the next year by the
move to a smaller dwelling meant that the home was no longer
the centre and resort for revolutionaries from every country,
while the other members of the family had flown—if not far—
away. Even "the French emigration has gone to pieces", wrote
Engels in September 1874. "All have fallen out with each other
and with everyone else on purely personal grounds—mostly
over money matters—and we are almost entirely rid of them."
Parallel to this attenuated social life ran Eleanor's lingering
engagement to Lissagaray, with no promise of personal fulfil-
ment in sight, though her interest in him and his affairs was
undiminished. Not that things were bleak at 41 Maitland Park
Road to which, particularly on Sundays when open house was
kept, friends old and new found their way, including many now
introduced by Eleanor herself. But the days of passionate
political involvement—the endless meetings and discussions at
the very heart of the international movement—were over.
Marx with continuing ill health seldom forsook his study.
He does not appear to have confided in Tussy his initial exertions
in connection with the German edition of the *History of the
Commune* for, towards the end of October 1876, Eleanor wrote
to Hirsch—thanking him for the cigarettes he had sent to
Carlsbad and for a second pair of delightful pince-nez—
confidently announcing that the book would be published in
both languages at more or less the same time in about a
month when in point of fact the translation was not so much as
under way.

That autumn she plunged into an entirely new activity:
working for the London School Board elections in the interest
of a Mrs. Westlake, the only woman standing for the Maryle-

bone division.* Eleanor explained in a letter to Hirsch that
these bodies were responsible for the control of the Board
Schools and that Mrs. Westlake, though basically a middle-class
lady—"like almost all Englishwomen", she oddly said—was
at least a free-thinking one and certainly of greater worth than
any of the male candidates. The main issue was the defeat of the
"Church Party" which "sought to abolish compulsory education altogether".

Mrs. Westlake had been the Treasurer of the Dispensary
and New Hospital for Women in the Marylebone Road. She
declared that she would give up all such work if elected, but
it was to this connection that she owed the support of Dr.
Garrett Anderson,† who, as Eleanor's doctor, may well have
pressed her into the campaign. Another influential backer was
Miss Buss of the North London Collegiate School and both
these well-known personalities were on the platform at Mrs.
Westlake's election meetings during the last two weeks of
November, while "The Only Lady Candidate" was well
publicised, her policy and her views regularly reported, by the
local press.

From the Committee Rooms at 157 Camden Road Eleanor
went canvassing from door to door. "You cannot imagine the
curious things I see and hear", she wrote to Hirsch. "In one
house they demand that 'above all religion should be taught',‡
in another I am told that 'schooling is the curse of the country,
that education will ruin us', etc., etc. Still, it is amusing,
though sometimes rather sad, as when one calls on a worker

* The School Boards, established under the 1870 Education Act, were elected for
three years. Women were eligible to sit on the Boards, as were representatives of the
working class. "The candidates were elected on a cumulative voting system under
which each rate-payer had as many votes as there were places on the Board."[130]
† Who had stood for the same division in the first School Board elections of 30
November 1870 and polled the highest vote (47,848), her nearest runner-up being
Professor Huxley (13,494). Dr. Garrett—as she then was—served only one term of
office and did not stand again. The new Hospital for Women was opened by the
Earl of Shaftesbury in 1872, replacing the St. Mary's Dispensary for Women that
had existed in Seymour Place since 1866. The Hospital moved to the site of the
Great Central Railway Hotel in the Marylebone Road in 1874 and in 1888 to 144
Euston Road, opposite St. Pancras Church. Since 1917—the year she died—it has
been known as the Elizabeth Garrett Anderson Hospital.
‡ In this, as in claiming Mrs. Westlake as "free-thinking", Eleanor was slightly
departing from her candidate's declared policy. "Mrs. Westlake approves of the
manner in which the religious question has been dealt with, as she could not
support an education from which the Bible was excluded," *The Camden & Kentish
Towns, Hampstead, Highgate, Holloway and St. Pancras Gazette* reported on 11 November 1876.

who says he wants to 'consult his boss' first."[131] The election was held on 2 December and Mrs. Westlake romped home at the head of the seven successful candidates with 20,231 votes.

Engels approved of this activity and of women's entry into public office, casting all his seven votes for Mrs. Westlake. Shortly after the Reichstag elections of January 1877 he wrote to a lady in Germany who, of course, was not franchised: "When we take power, not only will women vote, but they will be voted for and make speeches, which last has already come to pass on the School Boards. . . . Moreover, the ladies on these School Boards distinguish themselves by talking very little and working very hard, each of them doing on an average as much as three men. Ought one to say 'new brooms sweep clean'? Though most of these 'brooms' are rather old."

With the turn of the year Eleanor embarked upon a fresh enterprise, translating a paper by Professor Nikolaus Delius of Bonn University on "The Epic Element in Shakespeare's Dramas"* which was printed in the *Proceedings of the New Shakespeare Society* where it earned general praise and Professor Delius's salute to a fellow-worker.

It was her mother's hope that this first entry into literary circles would lead to her finding remunerative work less strenuous than that of teaching, for, since the Brighton days, it had been accepted that, unlike her sisters, Eleanor was not going to be either a dependant or her father's unpaid secretary. Mrs. Marx had found her "pale and emaciated" on her return from Carlsbad and continued to regard her as of a peculiarly delicate constitution, though it is doubtful whether so frail a creature as she was thought to be could have done the election canvassing, than which activity nothing demands more physical and moral resilience.

It was, in fact, the health of two quite other people that became a genuine cause for anxiety in 1877: that of Lizzie Burns and of Mrs. Marx herself.

A real if incongruous friendship between these two had ripened since Engels moved to London. Though he and Marx might wish to meet daily, to go for long walks together and spend each evening at one another's houses, there was no

* The original was published in the *Jahrbuch der Deutschen Shakespeare-Gesellschaft* 12 Jg. Weimar 1877.

necessity for the ladies to strike up an intimacy. Yet they did. Despite Tussy's devotion to Lizzie Burns and her own sense of what was owing to Engels' companion—expressed with warmth in the first letter she had written to him on finding the house in Regent's Park Road—Mrs. Marx had no reason on earth to spend holidays with Lizzie unless she had chosen to do so and enjoyed her company. In 1873 she had proposed to stay with her at the seaside and two years later she went with Lizzie to Shanklin on the Isle of Wight, while in 1876, when Marx and Tussy were in Carlsbad, she elected to leave Hastings where she had gone for her health in order to join Lizzie and Engels in Ramsgate. Each morning he took the ladies to the railway station bar to fortify them with a small glass of port before leaving them to their own devices. They strolled together on the beach and rejoiced that they had nothing to do and no letters to write.*

But in all these years Lizzie had not been well: even when she first came to London in 1870 she had what she called "a gammy leg"[132] and then, as time went on, complained of "pains all over".[133] By 1876 Engels† had to admit that she was "always ailing in the spring", for which the only cure was sea air, while, as the years advanced, he took her away for long periods—to Scotland, Ramsgate, Brighton, Germany—in the hope that "it would see her through the winter".

In the autumn of 1875, the couple went to Heidelberg to place Lizzie's niece Pumps in a finishing school under a Fräulein Schupp. The girl, now 15 years of age, was to remain there for a couple of years to be licked into shape and, indeed, after a few months she wrote a long letter to Mrs. Marx and Tussy upon which Marx commented that "if the spelling is a little uncertain here and there, in style and in facility of expression, which are far more important, she has made truly astounding progress". Engels, too, was struck—though rather less—

---

* It is not clear why Lizzie, who could not write, should have found this so singular a blessing.

† At which time he began writing *Anti-Dühring*, published in an unsatisfactory way—as a "space-filler"—in *Vorwärts* from 3 January until 13 May 1877. Later, translated into French by Paul Lafargue with Laura's help, that part known as *Socialism, Utopian and Scientific*, appeared in the *Revue Socialiste* (Nos. 3, 4 and 5) of 1880. The English translation of this, by Edward Aveling, appeared in 1892. Engels finished the book in the spring of 1878, when he took up again the writing of *Dialectics of Nature*, begun in 1873, on which he continued to work until Marx's death in 1883, leaving it uncompleted.

by the improvement shown. Throughout Pumps' stay abroad the family of Philip Pauli—the owner of a chemical factory in Rheinau, near Mannheim, and a friend of Schorlemmer's—promised to keep an eye on the girl. This they did to such good purpose that Engels became a regular and cordial correspondent, writing in April 1876 that if in years to come Pumps were to remember her schooldays as the happiest time of her life it would be thanks to Pauli and his wife. In August 1876 Lizzie and Engels broke their seaside holiday to visit Pumps in Heidelberg, at which time the Paulis invited Marx and Tussy to stay with them in Rheinau when they left Carlsbad. Tussy's sudden fever and the engagement to go to Prague prevented their acceptance, but Pumps' fortunes had now involved the entire circle in friendly intercourse and some years later, in May 1881, Mrs. Pauli visited Engels in London.

The two years that the girl was to have been at school did not run their full course, for, though Lizzie had withstood the tests of winter—including the Christmas season, which represented all bibulous jollifications rolled into one—"in the last six weeks", Engels wrote to Mrs. Pauli on 14 February 1877, "we have had all manner of servant troubles and just now, when she should rest, she has to exert herself beyond her strength, working her fingers to the bone". He had reckoned with this possibility and informed the school that he might have to recall Pumps at any time. That point had now been reached and, since he could not leave London to fetch her, he would avail himself of offers made to escort Pumps back to England by the beginning or, at the latest, the middle of March.* He himself was doing all he could—"if you had seen me making the bed last night and lighting the kitchen stove this morning, you would have laughed"—but the burden of housework absolutely must be taken off Lizzie's shoulders. She went with him to Brighton for a fortnight while awaiting Pumps' homecoming. It was not a success.

Pumps was—and remained—a thoroughly tiresome creature. Despite her kindly upbringing and the Heidelberg veneer she was an ill-conditioned and a flighty girl. It could have been said of her that "with all her sail she carried not an ounce of ballast"

---

* Lina Schoeler travelled with her.

and it is wonderful that anyone should have bothered to take her seriously. But however badly she behaved she was Engels' protégée and was shown a degree of consideration that, in her own right, she had not earned. Never was this more so than when the wind was taken out of her sails, as it shortly was, for, on her return to London, she quarrelled with Lizzie, thereby affronting Engels, both of whom had been as parents to her and, turning her back on their needs, she left for Manchester to live with her own people. Whatever the cause of the break— and while Lizzie's health deteriorated so badly that Engels had to take her away from home for weeks on end—Pumps' life in Manchester proved a hard school that did nothing towards improving her literary style. Her father, Thomas Burns, made it clear that he could not afford to let her stay for any length of time, or to support her at all: she worked in her brother's fish-shop all day and every day, while in the home she had the care of three tiny children, including a new-born infant, whose mother, Mrs. Renshaw, was still unable to leave her bed.[134] Pumps was not, therefore, averse from returning to London but she refused to eat humble pie or apologise to her aunt and "uncle". Engels, who had not answered her one un-repentant letter, was disinclined to make the first move and deadlock was reached.[135]

This did not, however, emerge for some months and then only because Mrs. Marx, who went to Manchester that autumn, reported on the unhappy state of affairs and took a deal of trouble to bring the girl round, though she was reluctant to meddle, since she believed hardly anything that either Pumps or Lizzie told her "and the only upshot would be rows".[135] Mrs. Marx's visit to Manchester was not of course primarily on Pumps' account: she was there to seek the ever dependable Dr. Gumpert's advice on her health, which had begun to trouble her afresh despite a foreign cure.

Though Marx had not been made aware of it at the time, the Austrian authorities had tried to expel him from the country when he had been in Carlsbad with Tussy in 1876. Rather than make the long expensive journey only to meet with an expulsion order, and also on medical grounds, he decided that, for his wife's sake as much as for his own, they must take a cure elsewhere. They set off, with Tussy, in the first weeks of August for Neuenahr. This little resort in the Rhineland on the banks of the river Ahr, whose thermal springs had not been tapped until 1854 nor the main source discovered until almost a decade later, was barely more than a village, without so much as a market, its railway still under construction in 1877.* Nonetheless, it had attracted good doctors for the annual influx of some 3,000 health-seeking visitors—though the trade slump in the year of the Marxes' stay had reduced them to no more than 1,700 or 1,800—and Marx trusted and liked Dr. Richard Schmitz, who had practised there since 1863 and gave Mrs. Marx to understand that she had come for treatment only just in time to avert a serious malady. Tussy's appetite improved —always the best sign in her case, according to her father— and they were advised to go to the Black Forest after the three weeks' cure which ended on 4 September.

About a month after her return to England Eleanor took to going to the British Museum,† where she worked for Dr. Furnivall in the interests of the Philological, the Chaucer and the Shakespeare Societies. But that her interests were somewhat dispersed is shown by the fact that she was busily reading the great naturalist Alfred Russel Wallace's "foolery"‡ on spiritualism and John Nevil Maskelyne's exposure of spiritualistic frauds at the end of the year 1877. It is also more than likely— though no record of this can be traced—that she now embarked upon her translation of Lissagaray's *History*, for she cannot have started it earlier than November 1877, when the second (unpublished) French edition which she used had been completed, nor later than 1880, when Lissagaray left England for good and Marx was unable to consult him—or advise Tussy—on the detailed revisions and rewriting of the English version which he is known to have done. It was a daunting task for a relatively prentice hand. Anyone reading it today—when the cottage industry of translating has reached a degree of excellence undreamt of until such practitioners as C. K. Scott Moncrieff

---

* By the end of the century it had developed into a stylish little town, with the grandest of its many new hotels built in the "English Gothic" style, its own railway station and fine Assembly Rooms. However, the little Hotel Flora on the left bank, where the Marxes had stayed, was still on the map.

† Her signature for 22 October 1877, the day of her first application for a ticket to the Reading Room, is reproduced overleaf.

‡ Engels' word.

appeared upon the scene—may well ask how it ever passed Marx's rigorous standards since, for all its fidelity to the original, it is grating, awkward and heavy-handed in its literalness. Notwithstanding, it remains a brave piece of work that has provided countless English readers with the earliest and the fullest first-hand account of embattled Paris in the days of the Commune.*

It was while Eleanor was daily occupied at the Museum that Mrs. Marx, the Neuenahr doctor's optimism having proved unfounded, felt so seriously unwell that she made her trip to Manchester. "The head and feet are all right", she wrote to Tussy, "but the centre of the machine, where the brewing goes on, is not yet in working order."[136] She stayed with Sam Moore and was made warmly welcome by all the old Manchester friends—many of whom sent greetings to the young Tussy they had known in former years—while Gumpert himself called for her each day to dine at his house. Marx had previously observed that the doctor had become commonplace and twaddling as a result of indulging in too much "town chatter". Mrs. Marx now found that, ageing and widowed, he had, by virtue of this constant intercourse with "dyed-in-the-wool Philistines", unconsciously allowed a "formal stiffness and English conventionality to creep into his manner".[135] But he could not have been more attentive to her, either professionally or socially and, while she described his ridiculous and pompous behaviour at table, she felt ashamed of mocking a man to whom she owed such endless kindness, consideration and, indeed, affection. He examined her with care, dispelled her fear that her condition might develop into dropsy—"it's more wind than water", she wrote[136]—and, so far as one may judge from the treatment he prescribed and the general state of medical knowledge at that time, he may well have diagnosed her carcinoma correctly. After a few days' freedom from pain, when she thought of returning home at once, she suffered a severe setback which caused him no surprise and he warned her that she must expect such "ups and downs", saying that much patience and medicine would be needed for some length of time, though the attacks might occur less often

---

* These words are written on the centenary of the Paris Commune: 18 March 1971.

MRS. MARX IN HER LAST YEARS

1877. Oct: 22nd

ELEANOR'S FIRST READING ROOM ENTRY AT THE BRITISH MUSEUM
22 OCTOBER 1877

and at greater intervals. Whenever she felt well enough she was taken sightseeing and to the theatre, while Schorlemmer showed her round Owen's College and she planned to go to a Hallé concert* to hear the new Wagnerian music, but in the end settled for the warmth of Moore's fireside where every evening they drank and chatted together for an hour. "Never", she wrote, "have I been so pampered in my life."[134] But conversation at dinner parties of the Manchester *beau monde* to which she was invited was more than she could stand. The Turco-Russian war was then nearing its end and, to her horror, even some of Marx's associates, in particular the geologist Dakyns, proved to be "out and out Russians".† Unaccustomed as she was to discussion with political dunces, she remarked that "one could be driven to imbecility in such a *milieu*".[135]

And then she saw Pumps. The girl, dispirited and coughing, sullenly declined to seek a reconciliation with Lizzie and Engels, though there was plainly no alternative but for her to go back to them. Sam Moore, who was present when she came to tea with Mrs. Marx, pressed the point and said she had only to write that she was sorry for what had happened and Engels would respond. "Her life in London must have been very hard", Mrs. Marx commented, "for it is far from a bed of roses here."[136] There was no question of running about or enjoying herself and although, through the Catholic connections of an amiable priest, a friend of the family, it was hoped that some suitable work might be found, her father was in no position

---

* Charles Hallé founded his orchestra in Manchester in 1858. Born in Westphalia he came to England from Paris, where he had given his first concerts, after the 1848 revolution.

† The "Christian humbug and hypocritical atrocity mongers" of the English press, which was overwhelmingly pro-Russian, disgusted Mrs. Marx.[118] In April 1876 a Bulgarian uprising against the Turks had been ferociously crushed in a matter of weeks. Russia declared war on Turkey in April 1877. Both Marx and Engels held the view that the Tsar's war was launched to strengthen Russian influence in the Balkans—where he had the backing of Serbia, Montenegro, Rumania and Bulgaria—combined with the need to divert attention from internal social problems. They were convinced that it would give fresh impetus to the Balkan national liberation movements to throw off the rule of the Crescent and lead to a revolution in St. Petersburg. Engels considered the strength and efficiency of the Turkish army—as against the disorganisation of the Tsar's forces—a sufficient guarantee of victory, in which prediction he was, for once, confounded, for the war ended with the military defeat of the Turks, freeing a large part of the Balkan peninsula from the Turkish yoke. The armistice was signed on 31 January 1878. Nevertheless, Marx believed that in Russia this futile war, followed by fresh impolicies, would bring about a revolution, and indeed a revolutionary situation did result.

to buy her new dresses and Mrs. Marx thought she was too
unpresentable to apply for a post with any chance of success.[134]
Several times a day Mrs. Marx called upon Mrs. Lydia Renshaw who was much concerned about Mary Ellen's wretched
situation. But Mrs. Renshaw, closely related to Lizzie, had no
intention of meddling either. With the husband, James Renshaw, Mrs. Marx went to the Roman Catholic Church to
hear the admirable music. She gave Tussy an amusing account
of the preacher—a boorish figure where she had expected a
resplendent Prince of the Church—who puffed and wheezed,
sweating as though he were already suffering the torments of
hell-fire and ceaselessly wiped his bald pate with his hand-
kerchief. "The worst part", said Mrs. Marx, "was the endless
kneeling which lasted close on an hour-and-a-half. Since not
a soul was seated and every soul knelt, I, old fool that I am,
knelt too . . ."[136] However, the painful experience did not
deter her from going again, taking Pumps with her, for the
sake of the music. She recovered from this pious exercise, but
came back to London with little hope of curing her disease.

Eventually, of course, Pumps was forced to swallow her pride
—or resentment—and return to Regent's Park Road, where
Engels thought that the Manchester lesson had done her a
power of good. By this time and during the whole spring and
summer of 1878 Lizzie was confined to her bed. Meanwhile
Mrs. Marx consulted an eminent specialist who pronounced her
condition incurable: all that could be done was to alleviate her
sufferings. In July, though Marx had supposed that "Her
ex-Ladyship the ex-Baroness von Westphalen"* might possibly
be allowed into Carlsbad as non-contraband, he was unwilling
to take the risk. Instead, she went to Malvernbury in Worces-
tershire. From there she wrote to Tussy, facing the fact that
she might never quite recover—her illness was too longstanding
and obstinate—but "all I know is that, had I come here earlier,

---

* In this, one of his rare references to his wife's origins and their potential snob
value abroad, Marx was being realistic. It must be admitted that there was one
droll occasion, in 1871, when he induced Mrs. Marx to write to the editor of
Public Opinion with her card bearing the words "*née* Baroness von Westphalen",
under the impression that this would make him quail, unaware that nothing im-
presses the English less than a minor foreign title, usually thought to be bogus
anyway and more particularly so when it is a lady claiming to be a Baroness in her
own right, than which there is no rarer bird in the whole flock of the true British
peerage.

at least I should have found great relief".[137] Gumpert's "whole-sale pills" of belladonna had not helped her much and she preferred the treatment she now received daily at the hands of a "quiet, unassuming, honest little doctor". She worried about the "Leighton Grove Institution"—the Longuets—for on 4 July 1878 Jenny had given birth to another son, Harry Michel, known as "Harra",* whose troubled little life lasted not five years, while Jean, now two, had been dangerously ill the summer before and was again far from well, so that when Marx went to Malvern on 4 September for ten days, Jenny, leaving the baby in Tussy's care, took Jean to join her mother, staying with her until Mrs. Marx's own return on 22 September.

Thus Marx, his wife and their eldest daughter were away when at half-past one on the morning of 12 September 1878 Lizzie Burns, after years of pain and indignity, died of a tumour of the bladder and exhaustion from haemorrhages. The evening before the Rev. W. B. Galloway, vicar of St. Mark's Church, a short step from 122 Regent's Park Road, came to the house to perform the marriage ceremony, by special licence, according to the rites of the Church of England in the presence of Charles Read and James and Lydia Renshaw, the last of whom, like the dying bride, being unable to write and entering her mark on the register. "To please her, Engels married her legally . . . on her death-bed", Eleanor recalled a fortnight before her own life ended.[25]

Immediately, in the very hour of Lizzie's death during that night, Engels wrote to Lessner to tell him the news and, on the same date, to his brother Rudolf in Barmen to say that his wife, "who had legally married me the evening before, died peace-fully after long sufferings". He also sent an announcement to *Vorwärts*: "I herewith notify my friends in Germany that my wife Lydia, née Burns, was torn from me by death during the past night."[138]

Thus he made the eleventh-hour marriage as widely known as possible, including to his family, and Lizzie lies buried in St. Mary's (Roman Catholic) cemetery in Kensal Green under a stone engraved with a delicate small Celtic cross enclosing the sacred monogram I.H.S., above the words:

---

* Like Jean, this child was born at 30 Leighton Grove, Kentish Town.

In memory of
Lydia
wife of Frederick Engels
born August 6th 1827 died September 12th 1878
R.I.P.

which tomb, now weather-worn, overgrown and hard to find, is also a monument to the man of feeling who honoured her wishes to the very last.

Eleanor and Mrs. Renshaw went to the funeral, as did Pumps, who was rigged out in mourning attire regardless of expense. This elicited from Marx the comment that her dress, added to the airs and graces she now gave herself, only served to emphasise her ill-concealed glee. Considering the bad relations that had existed between the girl and her aunt before the end and Pumps' seedy life in Manchester, her behaviour seems excusable; the more so since she was immediately elevated to the head of Engels' household—"knighted", as Marx called it, with the title of "Pumpsia"—where she reigned with some ineptitude for several years, earning Engels' affection and ever-increasing admiration, not shared by the Marxes.

It was during these years that Eleanor began to spread her wings. In the Reading Room of the British Museum she made several new acquaintances, including the young Irishman, George Bernard Shaw, her junior by 18 months, who had come to England in 1876 and to whom she was to draw much closer in years to come, not only by reason of their shared—then amateur—interest in the theatre, but also because he later claimed to have been completely converted by reading Marx's *Capital*—"the turning point in my career"[139]—and prided himself on being the only one of Hyndman's disciples in the Democratic Federation* to have read it, which he did in Gabriel Deville's popularised French version† "then accessible only . . . in the British Museum Reading Room, my daily resort".[141]

Another place where Eleanor found a congenial circle was at the meetings of the New Shakespeare Society, held in the

* Founded in June 1881.
† Deville's abridged translation, published in August 1883, had been approved by Marx in its earlier and by Engels in its later stages. As a matter of fact Shaw himself says that he read it in 1885 when "William Archer found me . . . poring over" it.[140]

Women's Reading Room of University College in Gower Street, out of which grew the "Dogberry", a little private Shakespeare Reading Club, whose members' subscriptions were devoted to buying tickets for Irving's First Nights, when he always let them have seats in the front row of the dress circle. One of its adherents, Mrs. Comyn,* has left a description[142] of these Club meetings which were most often held at the Marxes' house since Eleanor "was the leading spirit". Marx himself, "who had a guttural voice and a decided German accent", sat at the end of the long double drawing room. "As an audience he was delightful, never criticising, always entering into the spirit of any fun that was going on, laughing when anything struck him as particularly comic, until the tears ran down his cheeks —the oldest in years, but in spirit as young as any of us. And his friend, the faithful Frederic Engels, was equally spontaneous. . . . Near him [Marx] sat his wife—a lovable and charming woman. She was said to have been beautiful in her youth, but ill-health and perhaps turbulent times had taken their toll. Her skin had faded to a waxen pallor, there were purplish stains under her eyes." Mrs. Comyn remembers that the company included Edward Rose,† Mrs. Theodore Wright,‡ "pretty Dollie Radford"§ and Sir Henry Juta.‖ The house

---

* Marian Skinner, as she was at the time, married Henry Ernest Fitzwilliam Comyn in 1884. Her husband became Assistant Solicitor to the Treasury.

† Edward Rose became a playwright and the Vice-President of the Playgoers' Club founded in 1884. In 1886 Shaw acted—for the second and last time—in one of Rose's plays (*Odd to Say the Least of It*). Another of Rose's plays, *Her Father*, written in collaboration with J. T. Douglas, was performed in a Double Bill with *Dregs* by Edward Aveling—under the pen-name Alec Nelson—at the Vaudeville Theatre on 16 May 1889. Rose adapted Weyman's popular novel *Under the Red Robe* for the stage in 1896.

‡ Mrs. Theodore Wright was the former wife of George Jacob Holyoake, the Owenite, Co-operator and Secularist who was the last Englishman to be gaoled on a charge of atheism. He was the editor of *The Reasoner* and, though his wife left him for another, she had mixed in socialist circles since the days of the International and she both married and became a Fabian. An amateur actress of talent though little known in the professional theatre, she played Mrs. Alving in the first production of *Ghosts* at the Royalty Theatre in 1891 and was hailed by Shaw as "the pluckiest of the lot" among those performing Ibsen[141] and, at the same time, he offered her the eponymous role in *Mrs. Warren's Profession* (eventually taken by Fanny Brough, though not until 1902).

§ Both the Maitland sisters, Caroline, known as "Dollie", and Clara, attended the Dogberry meetings at 41 Maitland Park Road in 1880–1881. Dollie had been a friend of Furnivall's since her schooldays when he had taken her regularly to theatre matinées. She published some dozen volumes of verse between 1897 and 1910 under the name of Dollie Radford. Ernest Radford, whom she married in 1883 when they were both in their early twenties, was also a member of this little band of Shakespeare enthusiasts, though not mentioned by Mrs. Comyn. Marx

in Maitland Park Road "was a very ordinary suburban villa", but the atmosphere "I suppose . . . was Bohemian in its open-handed hospitality, its gracious welcome to strangers within its gates. And the strangers were numerous and shared the classic charm of great variety. There was one point of resemblance between them—for the most part they were impecunious. Shabby as to clothes, furtive in movement, but interesting, always interesting . . . Dr. Marx's manners to his family were altogether delightful."

One revealing passage in Mrs. Comyn's recollections* relates to Lenchen, who was so much taken for granted by the family as barely to have figured in all these years,† while no one either before or since ever described her relations with Eleanor from personal observation. "The nice-looking old German cook-housekeeper . . . was an excellent cook", wrote Mrs. Comyn. "She was a fresh-complexioned old woman, who wore gold ear-rings, and a chenille net over her hair, and who reserved to herself the right of 'speaking her mind' even to the august doctor. Her mind was respectfully, even meekly, received by all the family, except Eleanor, who frequently changed it. . . ."[142]

On Jenny's return from Malvernbury she found Harry "flourishing" and claimed that Eleanor had "*changed him—he is not the same at all. You have given him excellent habits at night . . .*". But poor Jenny, who had continued her teaching during her pregnancy and the suckling of her new-born infant, was now so harassed that she wrote in desperation to Tussy on

wrote to Jenny in April 1881: "Tussy has discovered a new *Wunderkind* among the Dogberries, a certain Radford; this youth is already a barrister-at-law . . . he looks well, cross between Irving and Lassalle . . . an intelligent and somewhat promising boy. . . . Dolly Maitland pays fearful court to him."

‖ Henry Juta, the son of Marx's sister Louise, came to London from Cape Town. In 1877, when his nephew was 21, Marx tried to obtain help for him to complete his law studies at the University of London and to be admitted to the Inner Temple. Juta became Attorney General of the Cape in 1894 and Speaker of the Cape House of Assembly from 1896 to 1898. He was knighted in 1897.

* Which she places "in the early 'eighties' " but which, though they certainly cover incidents up to and including 1883, and are much bolstered by hindsight, must in fact refer for the most part to the period before October 1881, from which time Mrs. Marx took to her bed.

† She appears in many reminiscences of the Marx household, in particular in Liebknecht's *Karl Marx zum Gedächtnis* where he recalls the young Lenchen as he first knew her, then "27 years of age and, while no beauty, she was nice-looking with rather pleasant and pleasing features. She had no lack of admirers and could have made a good match again and again."

23 September that it was "with great reluctance and regret that I send you these lines to ask you to replace me at Clement Danes tomorrow and Tuesday. I know you have already too much work on hand . . . it pains me . . . to burthen you with work of mine. . . ."[143]

Eleanor was, indeed, busy. She did not go away at all that summer and when Hirsch invited her to contribute to his journal in early June 1878—at which time Lissagaray had again gone to Jersey—she had to refuse "because my whole day is taken up by my work at the Museum".

But however absorbed she might be in her literary activities, one burning issue affected the entire family: the amnesty for the Communards in banishment and exile. The fight lasted for nine years, having been begun at the start of the proscriptions in 1871. The French Assembly threw out Bill after Bill until its dissolution in 1875, when the new government went no further than to grant a partial amnesty to those condemned after Bloody Week. François Grévy became President on 30 January 1879, by which time some of the Communards were beginning to return, though thousands remained in New Caledonia and hundreds who had fled were under sentence. A full amnesty was still withheld, but now popular sentiment began to assert itself and the people were recalling their old representatives by voting for them at every opportunity. Blanqui's election for Bordeaux in April 1879 was annulled by the government which, however, was obliged to extend the "pardons". The agitation, greatly strengthened by the organised forces of the new French Workers' Party,* took public forms: on 18 March 1880 the anniversary of the Commune was openly celebrated in Paris; on 23 May, despite police obstruction, enormous crowds flocked to the Père Lachaise cemetery to lay wreaths at the foot of the *mur des Fédérés*† and in July 1880 the ban on the proscripts was lifted.

Of the members of the family circle—if such he may be

---

* This "genuine workers' party", as Marx called it, had emerged from the decision taken at the 3rd Socialist Congress at Marseilles in October 1879 to form a Federation of Workers' Socialist Parties. A letter to the Congress supporting the motion was written by the London Communard exiles Longuet, Lissagaray, Johannard and Theisz. The Rules were adopted in July 1880 at a Paris Regional Congress attended by 24 Federations and nationally approved at the Havre Congress in November of that year.

† The wall against which 147 people had been shot by the Versailles troops.

called—Lissagaray was the first to avail himself of the amnesty, returning to Paris on 4 July 1880. He was followed that autumn by Longuet, whom Jenny rejoined in March 1881, while Paul Lafargue delayed his departure until April—and Laura until July—1882.

REFERENCE NOTES

Abbreviations

Andréas — *Briefe und Dokumente der Familie Marx aus den Jahren 1862–1873* by Bert Andréas in *Archiv für Sozialgeschichte*, II. Band, 1962. Verlag für Literatur und Zeitgeschehen, Hanover.

BIML — Institute of Marxism-Leninism, Berlin.

Bottigelli Archives — Letters in the custody of Dr. Emile Bottigelli, Paris.

Bottigelli L & D — *Lettres et Documents de Karl Marx 1856–1883*. Previously unpublished texts edited by Dr. Emile Bottigelli. Annali dell' Istituto Giangiacomo Feltrinelli, Anno Primo. Milan, 1958.

ELC — *Frederick Engels Paul and Laura Lafargue: Correspondence*, Volumes I–III. Lawrence & Wishart, 1959–1963.

IISH — International Institute of Social History, Amsterdam.

IWMA — *Documents of the First International*, Volumes I–V. Lawrence & Wishart, 1963–68.

Liebknecht — *Wilhelm Liebknecht Briefwechsel mit Karl Marx und Friedrich Engels*. Edited by Georg Eckert. Mouton & Co., The Hague, 1963.

MEW — *Marx Engels Werke*. Dietz Verlag, Berlin, 1956–1968. Unless otherwise stated Volumes 27–39.

MIML — Institute of Marxism-Leninism, Moscow.

(1) *La Commune de 1871* under the general editorship of Jean Bruhat, Jean Dautry and Emile Tersen. 2nd edition. Editions Sociales, Paris 1970.
(2) Laura to Eleanor, January 1870. Bottigelli Archives.
(3) *The Civil War in France.*
(4) To Mrs. Marx, 31 March 1869. Bottigelli Archives.
(5) 26 April 1869. MIML.

(6) To Jenny, 2 June 1869. Bottigelli Archives and Bottigelli L & D.

(7) Letter to Vera Zasulich, 23 April 1885. MEW.

(8) Engels, 1895 *Introduction* to Marx's *Class Struggles in France 1848 to 1850.*

(9) *The Eighteenth Brumaire of Louis Bonaparte.*

(10) 25 March 1868. ELC, Vol. I.

(11) First preface to *Anti-Dühring.* June 1878.

(12) John Smethurst. *Ermen & Engels. Marx House Bulletin* No. 41. January-March 1967.

(13) Published in English in the first German edition of 1845 and again in that of 1892, but not included in any English (or American) editions until 1958 with the publication of a translation by W. O. Henderson and W. H. Chaloner, Macmillan, New York, and Blackwell, Oxford.

(14) 4 April 1869. MEW.

(15) 21 October 1870. MEW.

(16) To Johann Philip Becker, 15 October 1884. MEW.

(17) *Sozialdemokratische Monatsschrift* Nos. 10–11. 30 November 1890. (In English in *Reminiscences of Marx and Engels.*)

(18) 10 June 1869. Original English MIML.

(19) Eleanor to Jenny, 2 June 1869. Bottigelli Archives.

(20) Engels to Marx, 23 May 1856. MEW.

(21) Marx to Kugelmann, 29 November 1869. MEW.

(22) *The Condition of the Working Class in England in 1844.* Trans. Florence Kelley Wishnewetzky 1892. George Allen & Unwin, 1936.

(23) Cecil Woodham-Smith. *The Great Hunger.* Hamish Hamilton, 1962.

(24) 4 November 1869. Address of the Land and Labour League (founded in October 1869) to the Working Men and Women of Great Britain and Ireland.

(25) To Kautsky, 15 March 1898. IISH.

(26) 8 March 1892. MEW.

(27) Eleanor to Jenny, 19 (misdated 20) July 1869. Bottigelli Archives.

(28) *Report of the Commissioners on the Treatment of the Treason-felony Convicts in the English Convict Prisons.* It was known as the Knox-Pollock Report after the investigators, Alexander Knox, a former *Times* correspondent turned Police Commissioner, and George Pollock, an army surgeon.

(29) To Engels, 27 June 1867. MEW.

(30) Engels in an unpublished manuscript wrtitten *c.* 5 July 1870

for a preface to a collection of Irish songs. First published in Italy (No. 2 of *Movemento Operaio* 1955), and then in France (*La Pensée* 1957), it appeared in English, translated from the manuscript by Angela Clifford, in *Frederick Engels: History of Ireland*. Irish Communist Organisation, London 1965. (2nd edition 1970.)

(31) First published in German and Russian in *Marx-Engels Archives*, Volume 10, 1948. (MEW, Volume 16). See (30) for English translation.

(32) 30 October 1869. Andréas.

(33) IWMA. Vol. III.

(34) To Marx, 29 November 1869. MEW.

(35) 29 November 1869. MEW.

(36) 5 March 1870. English Original MIML.

(37) Postscript to letter from Marx to Engels, 10 February 1870. MEW.

(38) IWMA Vol. IV.

(39) 13 December 1870. MEW.

(40) Jenny to Kugelmann, 19 November 1870. Andréas.

(41) 12 August 1870. English Original MIML.

(42) Frank Jellinek. *The Paris Commune of 1871*. Gollancz, 1937. Lissagaray estimated the victims of the Commune, apart from dependants, at 100,000 compared with 140,000 killed in the entire Franco-Prussian War.

(43) *History of the Commune of 1871*. Translated from the French of Lissagaray by Eleanor Marx Aveling. Reeves & Turner, London 1886.

(44) Mrs. Marx to Kugelmann, 12 May 1871. Andréas.

(45) Letter in *The Irishman* of 29 April 1871 over Jenny's pen-name "J. Williams", published, following the obituary notice on Flourens, to give a fuller account of his devoted championship of the Irish cause.

(46) Jenny to Kugelmann, 18 April 1871. Andréas.

(47) 15 April 1871. *Réimpression (in extenso) du Journal Officiel de la Commune*. Victor Bunel, Paris 1872.

(48) *Ibid.*

(49) Marx to Jenny, Laura and Eleanor, 13 June 1871. English Original MIML.

(50) Eleanor to Liebknecht, 29 December 1871. Liebknecht.

(51) Marx to Kugelmann, 18 June 1871. MEW.

(52) English Original BIML.

(53) Jeremiah O'Donovan Rossa. *My Years in English Jails*. Originally published by the American News Company, New

York, in 1874. English edition edited by Sean Ua Cearnaigh, Anvil Books, Tralee, Co. Kerry 1967.

(54) 12 April 1871. MEW.

(55) Mrs. Marx to Liebknecht, 26 May 1872. Liebknecht.

(56) 29 December 1871. Liebknecht.

(57) Jenny to Kugelmann, 21 December 1871. Andréas.

(58) Engels to Sorge, 17 March 1872. MEW.

(59) Eleanor to the Aberdeen Socialist Society, 17 March 1893. The original letter was lent by William Diack, former secretary of the Aberdeen Socialist Society, to Mr. G. Allen Hutt in 1939 and was published in *Labour Monthly*, March 1940.

(60) Henri Perret to Marx from Geneva, 8 October 1870. Original French MIML.

(61) Paul Lafargue to Engels, 26 December 1871. ELC, Vol. III.

(62) Volume I, Barcelona 1923. (English in *Reminiscences of Marx and Engels*.)

(63) This letter was one of those sold at Sotheby's on 15 May 1967 to the Soviet Embassy where I was allowed to read it before it went into the archives in Moscow.

(64) Marx's *Civil War in France* was published on 13 June 1871.

(65) *Programme and Rules of the International Alliance of Socialist Democracy*. November 1868.

(66) *Progress*, May 1883. A second article appeared in June. Curiously enough Eleanor misdated the climactic Hague Congress 1873.

(67) Eleanor to Kautsky, 3 December 1897. IISH.

(68) Engels to Philip Patten in New York, 18 April 1883. MEW.

(69) 12-17 September 1874. MEW.

(70) 27 June 1872. Andréas.

(71) 9 November 1871. MEW.

(72) *Eastern Post*, 16 and 23 December 1871.

(73) 26 May 1872. Liebknecht.

(74) 11 March 1872. ELC, Vol. I.

(75) 26 May 1872. Liebknecht.

(76) Mrs. Marx to Sorge, January 1877. MEW.

(77) 7 November 1872. MIML.

(78) Andréas.

(79) 10 September 1872 from 134 Harley Street. Bottigelli Archives.

(80) Jenny to Kugelmann, 23 December 1872. Andréas.

(81) 7 November 1872. Bottigelli Archives.

(82) Mrs. Marx to Eleanor, 25 March 1873. MIML.

(83) Mrs. Marx to Eleanor, 3 April 1873. MIML.

(84) Eleanor to Marx, 3 May 1873. Bottigelli Archives and IISH.

(85) Mrs. Marx to Eleanor, before 3 May 1873. MIML.

(86) Mrs. Marx to Eleanor, late April 1873. MIML.

(87) Privately communicated.

(88) Eleanor to Mrs. Marx, 31 May 1873. IISH.

(89) Mrs. Marx to Eleanor, n.d. probably June 1873. MIML.

(90) Mrs. Marx to Eleanor, c. 22 May 1873. MIML.

(91) Quoted by Mrs. Marx in letter to Eleanor, c. 31 May 1873. MIML and IISH.

(92) Mrs. Marx to Thomas Allsop. 12 September 1874. (See Ref. 63.)

(93) A good, if biased, start has been made by Paul Mayer in *Die Geschichte des Sozialdemokratischen Parteiarchivs und das Schicksal des Marx-Engels Nachlasses. Archiv für Sozialgeschichte*, VI./VII. Band 1966/67. Verlag für Literatur und Zeitgeschehen, Hanover. As this book was about to go to press the researches of two journalists, Messrs. Heinz Stern & Dieter Wolf, into the fate of Marx's unpublished MSS. appeared in the German Democratic Republic. Unfortunately their findings, even where relevant to a biography of Eleanor Marx, cannot be incorporated in this volume.

(94) Written in 1928. English in *Reminiscences of Marx and Engels*.

(95) Bottigelli Archives and IISH.

(96) Some of the biographical details are given in *Notice sur Lissagaray* by Amédée Dunois in a preface to *L'Histoire de la Commune de 1871*, Librairie de Travail, Paris, 1929; others from (1).

(97) Dossier on Carl Hirsch in the archives of, and officially stamped by the Secretariat General of the Paris Prefecture of Police found by Professor Dr. Bruno Kaiser in Switzerland and presented to the Berlin Institute of Marxism-Leninism in November 1963.

(98) Bertall. *The Communists of Paris 1871*. Buckingham & Co., Paris, London and Dublin 1873.

(99) In addition to information extracted from intercepted correspondence, there are nine complete letters from Eleanor and one from Mrs. Marx to Hirsch, written between 1875 and 1878. These could have been confiscated with such other items as his address book when Hirsch's rooms were searched by the police who did not then enjoy photocopying facilities. Three of Eleanor's letters—dated 25 October 1875, 25

November 1876 and 8 June 1878—are published in MEW, Volume 34; five, including the above three, in the possession of the Ohara Institute for the Study of Social Problems attached to Hosei University, Tokyo, were published in the original French by Dr. C. Tsuzuki in *Bulletin No. 8* of the Society for the Study of Labour History, Spring 1964. The two additional letters from this source are dated 12 May and 18 July 1876. Three further letters from Eleanor of 16 and 27 July and 20 October 1876, and one from Mrs. Marx to Hirsch in early May 1876 have not been published hitherto. The originals, owned by Professor Dr. Sakasaki of Japan, were given in photostat to BIML, by whose courtesy I was permitted to use a copy. While Eleanor wrote to Hirsch in French, his letters to her were in German. MIML.

(100) 12 May 1885. ELC, Vol. I.

(101) Jenny to Marx, 24 February 1882. MIML.

(102) Jenny to Eleanor, 1 September 1875. IISH.

(103) Mrs. Marx to Thomas Allsop, 12 September 1874. (See Ref. 63.)

(104) This document, in the archives of the Public Record Office, had been mislaid when searches were made. A photocopy was kindly provided by the IISH.

(105) An article of that title by W. Fraser Rae appeared in *The Nineteenth Century*, Vol. XVI, July–December 1884.

(106) Egon Erwin Kisch. *Karl Marx in Karlsbad*. Aufbau Verlag, Berlin, 1953.

(107) *Marx House Bulletin*, No. 39. July–September 1966.

(108) Eleanor to Jenny, 5 September 1874. Bottigelli Archives.

(109) Published in English as *Letters to Kugelmann*. Lawrence & Wishart, 1936.

(110) Liebknecht.

(111) To Natalie Liebknecht, 23 October 1874. Liebknecht.

(112) To Natalie Liebknecht, 1 January 1875. Liebknecht.

(113) Jenny announced the appointment to an unknown French correspondent on 25 December 1874. BIML.

(114) Information supplied by the Historical Research Department of the Greater London Council Record Office.

(115) Mrs. Marx to Hirsch, n.d. From internal evidence late April or early May 1876. BIML.

(116) *Frederick James Furnivall. A Volume of Personal Record* edited by Henry Froude, O.U.P. 1911.

(117) Quoted by her son, Compton Mackenzie, in *My Life and Times. Octave 7*, 1931–1938, Chatto & Windus 1968.

(118) Mrs. Marx to Sorge, 20 or 21 January 1877. MEW.

(119) G. Bernard Shaw. *The Perfect Wagnerite*. Constable, 1898.

(120) Mrs. Marx to J. P. Becker, n.d. after 20 August 1867. MEW.

(121) Published in the *Deutsch-Französiche Jahrbücher*, Paris 1844. *On the Jewish Question* appears in English in *Karl Marx: Early Writings* translated and edited by T. B. Bottomore. C. A. Watts, 1963.

(122) *Karl Marx and Friedrich Engels. Correspondence 1846–1895.* Translated and edited by Dona Torr. Martin Lawrence, 1934.

(123) Eleanor to Mrs. Marx, 19 August 1876. Bottigelli Archives.

(124) 1 February 1877. IISH.

(125) MEGA I.1.

(126) Luise Dornemann. *Jenny Marx*. Dietz Verlag, Berlin, 1968.

(127) Marx to Lavrov, 24 February 1877. MEW.

(128) 6 November 1876. MEW.

(129) Liebknecht to Engels, 20 October 1878. Liebknecht.

(130) Brian Simon. *Education and the Labour Movement 1870–1918.* Lawrence & Wishart, 1965.

(131) 25 November 1876 (misdated September in the *Bulletin* of the Society for the Study of Labour History, Spring 1964).

(132) 16 November 1889. ELC, Vol. II.

(133) 9 August 1887. ELC, Vol. II.

(134) Mrs. Marx to Eleanor, 20 November 1877. MIML.

(135) Mrs. Marx to Marx, 25 November 1877. MIML.

(136) Mrs. Marx to Eleanor, n.d. probably November 1877. MIML.

(137) August 1878 from Malvernbury. MIML.

(138) Published on 18 September 1878.

(139) Quoted in Hesketh Pearson's *Bernard Shaw, His Life and Personality*. Methuen, 1961.

(140) G. B. Shaw. *Sixteen Self-Sketches*. Constable & Co., 1949.

(141) To William Archer, 23 April 1891. G. B. Shaw. *Collected Letters 1874–1897*. Edited by Dan H. Laurence. Reinhardt, 1965.

(142) *The Nineteenth Century and After*. Vol. 91, No. 539 January 1922.

(143) IISH.

PART III

BREAKING POINTS

Eleanor has been described by many of those who knew her in these or later years—by Will Thorne, the founder and General Secretary of the Gas Workers' and General Labourers' Union; by Henry Mayers Hyndman, who formed the Social Democratic Federation; by William Collison, employers' spy and strikebreaker who called himself "the Apostle of Free Labour"; by Henry Havelock Ellis, the first Englishman to bring sex out of the private into the public sector and by Beatrice Potter,* to mention but a few of whom more will be heard—but there are two accounts, admittedly written in retrospect, that show her as she was in her mid-twenties before she had broken out of the shell of family life.

They are of especial interest if only because the impression she made upon these observers, whose vantage points could not have been more disparate, is strikingly in accord.

Marian Skinner, the young lady who frequented 41 Maitland Park Road as one of Eleanor's literary-minded friends to whom Marx played host when his arcane studies permitted, says that he "treated Eleanor with the indulgent affection one bestows on a beloved but wilful child. Wilful indeed she was, but she was also an unusually brilliant creature, with a clear, logical brain, a shrewd knowledge of men and a wonderful memory. . . . She either passionately admired or desperately scorned, she loved fervently or she hated with vehemence. Middle courses never commended themselves to her. She had amazing vitality, extraordinary receptivity, and she was the gayest creature in the world—when she was not the most miserable. Her appearance was striking. She was not really beautiful, but she somehow gave the impression of beauty by reason of her sparkling eyes, her bright colouring, her dark locky mass of hair. . . ."[1]

* Although mentioned earlier as one of the collaborators in Charles Booth's *Labour and Life of the People* (see fn., pp. 174–5), Miss Beatrice Potter (1858–1943), who became Mrs. Sidney Webb in 1892, is not to be confused with the even more widely read Miss Beatrix Potter (1866–1943), later Mrs. Heelis, of *Peter Rabbit* fame.

Eduard Bernstein* met Eleanor for the first time in 1880 when he came to London for a week in November. His was no ordinary social visit. As private secretary to and one of the German socialists grouped round the wealthy publisher Karl Höchberg† who had emigrated to Switzerland in 1878, Bernstein had come under heavy fire from Marx and Engels. With August Bebel‡ he at last decided to clear the position by bearding the lions in their den: "Going to Canossa", Bebel called it.[2]

To Bernstein, then, on his political mission, Eleanor was simply the daughter of the house of whom he left two separate descriptions. In the earlier one[3] he referred to her at this first meeting as "a lively young girl of slender build with beautiful black hair and fine dark eyes. . . . At that time she was already working hard at the British Museum, partly for her father,§ partly 'devilling', that is, taking excerpts or doing research for a pittance to save well-to-do people who wanted to write books the trouble of looking things up for themselves."

At a Benefit Concert for the widow of a Communard, Bernstein—startled to find that the list of subscribers was headed by Queen Victoria with a donation of £10—heard Eleanor recite *The Pied Piper of Hamelin* and was much struck by her "tremendous verve and wonderful voice". The occasion, despite its regal patronage, was graced by the presence of Marx, Engels, Bebel, Carl Hirsch, Leo Hartmann and a pack of "other Reds".[3]

In his later reminiscences, written in 1915, he repeated his commendation of her striking appearance and "exceptionally musical voice", adding: "She was unusually vivacious and took part, in her sensitive and emotional manner, in our discussions of party matters. With much greater devotion than her two

* 1850–1932. From 1881 to 1890 Bernstein edited the German Social Democratic Party's official organ, the *Sozialdemokrat*, issued in Zürich until 1888 and, from October of that year until the following September, in London.
† The pseudonym of Dr. Ludwig Richter.
‡ 1840–1913. One of the founders of the German Social Democratic Party at Eisenach in 1869, Bebel remained continuously the Chairman of its Central Committee.
§ There is no contemporary evidence that Eleanor was working for Marx at this time, apart from dealing with some of his vast correspondence when he was unwell. She herself wrote to Jenny a few months later to say that she had been offered the job of précis writer for a scientific journal. "I suppose you know that in literary slang a précis writer is one who summarises articles, books, etc. It is a mere trick to do it but . . . I have never tried it and don't know if I can do it . . . if I can I shall earn £2 a week and not have much work—about a quarter of what I'm doing now . . ."[4]

elder sisters, Tussy . . . had dedicated herself to the socialist movement . . . On my first visit this girl was . . . the pet of the family."[5]

It was natural that Marian Skinner should see only the "brilliant creature", whose diverse talents were to include speaking at socialist meetings, while Bernstein regarded her first and foremost as the "perfervid socialist".

Yet socialism in England was almost non-existent at that time.

It was to Bernstein, before he had met him, that Engels wrote: "For years the English working class movement has revolved hopelessly in a narrow circle of strikes for higher wages and shorter hours, not as a makeshift* nor as a means of propaganda, but as an end in itself. The Trades Unions in fact exclude on principle and in their rules all political action and thereby debar the working class from taking part in any general activity as a class. . . . So one can speak of a workers' movement here only insofar as there are strikes which, successful or not, advance the movement by not a step. To inflate such strikes—which, moreover, during the recent bad trade years have quite often been deliberately engineered by the capitalists to furnish a pretext for closing their factories—strikes by which the working class makes no headway, into struggles of world importance . . . can, in my opinion, only do harm. It should not be concealed that at present no real workers' movement, in the Continental sense, exists here. . . ."[6]

The population of Great Britain had reached nearly 30 million in 1881, an increase of 28 per cent in 20 years. 12,731,000 were "occupied persons", of whom one-third were females, with nearly two million in domestic service—"useless persons, eating their heads off and producing nothing"[7]—while in 1880 a mere quarter of a million were estimated to be organised in 34 trade unions.† Thus, in disparaging the trade unionists' futile

---

* Engels uses the word *Notbehelf*, generally translated as "expedient" in this context, which does not precisely convey the meaning.

† The Webbs' *History of Trade Unionism* (1919 edition) states that "until the appointment, in 1886, of John Burnett as Labour Correspondent to the Board of Trade, no attempt was made to collect any statistics of the movement, and the old Unions seldom possess a complete series of their own archives. No total figure can be given with any confidence." The estimated number of trade unionists in 1880 showed a slight decline from that of 1875—when it was nearer to 300,000— reflecting the first wave of the economic crisis in the period 1873 to 1879. With intermittent years of recovery, notably 1880 to 1882 and 1887 to 1890, the great depression lasted until 1896.

round of strikes, sometimes instigated by the factory owners themselves, Engels was referring to class conflicts which were not only without political significance but which left the mass of the workers untouched.

As for "real workers' movements in the Continental sense", they were genuine and formidable enough for the German Reichstag to have passed the Anti-Socialist Law,* under which Liebknecht was gaoled yet again for three months at the end of October 1878 and whose long arm extended to Germans abroad, so that Carl Hirsch was arrested in Paris on 16 August 1879,† while a fresh stream of socialist refugees flowed into England.

But, dangerous as the workers' party appeared to the German ruling class, Marx saw it as increasingly under the influence of doctors, students and what he called "professorial socialist riff-raff . . . nonentities in theory and useless in practice" who were eroding the movement by a brand of socialism "concocted according to university recipes", palatable to the petty bourgeoisie. Marx and Engels jointly drafted a circular letter to the leaders of the German Social Democratic Party analysing its position, making their own attitude towards it clear. "For almost 40 years", they wrote, "we have stressed the class struggle between bourgeoisie and proletariat as the main lever of modern social revolution; it is therefore impossible for us to co-operate with people who seek to expunge this class struggle from the movement. When the International was founded we explicitly formulated the battle-cry: The emancipation of the working classes must be brought about by the working classes themselves. We cannot therefore associate ourselves with people who openly state that the workers are too uneducated to emancipate themselves and must be freed from above by philanthropic big bourgeois and petty bourgeois . . . for which purpose the working class must place itself under the leadership of 'educated and propertied' bourgeois, who alone possess the

---

* The Bill was put before the Reichstag on 8 September 1878, debated for six weeks and passed by 221 to 149 votes on 19 October. The Act came into force two days later, was constantly renewed and not finally repealed until October 1890.
† He was picked up in the street, taken before the Police Commissioner and then left for two days in the Prefecture before being sentenced to a month's imprisonment for "unauthorised re-entry" to France, which he left forthwith, arriving in London on 23 August.

'time and opportunity' to acquaint themselves with what is good for the workers."

In contrast to this view, Hyndman in England expressed the opinion "that the emancipation of the workers must be brought about by the workers themselves is true in the sense that we cannot have Socialism without Socialists. . . . But a slave cannot be freed by the slaves themselves. The leadership, the initiative, the teaching, the organisation must come from those who are born into a different position and are trained to use their faculties in early life."[*8]

For a period of a few months from the end of 1880, Henry Mayers Hyndman—introduced, according to his own account[8] by Carl Hirsch, but according to Engels' by Rudolph-Hermann Meyer†—enjoyed an acquaintance with Marx. The families visited each other, Eleanor accompanying her father to dine with the Hyndmans at 10 Devonshire Street, Portland Place, when her mother was not well enough to go, while the Hyndmans called—sometimes uninvited—at the Marxes' "modest dwelling in Haverstock Hill".[8] Though Hyndman was never shaken in his conviction that at this period the regard was mutual and that he was indeed favoured by a special intimacy with Marx "accessible to very few outside the immediate family circle", attributing to Engels—upon whom he never set eyes but called "the Teutonic Grand Lama of the Regent's Park Road"[8]—a jealousy and arrogance that severed this beautiful friendship, his belief was false. Marx did not take to him, thought him smug and overweening, resented the way he forced himself upon him and stole "many of my evenings to pick my brains and thus to learn things by the easiest means". In a letter to his daughter Jenny in April 1881 he wrote of "an invasion" by the Hyndmans on which occasion they so outstayed their welcome that Mrs. Marx was completely exhausted

---

* The interesting point here—for no one would deny that both Marx and Engels were "born into a different position" from that of the average worker—is Hyndman's blurring of the distinction between theory and practice: to lead and to teach slaves who have no initiative or organisation of their own would seem to be not a means to socialism but a perfect waste of time. "Hyndman's bourgeois mentality made it impossible for him to estimate the worth of industrial organization correctly", wrote Tom Mann who nevertheless admired his ability to address working men on socialism and "to state the case comprehensively, logically and argumentatively".[9]

† A German émigré economist and journalist who frequented the Marxes, Engels and the Lafargues.

and had to retire. "I quite like the wife for her blunt, uncon-
ventional and decided manner of thinking and speaking, but the
admiring way she hangs on the lips of her self-satisfied, garrulous
husband is comical", wrote Marx.

Although his talks with Marx undoubtedly fired Hyndman's
resolve to establish "a really democratic party in opposition
to the monstrous tyranny of Mr. Gladstone and his Whigs in
Ireland and their equally abominable policy in Egypt,* with
the object of bringing about democratic changes in England", [8]
the wide political differences between the two men were thereby
brought to light.

The inevitable breach between them—ascribed by Hyndman
to Marx's resentment at his name having been omitted and
Hyndman's debt to him unacknowledged in the little book
England for All†—has been finally and fully documented by
Dr. Emile Bottigelli.[10] Marx's objections were not to the half-
baked plagiarism of *Capital*; certainly not to the fact that he
received no personal credit, for, as he wrote to Hyndman,
"Party programmes ought to be kept free of any apparent
dependence upon individual authors or books"; and not even
to the foolish excuse—as applied to the friend of the Chartists
and the leader of the International—that his name "was so
much detested" and "Englishmen have a dread of being taught
by a foreigner", but quite simply—apart from Hyndman's

---

* This refers to the Coercion Act of 1881 whereby the leaders of the Irish Land
League suspected of "seditious conspiracy" could be arrested. It followed upon the
workings of the 1870 Land Act which gave no security from eviction for tenants
who did not pay the rent laid down by the landlord. A Bill mitigating these conditions was thrown out by the Lords and, in 1880, Lord Ernle's steward, Captain
Boycott, refused the fair—but not full—rent offered by his tenants, and issued
eviction notices, whereupon the entire tenantry, including his parish priest, shopkeepers, postmen, laundresses, blacksmiths, farm-hands and domestic staff refused
to serve him. A new word was added to the English language, while Irish M.P.s,
notably Parnell, were sent to prison.

Britain and France between them had succeeded in bringing Egypt to a state
of bankruptcy by means of loans for the building of railways, bridges, canals and
docks paid for by the peasants, who had least need of these improvements which
were of vital importance to Britain in particular, both for the control of the
Suez Canal (opened in 1869) as the route to India, and as the chief importer of
Egyptian cotton vastly developed at the time of the American Civil War. In 1881
the nationalist movement under army command seized power, whereupon the
British and French sent battleships to Alexandria and, in the following year, the
British bombarded the city and landed an army which, by September 1882, im-
posed military control over the whole country.

† Published June 1881. Hyndman claimed it to be the "first socialist work that
appeared up to 1881 in English".[8]

disingenuousness in approaching him only after the booklet was in the press—to the fact that borrowings, however distorted, from *Capital* had no place in a programme whose professed aims were wholly at variance with its theories.

The Democratic Federation, founded in June 1881,* was composed on Hyndman's own showing of Comtists, Tories, middle-class Radicals and M.P.s, with a sprinkling of ancient Chartists, none of whom could have agreed on any but the mildest of social reforms. "What can you expect", wrote Engels, "of a set of people who take in hand the task of instructing the world about matters of which they themselves are ignorant? There is not a single burning question which they know how to tackle; Hyndman combines internationalist phraseology with jingo aspirations."[11]

In fact Hyndman had not picked Marx's brains thoroughly enough to arrive at the fundamental concept of an independent workers' party. He had read the French edition of *Capital* before he met Marx but "did not at the time"—nor ever after—"fully grasp all the significance of his theories"[8] and to have used them—however rightly or wrongly presented—for the embellishment of a programme acceptable to "*the* Englishmen"[10]—without distinction of class—was something Marx could not condone. He wrote to Hyndman on 2 July 1881 from Eastbourne where he was staying with his wife, having given himself time to turn the matter over. "On Saturday", Mrs. Marx reported to Laura, "the pale-eyed Hyndman received his blow on the head. He is not likely to prop up the letter on his looking-glass, although, for all its pungency, it was so wittily worded that anger was barely perceptible. I think Mohr was rather happy in this opus."†[12]

From this letter it would appear that the "refined and highly intelligent woman" of Hyndman's reminiscences, whose "great charm of manner and conversation"[8] had fed the conceit that he was the most welcome of guests at Maitland Park Road, did not reciprocate this high esteem.

Nevertheless, Hyndman's Federation, which Eleanor joined,

---

* Subsequently the Social Democratic Federation.

† Far from putting this letter on show, Hyndman did not even keep it. Thus, were it not for Mrs. Marx's (unpublished) letter to Laura,[12] there would be no trace of it and Hyndman's version[8] the only explanation of the breach until Dr. Bottigelli discovered the original draft of Marx's letter among the Longuet papers.[10]

was to play a major part in the revival of socialism and the
development of the labour movement in Britain at a time when
America, France and Germany had begun to break England's
monopoly of world trade.* But for the hostility between Engels
and Hyndman, born of the latter's irrational conceit that he
was regarded as a rival who had threatened to supplant Engels
in Marx's life, the whole course of British socialism, Eleanor's
part in it and her personal fate might have taken a different
turn in the years to come.

In the meantime, she was not only participating in political
discussions with Bernstein and Bebel at her parents' table and
dining with the Hyndmans but she associated with Helen
Taylor† and Joseph Cowen,‡ both of whom were among the
founder members of the Democratic Federation, writing to tell
Hirsch of her various dealings with them,[14] though it is not
clear from the context whether this was in connection with Miss
Taylor's keen interest in the Irish question or another crusade
on which Eleanor was now embarked.

In November 1880 she sent out two letters to 38 London and
provincial papers§ drawing public attention to the state of
siege declared under the Anti-Socialist Law and the expulsion
of citizens from Hamburg, Altona, Ottensen, Blankenese, Wedel
and Lauenburg (which included some of Bismarck's own landed
property). "Of course", she wrote to Liebknecht, "very few—
if any will take notice of it—but at least I wish to *try* and do
something. . . . I am also going to try with Hirsch to get up
a committee here to collect funds for the families."[15] She was
so far successful that in October 1881 she sent Karl Kautsky,

---

* It may also be said that the character of the British labour movement was determined by the fact that, following the challenge to its position as the leading capitalist
country, England entered the stage of exporting capital to its expanding Empire.
The effects of this trend, which were not—and perhaps could not be—analysed
until several decades later, were to give certain sections of workers a privileged
position, damping down their need and desire for any basic social changes. One
writer rammed home the point in the phrase: "There is not a more contented
community, nor one less likely to be influenced by Communistic or Socialist
ideas, on the face of the earth, than the British working class."[13] Since these skilled
workers were also the most powerful and best organised sections, the unskilled and
unorganised were in a peculiarly vulnerable position and it was they who displayed
the militancy otherwise so markedly lacking during the late '80s and the '90s.

† J. S. Mill's stepdaughter.

‡ M.P. for Newcastle, where he had organised meetings for Garibaldi in 1864.
An old Chartist, Engels characterised him as "half if not a whole Communist
and a very good chap".

§ See Appendix 4, p. 301.

then in Zürich, 40 marks subscribed by Helen Taylor for the families of the persecuted socialists.[16]

At the beginning of February 1881, Michael Davitt, who had founded the Irish Land League in 1879, was arrested*: "an act of cowardly retaliation and petty spite". Knowing that he was to appear at Bow Street on 11 February, Eleanor went to the Police Court "and found a large—and angry—crowd assembled outside the station". The crowd was angry because, contrary to all precedent, the prisoner had been brought before the magistrate at 8 a.m. "The government feared to face the public", was Eleanor's comment. She asked a policeman whether Davitt was still in Court and was told in a strong Irish brogue " 'No, it's meself put him in the van' ", whereupon she " 'went for him' " and asked "if there weren't enough Englishmen to do such dirty work that an Irishman must help 'put in the van' a man who like Davitt had done so much for his country". As she turned away in disgust an Irishman standing in the crowd came up to her and said: "Allow me to shake hands with you and thank you."[17] In the same letter to Liebknecht she asked him to send her any information he had about working-class opposition to the Jew-baiting in Germany: "I might get something about it into the press."

It will be seen that at this stage of her life, whatever other interests she pursued, Eleanor was involved in every social issue at home and abroad and was, indeed, as her mother had earlier pronounced her, "political from top to bottom".

* He had previously served a seven year sentence (1870 to 1877) as a Fenian convict.

§ 2

One feature of Eleanor's personality, seldom if ever described by her contemporaries, was her intense love of children. Not the least of her tragedies was that she had none of her own. Everybody's babies interested her. She never wrote to young parents without making the closest enquiries about their off-spring, but her most passionate maternal feelings were centred on her nephews.

On 17 August 1879, with Lenchen in attendance at 6 Artillery Road, Ramsgate, Jenny had given birth to another son, Edgar Marcel, nicknamed Wolf. When she left England in February 1881 to rejoin her husband in Paris she was in her eighth month of pregnancy with the fourth son, Marcel Charles, known as Par.*

In a letter to Natalie Liebknecht written at that time Eleanor described these little boys: "Harry . . . is a very backward and very delicate child . . . and requires much care and attention—so much in fact that it is difficult for him to get it as the next child (who is very forward) is only 13 months younger than he and Jenny expects another baby in March! This last expectation is not altogether a blessing . . . it is difficult to attend to three—one might almost say four babies, for of course Johnny is still only a baby . . . five next May . . . a dear little fellow . . . a very beautiful boy . . . the second boy—*my* boy—Harry is not pretty . . . but I love him best of all because I think his nature is by far the sweetest of the three, and he is one of those children who seem destined to suffer. . . ." The youngest, Edgar, was his mother's favourite: "not so handsome as Johnny" in Eleanor's view, but "strong and healthy, bright—and terribly spoilt".[18]

One of the reasons why Longuet had gone back to France ahead of his family—apart from the Marxes' strong desire to keep Jenny and the children with them for as long as possible—

* Including the first child who did not survive, Jenny bore in all six children—five boys and a girl—between September 1873 and September 1882.

was that his mother had written to her daughter-in-law in March 1879 complaining of her solitude and repeating the rather individualist argument, expressed on her last visit to England, that if she longed for an amnesty it was not that she wished to deprive Charles or Jenny of their employment in London but to enable her son to come to France where his property was being sequestrated, running her into losses to the tune of thousands of francs.[19]

Although Madame Longuet senior does not appear a very sympathetic character, she did at least show genuine concern for Mrs. Marx's health and was perturbed when no news came, while her interest in her grandchildren, though not overpowering, was enough for Longuet to send her reports on their characters, teething troubles, and locks of Johnny's and Harry's hair (Edgar's he could not send because, owing to eczema, the poor child was bald at six months).[20]

There is no question but that Jenny loved her husband dearly, particularly in his absence, when she wrote that she realised "how lonely my life would be without you" and found herself waiting impatiently for the postman's knock to announce a letter from him.[21] Her departure for France—where for the short time that remained to her she lived in a house at Argenteuil* once a rich man's summer residence—caused the family great unhappiness. Mrs. Marx had been dreading it.

When the amnesty was granted in the summer of 1880, before setting out for a last seaside holiday with the Longuets and Lafargues to Ramsgate, she had been to Manchester to consult Gumpert once again, accompanied this time by Marx who, not satisfied, wrote at the end of September to Dr. Ferdinand Fleckles in Carlsbad appealing for advice. Never having seen or examined the patient, the doctor set out a list of questions for her to answer. Instead of replying to these in detail she sent him a letter—unread by Marx—giving a comprehensive account of her state of mind and health in which she said: "What has made my condition worse recently perhaps is a great anxiety which weighs heavily upon us 'old ones'. The

---

* This, the cradle of impressionist painting, was later to be the constituency for which Gabriel Péri was the Deputy from 1932 until his arrest in May 1941, when he was handed over by the Vichy government to the Nazis who executed him on 15 December 1941.

French amnesty will in all probability be synonymous for us with the loss of our children and grandchildren. And my own removal to Paris in my present condition frightens me . . . So I clutch at every straw. Dear, good Doctor, I should so like to live a little longer. How strange it is that the nearer the whole thing draws to an end, the more one clings to this 'vale of tears'." The whole household was topsy-turvy with the imminence of his eldest daughter's leavetaking, Marx wrote. The grand-children were "an inexhaustible source of joy to me and my wife in whose present circumstances this separation is most painful". They had dearly hoped that Harry, at least, would be left with them because, as Marx later wrote to Jenny, "he is a child who wants a whole family's attendance being singly, exclusively concentrated upon him. As it is, with so many other little ones requesting your care, he is rather an impediment." Eleanor, who also missed her nephews sorely, wrote: "This is a sad blow for Papa and Mama, as they are so devoted to the children"[18] and, indeed, a month after the young family had left Marx wrote to Jenny: "I often run to the window when I hear children's voices . . . forgetting for the moment that the little fellows are across the Channel."

The parting, however, was not final for there were visits to Argenteuil while, to the end of Jenny's days, Eleanor kept up an intimate correspondence with her, showing a love that was heightened not only by separation but also perhaps because, for reasons that remain obscure, there was a great coldness between Eleanor and Laura in these years.* Indeed, as early as 1879, while the parents were in Ramsgate with Jenny after her confinement and the two sisters in London, Engels was hard put to it to contrive that they should not meet at his house for the usual Sunday dinner. He communicated his stratagems to Marx and it was clearly understood on both sides that they were necessary. The antagonism of the Lafargues to Lissagaray—manifested at their first meeting and exploding into a quarrel between him and Paul—does not account for the

---

* In the summer of 1882, when Eleanor rejoined Marx in Argenteuil and the Lafargues were living in Paris (see p. 237), he wrote to Engels "Tussy and Laura have not yet seen each other and are hardly yearning to do so." For the sake of decency, he went on, they would have to meet at least once while he was there. In later years they corresponded in friendly terms on practical matters, and there was some warmth in the relationship towards the end, though Laura did not attend Eleanor's funeral. According to *Justice* she was too "prostrated by grief".[22]

estrangement between the sisters since Paul never evinced any ill-feeling towards Eleanor.

As the months passed Mrs. Marx's health grew ominously worse. Yet her cry from the heart to Dr. Fleckles was the only sign she gave of her knowledge and fear that she was dying. In her last decade Mrs. Marx became the gracious and serene figure recalled in so many reminiscences as to leave no doubt that this was her abiding image to all who knew her at the close of her days. Having weathered the storms of middle life during Eleanor's childhood, she developed with advancing age and despite sufferings that failed to crush her "bright spirit and great heart",[23] a gentle irony and self-mockery, a capacity to make light of her troubles, which had been lacking in the early years of struggle when they would have stood her in good stead.

In February 1879 she had so severe an attack that it was thought she could not recover. Two years later, Marx wrote to Danielson* that his wife's condition was daily becoming more dangerous though he had called in the most renowned consultant in London. The new doctor in regular attendance, Horatio Bryan Donkin,† a relatively young man who had qualified in 1873, "pleased both her and Mohr extremely, though he is still very doubtful as to the real nature of Mama's illness" wrote Eleanor.[25] Engels confirmed to Jenny at the end of May that her mother was unaware of the nature of her illness and he was inclined to agree that the doctors were groping in the dark, but she was visibly growing thinner and weaker, while what she had called her "ups and downs" were more marked: there were times when she was active from morning till night—in the course of June she went to the play several times a week—then again she would be laid low by pain, obliged to spend days in bed.

Her dearest wish was to see her grandchildren again and Dr. Donkin encouraged, even insisted upon the visit to France, though Marx thought it out of the question. In July he took her to Eastbourne for three weeks from where she wrote to Laura, who had done everything to keep up her mother's

---

* Nikolai Frantsevich Danielson (1844–1918), Russian writer and economist who had long been in correspondence with Marx, Engels and Eleanor. He translated the three volumes of *Capital*, the first volume in collaboration with Lopatin.
† He was deeply devoted to Olive Schreiner, "long cherishing the hope that she would become his wife".[24]

spirits: "I know how you long for good news of your old
Möhme. Alas, I have none to give. In spite of the propitious
circumstances, I do not feel better and have therefore written
to Donkin again. Just imagine, I have actually sunk to a Bath-
chair, a thing that I, the pedestrian *par excellence*, should have
regarded as beneath my dignity a few months ago."[12] Tussy
joined her parents for a few days at the end of their stay, but
whether her mother could go abroad was still unsure. Immediately on her return to London Donkin examined the patient
and, four days later, on 26 July 1881, she, with Marx and
Lenchen, left for France to stay with the Longuets at 11 boulevard Thiers in Argenteuil. "I never knew how dear you are
to me till now", wrote Jenny on hearing the news that "her
dearest Mama" was definitely coming. "The whole night I
could not close an eye dreading the announcement that you
would not come, because the promised telegram did not arrive.
. . . I do not know how I shall manage to live till Tuesday. . . .
Longuet who is always frightened when his mother comes is
almost as pleased as Johnny to have you here."[26]

The journey was trying enough for Mrs. Marx but, once
settled, she was subject to attacks that deprived her of her
greatest pleasure, the children's company, and caused Jenny's
doctor, Gustave Dourlen, to administer the pain-killing drugs
Donkin had held in reserve. Marx was under no illusions about
the character of the illness and, though thankful for intermittent
improvements, wrote to Engels: "they do not stop the natural
progress of the disease but they deceive my wife and confirm
Jenny—despite my objections—in her belief that the stay at
Argenteuil should be as long as possible. I know better and thus
have the greater fear."

Lenchen, whom the little Longuet boys called Nym, or
Nimmy—a nickname which, with variations, stuck to her for
the rest of her days—was of the greatest comfort to Jenny.
The more so when, upon receiving a letter from Dollie Maitland
to say that Tussy was desperately ill, Marx left abruptly on the
same day—16 August—taking an express train for London and
leaving his wife to follow. A couple of days later Mrs. Marx
and Lenchen set out to travel, first class, by slow stages, staying
overnight at Amiens and then resting for a day or two at
Boulogne before crossing to Folkestone where, again, they

halted until Mrs. Marx felt able to complete the journey to London. "Naturally", wrote Marx, "it is painful for me to separate from her, but her real support is Helen, my own presence was not absolutely necessary."

Early in October Eleanor wrote to Jenny: "dear Mama is very ill—the *worst* is we can do absolutely nothing. It is a beastly illness . . . in all other respects Mama is, Dr. Donkin says, so strong. All her organs are perfectly healthy. Is it not monstrous that . . . so terrible an illness should have come to her?"[27]

At this juncture Marx fell ill with pleurisy. Eleanor stopped Jenny from rushing to London. "You must not leave the children", she wrote. "It would be the merest madness and would cause Papa more anxiety than your being here could give him pleasure or do him good—much as we all wish you were here."[27]

For a time, while pneumonia threatened, Eleanor did not stir from her father's bedside until, upon Donkin's orders, Lenchen relieved her on duty and she took a night's rest. Meanwhile, her friend Clementina Black and others sat with and read to Mrs. Marx who had now lain for weeks in the adjoining room, so wasted that, to "give her a *little* change Dr. Donkin says we are to lift her—in her sheets—from her bed to the chair-bed".[28] "Engels", wrote Eleanor, "is of a kindness and devotion that baffle description. Surely there is not another like him in the world—despite his little weaknesses."[29] She described her father as a "cranky patient", but once he was out of danger at the end of the month, he was able to get up and see his wife, by now in such unendurable pain that Donkin was prepared to give her the morphine injections he had withheld for fear that when this stage was reached she should have developed a tolerance to the drug, making it ineffective. He suggested that Eleanor should administer the injection, but she was repelled by the idea and thought that a nurse would be needed.[28] "It was a terrible time", Eleanor recalled later. "Our mother lay in the large front room, Moor in the little room behind. And the two of them, who were so used to one another, so close to one another, could not even be together in the same room. Our good old Lenchen . . . and I had to nurse them both . . . Never shall I forget the morning when he felt strong enough to go into mother's room. When they were together they were young again—she a loving girl and he a loving youth, on the threshold of life, not an old man devastated by illness and an old dying woman parting from each other for life."[30]

During that last month, when Mrs. Marx "suffered all the terrible tortures that cancer brings with it . . . her good humour, her inexhaustible wit . . . never deserted her for an instant. She enquired as impatiently as a child for the results of the elections then being held in Germany. . . . Up to her death she remained cheerful and tried to dispel our anxiety by joking. Yes, in spite of her fearful suffering she joked—she *laughed*—she laughed at the doctor and all of us because we were so serious. She remained fully conscious almost until the last moment, and when she could no longer speak . . . she pressed our hands and tried to smile",[30] but "the last word she spoke was to Papa: 'Good'."[31]

During those weeks of agony her mother wrote to Jenny. She rejoiced that she had made the journey to Paris and relived the happiness it had given her and "to the *very last* she thought of you and the children more than of anyone", Eleanor told Jenny.[31]

Mrs. Marx was just under 68 years of age when she died on Friday, 2 December 1881. Laura, who had been present, notified the death of her mother.* She was to be buried on the 5th and on the day before the funeral Eleanor wrote to Jenny: "I do dread it—but of course Papa cannot go. He must not yet leave the house and I am glad of this in every way. We have asked all the people Mama liked. . . ."[31]

Her mother's resting-place, as Jenny had wished, was near to that of her first-born son Charles Longuet in Highgate cemetery. The funeral was conducted with all simplicity. A few days before her death Mrs. Marx had told her nurse that she wanted no pomp or ceremony: "We are no such *external* people", she had said. Engels made a short oration, recalling her life, her "noble heart", with admiration and respect. He ended with the words: "What she did is known only to those who lived with her . . . There is no need for me to speak of her personal virtues. Her friends know those virtues and will

---

* The death certificate gives Mrs. Marx's forenames as Jenny Julia Joan Bertha, the cause of death as cancer of the liver.

never forget them. If ever there was a woman whose greatest happiness lay in making others happy, this was she."[32]

An obituary notice appeared on 7 December in Clemenceau's *La Justice* of which Longuet had been joint editor since his return to France. It contained a passage saying that there had been great prejudice against the marriage to Marx mainly on the score of his Jewish origin, which angered him beyond measure. He wrote to Jenny on the same day: "I suppose I am not mistaken in crediting Mr. Ch. Longuet's inventive genius with this literary embellishment . . . Longuet would greatly oblige me in never mentioning my name in *his* writings."

Although Laura and Eleanor had prepared her for the inevitable, Jenny was stunned by the news and could not resign herself to the death of "one who could so intensely enjoy life when there are so many creatures living whose dreary existence is only a burden to them. . . . Only last week I had a letter from Mama. . . . though far away I was not forgotten. Poor Mama's heart was large enough for all of us. . . ."[23]

Eleanor wrote to Jenny now—sending her a piece of her mother's "dear hair . . . as soft and beautiful as a girl's"—to recall the "sweet expression as she saw and recognised us, which she did at the end",[31] while later she was to say: "My mother and I loved each other passionately . . . One of the bitterest sorrows of my life is that my mother died, thinking, despite all our love, that I had been hard and cruel, and never guessing that to save her and father sorrow I had sacrificed the best, freshest years of my life."[33]

§3

Exactly what had precipitated Eleanor's illness, causing Marx to dash back to England in mid-August *1881*, cannot be known with any certainty, but that it was in some way connected with her mother's decline is beyond doubt. Looking back and claiming that Mrs. Marx had died thinking her "hard and cruel"—when she was neither—is but one clear indication of the guilt she felt. Another is the nature of her illness.

While alone in London that summer she wrote cheerfully to her parents, saying "I get on capitally",[34] and sent a "jolly letter" to Engels in Bridport, but in fact she was unable to sleep and had stopped eating altogether,* until she reached a state of near collapse so alarming that Dollie Maitland, whose help she rejected, felt it necessary to summon Marx.

Eleanor had declined to see a doctor, but her father immediately sent for Donkin in whose opinion there was nothing organically wrong with her except for "a perfect derangement of the action of her stomach" owing to her obstinate fasting. Nor did he think she stood in any danger so long as she obeyed his strict injunctions to feed herself rationally. Marx reported to Engels and to Jenny that her "overwrought nervous system" manifested itself in trembling hands, a facial tic and convulsive spasms.

Yet only on 5 July—a bare three weeks before her parents had left for Paris—she had made a brilliant appearance at the Dilettante Club theatre in two one-act plays with friends, including Ernest Radford and Dollie Maitland—who, as Engels reported, showed great self-possession and looked adorable on the stage—while Tussy had been "very good in the passionate scenes, though it was rather obvious that she modelled herself

---

* Psychopathology recognises this type of *anorexia nervosa*, the refusal to eat, as a form of self-inflicted punishment: in extreme cases, capital punishment by starving to death. It most often occurs in adolescent girls and is thought by some to be a symptom of undisclosed feelings of guilt or aggression in relation to the mother as the giver of food. A notable feature is that such patients may remain in high good spirits while they waste away.[35]

on Ellen Terry, as Radford on Irving. However, that will soon wear off; if she intends to make an effect in public she must undoubtedly strike out a line of her own, as she certainly will."

Not only Dollie but also Ernest Radford, whom Eleanor deemed "a very nice fellow",[34] going with him to see Irving's *Hamlet* in July, had tried his best to help her in her depression.* Marx was reassured by her promise to change her way of life: "Once she gives her word, she keeps it", he said.

Sometime in the spring of 1881, before she went to Jersey,† Leo Hartmann‡ proposed to Tussy. She still considered herself affianced to Lissagaray, but this—unacceptable—offer may have jolted her into reviewing her situation, for it was in these years leading up to and immediately following her mother's death that Eleanor went through the second personal crisis in her life. But, unlike the earlier one when she had been a mere girl, childlike in many ways, and half in love with all Communards, she was now a young woman who, though to all appearances immensely occupied, was more and more dissatisfied with her life.

Objections to a relationship have a way of making it become objectionable. It is idle to speculate what might have happened had the Marxes approved of Lissagaray and Eleanor had married him. The defiant engagement had by now lasted for many "long miserable years",[33] casting a shadow between her and her father, until the romance was nothing but an oppressive weight.

* She sent him some books inscribed on 6 August 1881: "Will you accept these volumes as a small mark of my gratitude for all your kindness during my illness? 'Beggar that I am, I am even poor in thanks—but I thank you'. Eleanor Marx."[36]
† Although it is known that Eleanor spent a holiday there with Marx in 1879, (a holiday cut short by the birth of Jenny's son in Ramsgate whither Marx immediately went), staying at the Hotel de l'Europe in St. Helier—after a few days at the Trafalgar Hotel in St. Aubin where the unvarying diet of lamb and mutton turned Marx into a vegetarian—there is no evidence of this later visit other than in a letter from Marx to Jenny dated 6 June 1881.
‡ Leo (or Lev) Nikolayevich Hartmann (1850–1908) was a Russian member of *Narodnaya Volya* (The People's Will) implicated in an attempt on the life of Alexander II in December 1879. Hartmann fled abroad, but was arrested in 1880 in Paris which caused an outcry, headed by Victor Hugo, leading to his release. Thereupon he went to England, where he worked at Siemens Woolwich factory for a few weeks. Immediately before going to America for six months early in June 1881, he wrote to Engels asking for Pumps' hand. This evoked Marx's indignation, for he was under the mistaken impression that Hartmann had formerly lived in "free marriage" with Sofia Perovskaya, one of the leaders of The People's Will who, following the assassination of the Tsar on 13 March 1881, was tried and, on 15 April, hanged. "From Perovskaya to Pumps is really a bit much", commented Marx.

For months after Lissagaray had left England in July 1880 she made no move. She was immersed in work and play and politics, and it was of these—when not of her nephews— that she wrote to Jenny when first she, too, went to France. In April 1881 her news was of the appalling situation in Ireland— "two men shot and many wounded, and now a girl of 20 shot and several women hurt"—of the "newest 'New Party' ", the Democratic Federation, which she did not think would amount to much and of the *Labour Standard*, a penny weekly about to be launched under the editorship of George Shipton,* to which Engels contributed from 7 May until 6 August 1881.[25, 37]

But by June, at which time Marx felt he must warn Jenny that her mother's illness was mortal,† Eleanor was writing in a different vein. She was resolved to take acting lessons from Mrs. Vezin‡ who had moved conveniently nearby to Highgate Road. "Even if, as I fancy will be the case—Mrs. Vezin finds that she has much overrated my powers the lessons will still be useful to me, and I can always make the recitation venture", she wrote to Jenny. She intended to start in July. "I feel sorry to cost Papa so much, but after all very small sums were expended on my education, compared at least to what is *now* demanded of girls—and I think if I do succeed it will have been a good investment. I shall try too, to get as much work as I can so that I may have a little money by the time I need it. . . . You see, dear, I've a goodly number of irons in the fire, but I feel I've wasted quite enough of my life, and that it is high time I did something. . . ."[4]

Her breakdown, for such it was, thus occurred at a time when she was plotting a new course to discover and develop such talents as she might have.

All these thoughts were pushed into the background by her parents' illness, culminating in her mother's death. That she stood the strains of nursing, albeit shared with Lenchen, showed

* Secretary of the London Trades Council 1871–1896.
† In a letter written on Bank Holiday Monday, 6 June. The day before, Parnell's great demonstration in Hyde Park had been ruined by hideously cold weather and heavy rain "one of the bad jokes the Heavenly Father always keeps in readiness for His plebeian London flock", said Marx, a sentiment echoed by countless drenched and freezing British working-class demonstrators ever since in the phrase: "God knows which side His bread's buttered."
‡ See fn., p. 44.

her powers of self-command. It carried her through the worst
period when, in addition to all else, she had to entertain her
cousin Willa Juta* who wanted to talk all the time. "I think
our family is going quite mad", she wrote to Jenny, for it turned
out that another cousin, Jettchen Conradi†, suffered from the
strange hallucination that she was the author of *Little Women*—
published when that young lady had been three years old—
and Eleanor had not only to correspond with Louisa Alcott,
who modestly admitted authorship, but to get a written assur-
ance that the 1868 edition of the work was in the British
Museum. To Eleanor's dismay, the hallucinated girl and her
mother arrived in London at this juncture. "Is it not a damned
nuisance", she wrote.[27]

However she still managed to put in a few hours at the
Museum, for she was desperately anxious not to lose the work
she had undertaken for Dr. Murray.‡ "You don't know how
many people—most far better qualified to do the work than
I am—try to get what I've been doing—and if I once give it
up I may whistle for something else."[29] Eleanor also put to
rights citations from *Capital* which had been mistranslated
in the first eulogy of Marx to appear in England.§

In all it was a period that would have tried the staunchest
and, though it took its toll of Eleanor's physical strength, so
recently undermined by her refusal to eat, her good sense—
and her good humour—did not waver. But once the abnormal
demands upon her were relaxed—the guests departed, her father
out of danger and her mother's sufferings at an end—then the
reaction set in.

On 29 December Marx, on his doctor's orders, went to
Ventnor with Tussy. She proved a poor companion: morose,
twitching with nerves and miserably self-absorbed. While
Marx wrote to Laura and to Engels, mildly complaining of
his unhelpful daughter, Eleanor confided her fear that she

* Daughter of Marx's sister Louise from Cape Town.
† Daughter of Marx's sister Emilie who had married Conradi, an engineer, in
Trier.
‡ Sir James Augustus Murray (1837–1915) a colleague of Furnivall's and an editor
of the *New English* (Oxford) *Dictionary*.
§ By Ernest Belfort Bax (1854–1926), a member of the D.F. who became a friend
of both Engels and Eleanor. The article was published in the progressive monthly
journal *Modern Thought* as No. 23 of a series entitled "Leaders of Modern Thought",
on 1 December 1881.

H

was on the verge of another breakdown to her friends Clemen-
tiṇa Black and Ernest Radford, who immediately took steps.
Radford went to Maitland Park Road to beg Lenchen to go
to Ventnor and, when this proved impracticable since she
was now in sole charge of the deserted house, Dollie Maitland
sped to the Isle of Wight.

It was an ill-judged move though well meant. In the first
place the Good Samaritan demanded unremitting attention—
"Dollie positively *groans* when she is left five minutes unenter-
tained",[38] wrote Eleanor as she hastily finished a letter to
Jenny—and, secondly, Dollie's sudden advent told Marx all that
Eleanor had striven to conceal from him, including that she
had turned to outsiders for help rather than to him. It made him
"angry and anxious", yet she had felt she could not bother
her "darling Mohr", who was still far from well. She knew that
he must think her "disagreeable and dissatisfied—but I can't
explain to him".[38]

Into his ear Dollie now poured endless gossip: "she tells
Papa that she believes me to be secretly married and a lot
of other cock-and-bull stories, that do far more honour to
her imagination than her veracity".[39] She also provided details
of the frightening hysterical symptoms Eleanor manifested
at night which Marx, not being witness to them, had to take on
trust. In one way and another, dear little Dollie whom everyone
loved—"it was *very* good of the child to come"[38]—was really
"worse than useless" in this situation, causing an amount of
trouble quite disproportionate to the length of her stay. Neither
father nor daughter regretted her departure, but it left them
face to face with each other, both suffering the grief and shock
of recent bereavement, each labouring under present difficulties
that, fearing to hurt each other, they could not communicate.

To Jenny Eleanor poured out her heart, and it was an unquiet
one. She diagnosed her own condition shrewdly enough: "What
neither Papa nor the doctors nor anyone else will understand
is that it is chiefly *mental worry* that affects me." She dreaded
beyond all things consulting doctors who could not or would
not see that this was "as much an illness as any physical ailment
could be". She was unable to sleep at night and "for a long time
. . . tried various drugs . . . and am loth to try them again. It
is not much better, after all, than dram-drinking and is almost

if not quite as injurious." Her father, puzzled and annoyed, scolded her "as if I 'indulged' in being ill at the expense of my family—or gets anxious and that worries me most of all".[38]

Her problem was twofold and acute. For some time now she had tried to end her engagement to Lissagaray, but could not bring herself to do it because there was nothing to warrant the break: he was "blameless" and had been "so very good and gentle and patient" with her.[39] At the same time she longed to make a career for herself on the stage, to win a true independence by this means, and realised that now, at 27 years of age, time was running out. "It drives me half mad to sit here when perhaps my *last* chance of doing something is going", she wrote to Jenny.[38]

It was this inner struggle—to behave well to the man to whom she had given her word, holding to it through years of general disapprobation, and yet to face her situation realistically— that had so worked upon her during the summer before. Once free of this now artificial tie she might still make something of her life before it was too late. "I am not young enough to lose more time in writing*—and if I cannot do this *soon*—it will be no use to try at all. But I've no money (I mean not enough to begin my lessons even)—and it *is* hard. . . . I think I *could* do something. I cannot believe Mrs. Vezin would have spoken as she did, nor offered to bring me out had she not thought I had *some* chance of success. For she can have no object in bringing out a failure. You know, dear, I'm not a bit vain and that if I err it is not from over confidence but from distrust in myself. . . . I have seen too often—and with such different people that I can *move* an audience—and that is the chief thing."[38] On the eve of her birthday she wrote again to Jenny: "much and hard as I have tried I could not crush out my desire to *try something*. The chance of independence is very sweet. . . . You see I'm not clever enough to live a purely *intellectual* life nor am I dull enough to be content to . . . do nothing." She felt heartily ashamed of herself for worrying her father by her disagreeableness and egoism. "How I love him no one can know—and yet— we must each of us, after all, live our own life."[39] She turned the question round and round, arguing with herself more than with Jenny. At last she " 'screwed her courage to the sticking

* This referred to her hackwork at the British Museum.

place' " and broke off her engagement. She told Jenny that not only had the burden become too heavy but she had "other reasons" which she could not write, and she asked her sister as a great favour to see Lissagaray from time to time, to "treat him just as an old friend". She hoped that he and she, too, might remain on good and intimate terms, to which end "nothing will help so much as if you and Longuet continue to see him. . . . Oh! it has been a terrible struggle. I sometimes wonder how I have lived through it all. . . ."[39]

However sympathetically Jenny received Eleanor's outpourings, she wrote to Laura, who was at this time alone in London "without any distractions and surrounded by the thousands of things" to remind her of her mother, to say that she was "very much alarmed by the news Tussy gives me from the Isle of Wight". It was Marx's situation that concerned her: "Tussy's health, it seems, is breaking down altogether, and I think with much grief of poor Papa, ill as he is, with an invalid." Something must be done to help them both and, in Jenny's view, Tussy's sufferings were such that "she would be better in London hard at work than doing nothing, a prey to her fancies. Poor Papa in his present state of health, after the troubles he has undergone, required a cheerful and even-tempered companion. It is a thousand pities you did not go with him instead of Tussy". She begged Laura to talk the matter over with "our good devoted Nim". She herself would have wished to fly to her father, but was tied by the children.[40]

A few days later Tussy made a lightning dash to London to appear in some dramatic performance but had barely returned to Ventnor when, owing to the bitterly cold weather, Marx decided he must leave. On 16 January they returned to London together and plans were made for him to go south for his now chronic bronchial catarrh.

The most painful side-effect of this crisis in Eleanor's affairs was the tension it had created between her and Marx. As so often happens when two people are very close and try to spare each other's feelings by being less than frank, they succeeded only in wounding. After her father's death Eleanor wrote "our natures were so exactly alike. I remember his once saying a thing that at the time I did not understand and that even sounded rather paradoxical. But I know now what he meant.

. . . Father was talking of my eldest sister and of me and said: 'Jenny is most like me, but Tussy (my dear old home name) *is* me.' It was true—except that I shall never be good and unselfish as he was."[33] At present they were finely aware, she of being preoccupied with self, he of not being taken into her confidence. By their very likeness each knew the nature of the other's injury, but was powerless to assuage it. Eleanor wrestled silently with her problems; Marx would not encroach upon her privacy and thus, while she penned her remorseful letters to Jenny, he wrote to Engels saying that, from observation alone, for Tussy was not open with him, he was convinced that no medicine, no change of scene or air could cure her sickness: "Madame Jung", as he called Mrs. Vezin,* was the only doctor who could help her, since she was burning with the desire to find an opening for herself and believed it to lie in an artistic career. Certainly in one respect she was right: at her age there was no more time to be lost and, of all things in the world, he would hate her to imagine that she was being sacrificed on the "altar of the family" to be nurse to an old man. He added that he could hazard a guess at the root cause of her emotional perturbation, but this was too delicate a matter to set down in black and white; from which it must be inferred that he attributed her disorder, rightly or wrongly, to her long-preserved virginity.

* Formerly Mrs. Young (see fn., p. 44).

§ 4

Trying companion Eleanor might be and Marx quite resolved that she should not be his escort on his further travels—he had rather do without one—nevertheless, in the first week of February 1882, she accompanied him to Argenteuil. He stopped there for a week on the first leg of his journey to Algiers, setting sail from Marseilles on 18 February to remain there and in the South of France until June, alone.

Eleanor stayed on with Jenny for a few extra days. On her last morning Lissagaray called and arranged to see her off at the Gare St. Lazare that night. It was barely a month since she had broken off her engagement. He had expressed a wish to see Marx too, but Eleanor had prevented this and "in doing so, I think acted with good taste", Jenny wrote to her father, for such a meeting at such a time could not have been agreeable to him. Lissagaray and Tussy "behave to each other as old friends and Tussy's manner seemed very cool and distrait* to her quondam fiancé". Jenny was more than satisfied by the upshot—"the very best one that could have been expected . . . and these present amicable relations are most fortunate". She considered that her sister had had "a narrow escape", and felt positively grateful and therefore well-disposed to Lissagaray for not having carried out his plan to marry her, for "French husbands are not worth much at the best of times— and at the worst—well, the less said the better."[41] She repeated these uncompromising sentiments to Eleanor herself: "I feel you have acted for the best—you were right to break off your engagement. Though I bear no ill will to L. I know you could never have been happy with him. These Frenchmen at the best of times make pitiable husbands!"[42]

Marx was relieved that Tussy had conducted herself so tactfully in this delicate situation. Without committing himself one way or another on the general proposition of Frenchmen

* In the holograph the word could possibly be read as "distant".

as husbands, he had some powerful things to say to and about
his French sons-in-law now that they were again active in the
politics of their own country: "Longuet as the last Proudhonist
and Lafargue as the last Bakuninist! The devil take them
both!"[43]

Eleanor's return journey to "murky old London" was not
sweetened by a lady reeking of alcohol who struck up an
acquaintance by asking Eleanor to lend her a corkscrew and
when she could not oblige, persevered with a pair of scissors
until she had opened a fresh bottle "and drank one *tumbler*
after the other of brandy", after which, since the train did not
stop between Rouen and Dieppe she "relieved herself" in the
carriage, causing Eleanor to take a vow that nothing on earth
would ever again induce her "to travel in a compartment for
dames seules".[44] She missed Jenny and the children so badly
that she felt almost sorry she had been to Paris. "I don't know
what I shall do without you all", she wrote,[44] and, indeed, the
feeling was mutual for, by her "just and kind behaviour"
Tussy had become "such a favourite that the little men have
had some difficulty to get over the parting",[41] Jenny wrote to
Marx and, to Eleanor herself: "You have so delighted the
children that I think they would go out of their wits with joy
if you were suddenly to appear".[45] "As you know . . . your most
devoted friend at present is the Wolf,* who since your departure
has not woke up one morning without asking Where is Aunt
Tutty? . . . Harry's feelings are I suppose too deep for words.
Johnny is old enough to know he must put up with the inevitable. . . ."[42] They talked of her constantly, Jenny reported, and:
"You cannot imagine what a deep impression you have produced upon the little ones and how eagerly they long to have
you again."[46]

No doubt during her stay in Argenteuil Eleanor disclosed the
"other reasons" that had made necessary her break with
Lissagaray. Whatever they were, they certainly did not include
the forging of fresh bonds to chafe her. In April Jenny began
to receive frequent visits from "the uncanny Mrs. Kaub",
the sister of Carl Hirsch, the object of which "feverish activity"
was to ask for Eleanor's hand. She had not seen Hirsch in

* Edgar, now two-and-a-half.

Paris at all, sending him a postcard from London to say that she had been there purely to be with her sister and apologising for having refused his offer to take her sightseeing.[47] "Though I have done all I could to explain to the enamoured Hirsch that his aspirations are doomed to remain unfulfilled, he insists upon hearing his doom from your own lips", Jenny wrote. The "fool" had gone so far as to settle his affairs in Germany and make preparations for his future home, whether in England or in France, according to Eleanor's preference. With infinite tedium and despite her "unseemly interruptions" Jenny had to listen to detailed accounts of his financial position while he, impervious to hints or advice, pressed his suit. "He is after all a true and devoted friend of the family", Jenny admitted, nor was it a crime to have a tender heart, so, in charity, Tussy must send him some sort of "*decent* answer" as soon as possible without offending or exasperating him.[48] Eleanor thereupon wrote a kind and courteous refusal which, according to Jenny, was "really more than the silly Jew deserved. . . . I hope it will preserve eternal rest to the perturbed spirit of your irrepressible admirer." Though she pitilessly mocked the "lovelorn" man, Jenny yet held him in some regard and could not understand why Tussy should feel so angry at the proposal: to her it appeared "simply in a comical light".[49] Indeed, Eleanor's fury seemed unreasonable on the face of it. She had never failed to treat Hirsch as a valued acquaintance, they had corresponded for seven years, during which period he had visited London many times, staying for some months both in 1878 and in the following year when he was often invited to dine at Maitland Park Road. Mrs. Marx had both received him in her house and written to him in the kindest manner. Marx had pronounced him "an absolutely reliable man of the utmost loyalty", his main weakness being that, a poor judge of character, he was easily duped, if not for long, by those who affected a devotion to the cause of socialism.[50] It is true that Marx thought he had behaved like an imbecile, inviting martyrdom, at the time of his arrest, but both he and Engels championed him hotly against the Höchberg crew in Zürich long after that episode and it was only as time went on that Marx found him increasingly tiresome and tried to avoid meeting him. Hirsch finally fell from grace when he was suspected of having collaborated with Franz

Mehring* in writing a perfidious article on Marx in the *Sozialdemokrat* for which "the party will never forgive him". That, however, did not occur till many months after he had proposed to Tussy and may even have been occasioned by the antagonism her treatment of him aroused for, however gently she declined him, Jenny had made it abundantly clear that he was scorned.†

Far from contemplating marriage, Eleanor now threw herself into her lessons with Mrs. Vezin, and into work to pay for them. It was as though, whatever inner conflicts had brought about her nervous derangement had been finally resolved, leaving her, all neurotic traces eliminated, full of energy and hope. Not that she was happy at her father's absence: she missed him sadly and concern for his health was never far from her thoughts. "We are very anxious and we are eagerly awaiting further details as to how you are", she wrote to him in Algiers on 23 March.[52] Marx had run into bad weather, was making no progress, and Eleanor asked Engels if she should not go to him, but was dissuaded. In point of fact, though he did not mention it to his family—"why frighten them?"—Marx had another attack of pleurisy while in North Africa, less severe though lasting longer than the first one, as he told Engels after it was over. Again and again Eleanor wrote "How I wish we had you here again",[52] "How I do *long* for a sight of your face".[53] Indeed the very strong family feeling—discounting Laura—seems to have been heightened by Mrs. Marx's death, all Jenny's letters, too, being full of regret that they were now so far apart from each other. In May she begged Eleanor to visit her again, but this was impossible though she had found time to knit red petticoats for her nephews which, surprisingly,

---

* Franz Mehring (1846–1919) had defended Lassalle and Bakunin against Marx and Engels in his early days and did not join the German Social Democratic Party until 1890. In 1918 he published his biography of Marx, having some years earlier been invited by Laura Lafargue to edit and publish the correspondence between her father and Engels. He came under severe attack for "anti-Marxism", "a breach of confidence" and "the basest betrayal of Marx" from both Kautsky and Ryazanov, but his *Karl Marx*,[51] allowing for the relative sparsity of research material available in his day, remains one of the most rewarding sources, while his political courage in the years before and during the First World War refutes any "betrayal of Marx" or of Marxist principles.

† On 8 July 1882 Hirsch married a Miss Lina Haschert in Paris, an occasion of so mournful a nature that, according to an eye-witness, one of those present at the ceremony had exclaimed: "This is a top class funeral!"

enchanted the boys who strutted about in them "like little peacocks".[49]

Since her return from Paris Eleanor had been "grinding at Juliet with Mrs. Vezin", an exercise that permitted her to comment on Ellen Terry's rendering of the part in the current performance, which was "*the* event" of the day, that it was "the most disappointing feature" of "an exquisite production": she "gets weaker and weaker as the tragic element appears till in the poison scene she collapses altogether".*[54]

Now 55 and in retirement, Mrs. Vezin no longer had many connections with the living theatre but gave Eleanor every encouragement. "Despite my absolute ignorance of stage business she would like me to try it publicly . . . she wants to give me a chance if it is possible. What I should prefer would be to go to some small provincial place and get some practical knowledge of the stage to begin with. But all these are dreams and ten to one . . . nothing will come of it all."[54] Jenny was full of enthusiasm and advice. She saw no reason why her sister's "ambition to live an artistic life" should not succeed. "Some lucky chance (you know my fixed idea is an interview with Irving) may turn up", she wrote, "and at the very worst should you never tread the boards, the fact of acquiring perfectly the art of elocution . . . will be a great gain to you through life and will repay any outlay your lessons now will cost you."[42] An introduction to Irving was, indeed, her "fixed idea": "It is nonsense to say he would . . . treat you as he does the thousand stage-struck simpletons who no doubt come to him. The superior cultivation of your naturally gifted mind would have at once raised you in his eyes . . . and last but not least there is always something in a name and yours is Marx—not Smith or Brown. . . ."†[49] Not only in Jenny's view should Eleanor solicit Irving's patronage but she should apply to Engels, who was so generous, for the money that was needed to further her ambitions. Eleanor followed neither of these courses, she simply persevered; but she was touched by Jenny's sincere joy in her "prospect of living the only free life a woman can live—the

---

* An opinion not shared by the critic of *The Times* who wrote on 9 March "Miss Terry's Juliet is an unmixed success."

† Jenny seemed to forget that it rather depends on what your first name is. If, for example, you had been called Adam or Ford Madox there is no earthly reason why you should not have been received by a Brodribb.

artistic one", thus realising that which for years and years had been Jenny's "own day-dream",[49] and enabled her to write at a time when she herself was in the depths of misery: "The only bit of good news that I have had these many days is . . . of your literary enterprises. I congratulate you with all my heart and rejoice to think that one of us at least will not pass her life in watching over a *pot au feu*."[55]

"Literary enterprises": not theatrical ones. Eleanor's aspirations had foundered. Exactly when this happened, and how long the experiment lasted, is not clear but Marian Skinner recollected that "she was dramatic to the depths of her being and I think one of the sorest disappointments of her life was that she never became an actress. . . . Mrs. Hermann Vezin . . . reluctantly told her that she would never achieve real greatness on the boards—the glory would always fall short of the dream. . . . She came to me on the day Mrs. Vezin had given her ultimatum—white, tragic, despairing. . . . 'It's damnably hard not to be able to get the one thing in the world you want'. . . ."[1] Olive Schreiner,* too, recalled this time and her protective feelings towards Eleanor.

These two friends may have done much to help her withstand this dashing of her hopes but, during that spring and summer, Eleanor's social life took on a new momentum and she fairly whirled. With nothing to keep her at home—even Lenchen had gone to Argenteuil—she discovered, almost overnight, that she was attractive to people outside her own circle and a success when she went among them. She was invited to picnics, parties and At Homes. During a single week in July she recited at a Browning Evening—"the place was crowded and as all sorts of 'literary' and other 'swells' were there, I felt ridiculously nervous—but got on capitally"—saw Modjeska† in *Odette*— ". . . liked her more than ever—but the piece is vile—simply idiotic, in fact, in this English version"—Ristori‡ in *Macbeth*—

---

* She came to London at the end of March 1882 and lived at 11 Guilford Street, Bloomsbury.
† Helena Modjeska, née Opido, (1844–1909), a Polish actress who emigrated to America in the mid-seventies and, despite her poor command of English, was a soaring success. She toured England and the Continent, for the most part in plays by Feuillet and Sardou.
‡ Adelaide Ristori (1822–1906), an Italian actress who went to Paris in 1855 where she became a serious rival to Rachel. Her performance as Lady Macbeth in London

"which she acts for the first time in English"—went to Toole's* benefit concert, where Mrs. Kendal and Irving performed and Ellen Terry recited Thomas Hood's "Bridge of of Sighs"—"which I look upon as a personal injury, that being one of my stock pieces"—and was "asked . . . to a 'crush' at Lady Wilde's . . . the mother of that very limp and very nasty young man, Oscar Wilde, who has been making such a d——d ass of himself in America. As the son has not yet returned and the mother is nice I may go."†[56]

She went down the river with the Furnivalls and dined with the Lankesters, while Mrs. Sutherland Orr, the sister of Sir Frederick Leighton, then President of the Royal Academy, proposed taking her to meet Browning that she might recite his poems to their author.

Her social circle, though it still contained and she saw much of the Black and the Maitland sisters, Radford and other members of the little Dogberry group, expanded vastly, as did her openings for employment. She did not allow her "dissipated evenings", as she characterised them, to interfere with her working life: she took on an "advantageous pupil", went regularly to the British Museum, was entrusted with the task of compiling a glossary, which she could do at home and was, as she declared, "hard at it" and "pretty well out all day".

It is probable, it is almost certain—though no written evidence exists to prove it—that her animated existence in the spring and summer of 1882 was not unrelated to those "other reasons" for having broken off relations with Lissagaray. It could also account for her outburst of indignation at Hirsch's pretensions. The name does not appear among the host of people with whom she was associating at the time, but since she was undoubtedly partnered on her several outings and the character of her interests, the places she frequented, were so

was highly praised, Mrs. Kendall acclaiming her as a better actress than Bernhardt. She retired from the stage in 1885.

* John Lawrence Toole (1830–1906), an actor chiefly famous for his playing of Dickens roles, was a close friend of Irving's. In 1879 he went into management at the Charing Cross Theatre and in 1882 gave it his own name. Toole's Theatre, in King William Street, was demolished in 1895 to make way for an extension of Charing Cross Hospital.

† Later, when he came up for trial, it was not Wilde whom Eleanor criticised but the howling hypocrisy of the press and public, and that of the theatre managers who continued the profitable run of his plays to full houses at the Haymarket and St. James's but deleted the author's name.[57]

"DOLLIE" MAITLAND
(*circa* 1883)

ERNEST RADFORD
(*circa* 1883)

MARX IN THE YEAR BEFORE HIS DEATH

similar to those of Edward Aveling, a married man, it is reasonable to assume that he had entered upon the scene.

Her outer gaieties did nothing to still the anxiety about her father. He had left Algiers, where his cough had been aggravated rather than cured, to stay in Monte Carlo at the Hotel de Russie from the first week in May until early June when he planned to go to Jenny's. While he reported in great detail on his state of health to Engels—whom he rather blamed for the unfortunate Algerian venture which had led to no improvement—it was clear that he took a pessimistic view of the outcome. "Naturally, at a certain age, it is altogether a matter of indifference how one is 'launched into eternity' ", he wrote from Cannes, rather comforted than otherwise by Garibaldi's death from bronchitis.* On 6 June he left for Argenteuil where he stayed for almost three months.

Lafargue, who had been living in Paris since April, went to see him and reported to Engels that he looked well but that the Longuet household was too boisterous for a man in his condition. This was not Marx's view. He had told Jenny before his arrival that she was not to announce it to either Paul or Hirsch, that what he needed was absolute peace and quiet, adding as a postscript that what he meant by this was family life and the "microscopic world of children's noises". It was to help Jenny during Marx's stay that Lenchen had gone to France at the end of June, but that summer both Laura and Eleanor travelled to Paris, though not together. Laura rejoined her husband, spending a week at 38 rue de Lille, a small hotel on the left bank until, early in August, they moved the furniture sent from London—including the armchair bequeathed by Lizzie Burns—into a flat of their own,† at Engels' cost. She had seen her father for but a few hours when she wrote to Engels "Papa seemed to be very well and . . . very lively",[58] so that Eleanor, when she joined the Longuet household, was taken aback by his changed appearance.‡

Marx wrote to Hirsch asking him to take Lenchen sightseeing

---

* On 3 June 1882 at the age of 75.
† 66 boulevard du Port-Royal, where they lived until 1887.
‡ Not because, in April, his head and face had been shaved in Algiers owing to the heat—for they had grown luxuriantly since, as contemporary photographs show —but because he had not made the progress she had been led to expect from Laura's report and found him looking aged and ill.

in Paris before she left. Now that she had gone, Jenny, in her
eighth month of pregnancy, was only too grateful to Eleanor
who won Marx's golden opinions for her kindness and helpful-
ness to the children and to "poor Jenny". The situation had
brought out traits in Tussy that were dormant in London,
he wrote to Engels. She was "an excellent disciplinarian" and
he dearly hoped that she would take Johnny back with her
to England for a few months: the boy was running wild and
giving more trouble than the three smaller ones put together,
but Longuet, who generally stayed in bed the whole morning
and left for Paris at five each afternoon, opposed the plan,
out of his "love" for him, though he did nothing about the
child himself, and seemed not to care whether Johnny were
helped or Jenny's burden lightened. Nevertheless, against the
father's wishes, Marx prevailed and when Eleanor left for
London on 21 August it was with Johnny, who was destined
to remain with her—and to submit to an unaccustomed regimen
of cold water from top to toe each day, regular schooling and
early bed-times—for many a month to come.

Quite soon after his return to Argenteuil in June Marx had
written to Laura, still in London, a letter marked "Private and
Confidential" in which he confessed that he could not risk
travelling alone again and that therefore "It's more or less your
duty to accompany the old man of the mountains" when he
went to Switzerland at the end of August. This plan, too, was
realised and, a few days after Tussy's departure, Marx and
Laura set out for Vevey by way of Lausanne, returning to
France on 28 September, by which time Jenny had given birth
to her only daughter.*

Eleanor, with Lenchen's help at home, was happily caring for
Johnny and sending regular reports to his mother. She had taken
him to Yarmouth where Engels was staying with Pumps and
her baby† and, back in London, he was doing excellently at
school.‡

---

* Jenny, known as Mémé, born on 16 September 1882.
† Pumps had married Percy White Rosher, an accountant and, later, unsuccessful
small businessman, on 8 September 1881 at the St. Pancras Register Office in the
presence of Samuel Moore and Paul Lafargue. A daughter, Lilian, was born on
25 March 1882, whose conversation at six months, according to Marx, was more
interesting than her mother's.
‡ He was enrolled on 11 September at a little dame-school opposite the Marxes'
old house in Grafton Terrace.

"I have just put my boy . . . to bed", she wrote to Jenny on 2 October. He was "very anxious to hear about his little sister. Having got over the shock he is taking more interest in her now". What troubled his aunt most was his English: "the way he speaks is awful, but I suppose in time he will grow out of it. I've no doubt we spoke Helen's English some time. The worst is when I correct the boy Helen is either offended or laughs."[59] Helen—or Lenchen—or Nimmy—played her full part, of course, in looking after the six-year-old for, though Eleanor postponed working on her glossary until the evenings, after he had gone to bed, she still had to go by day to the Museum where she was accorded the exceptional privilege of being admitted during Closed Week: "when the Reading Room is shut and the books are dusted, re-arranged, etc." She owed this to the intervention of Richard Garnett,* in whose room she was allowed to work, and to "some half dozen of the head men. . . . It is an immense favour which I was told today had been extended to no one since some years ago Gladstone was allowed to go and finish his pamphlet on 'Atrocities'† there!"[59]

Marx, when he arrived back in London in the first week of October, thoroughly approved of Eleanor's ways with Johnny who was cheerful and happy, he wrote to Laura. The little boy talked a great deal of his mother and Harry, whom he obviously missed, but his progress left nothing to be desired. At the end of the month, warned not to remain in London during the season of damp and fog, Marx set off for Ventnor again, where Eleanor and Johnny visited him for a few days in November, leaving on the 20th. Thereafter Eleanor kept in constant touch with him and he wrote on 9 January that he was grateful to "his dear good child" for writing so often and at such length, which encroached upon the little free time she had. The intention was that Marx should remain on the Isle of Wight until the spring. But that was not to be.

* An official at the Museum, later Keeper of Printed Books (1890–1899), whose son, Edward, married Eleanor's friend Constance Black, better known under her married name as the translator of the great Russian classics.
† *Bulgarian Horrors and the Questions of the East*, published in 1876.

§ 5

Eleanor had long realised that Jenny had reached breaking-point. What she did not, could not know, for it was never mentioned, was that ever since April her sister had been in terrible pain with a disease of the bladder* which, then, she attributed to her three months' pregnancy.

After Eleanor had left Argenteuil in March Jenny, who apologised for having "been so dull" during her stay,[42] wrote to her on a note of mounting despair. Though she forebore to speak of her physical ailments, she felt exhausted by her family cares. As early as January, still bitterly mourning her mother's death, she had complained that "when night comes I feel quite giddy from the exertion of having looked after four babies, three of whom no longer sleep in the day",[61] while to Laura, at the same period, she wrote that "what with carrying, washing, feeding, driving three babies and looking after Master Johnny who is not the least troublesome one of the lot, I feel physically and mentally worn out. I am often too tired to get repose at night and feel like Don Quixote did when he had been well thrashed."[40] Mother-in-law and servant trouble loomed large in her letters to Eleanor but the bane of her life was Longuet: "The cruelest (*sic*) of it all is that though I drudge like a nigger [he] never does anything but scream at me and grumble every minute he is in the house."[48] His "present mode of life", she wrote to Eleanor again in May, "makes matters 50 times worse than they were when we lived in London". He perpetually nagged and was never satisfied with her, though "I assure you I do all in my power to do the work for house and children for weeks and weeks not permitting myself the luxury of taking up a newspaper, not to speak of a book."[60] Her husband's worst offence, however, was that he constantly postponed taking the children on holiday, a move so essential for Harry "whose condition *absolutely* requires

* In all probability cancer.

change of air".[49] It was for the sake of this daily expected, daily deferred vacation—which did not finally materialise until September—that Johnny had been kept from school since February, to become "not only a torment to me but also to himself, all day at home in a nursery, where the noise of three other babies prevents him from learning his ABC",[61] while Harry—"the best and sweetest little creature under the sun"[46] who knew "nought of life but pain and sorrow"[49]—was left to linger in a state that filled Jenny with foreboding.

Added to these trials was an acute shortage of money. Longuet's paper, *La Justice*, paid him less and less regularly, while Madame Longuet senior, convinced of the wilful parasitic idleness of her daughter-in-law, wrote eight-page letters to her almost daily exhorting her to resume her teaching to contribute to the family exchequer, depleted by the lady herself who had cut off the small allowance remitted to her son in England. To go out teaching, Jenny wrote to Eleanor, "would be madness, as such lessons would not pay the cost of a servant to watch over the children during my absences",[61] yet she was haunted by the unpaid debts which weighted upon her "like crimes, by day and night".[46] She blamed her insolvency for depriving "our dear Nim" of her projected trip to Germany and saw but one way out of it: "to get some children from London, Indian* or others", to bring up with her own. The house—where adult boarders would never stay with so many babies about—was "excellently adapted" for the purpose: the young paying guests would have the advantage of learning three languages and at the same time provide Johnny with the much needed society of his coevals to correct the "habits of indolence into which neglect and a naturally lazy disposition" had plunged him. "Pardon me, dear Tussy", she wrote "for troubling you. . . . I must somehow get out of this plight. Pray give me your advice. . . ."[61] It is almost incredible that Jenny, who felt so "overdone, so jaded and worn out by every sort of worry and fatigue", should have entertained the notion of adding to her problems in this way. She was five months pregnant—and ill— when she proposed it, but she felt she must find some means to earn money. She hated her "uncongenial life", felt more sick of it than she could say, cursed her poverty and was at her wits'

* That is, English children sent home for their education by parents in India.

end; "I am dead beaten", she wrote to Tussy.[61] Never wholly reconciled to the loss of the warm family life she had known throughout her youth—"I cannot get used to this separation— it is as if my heart were cleft", she wrote[60]—she took comfort from her father's long stay in the summer of 1882—grievously changed though she found him—coupled as it was with the familiar presence of first Lenchen and then Tussy. Small wonder that Paul should write to Laura in June "Jenny is much better, mentally and physically".[62]

There was little indeed to prosper her in the months to come, though she wrote to Laura in Switzerland making the most of the fact that, at long last, Edgar and Harry had gone to St. Aubin in Calvados with their Papa and that she was "having a holiday", alone with little Par (Marcel). Unfortunately, her mother-in-law, who had promised to join the family at the sea to keep an eye on the children, "left them in the lurch, pretend- ing important business in Caen",[63] her home-town some 18 kilometers away, exciting Jenny's pity for her husband, always nearest to her heart when he was furthest from her.

During Marx's brief return to Argenteuil at the end of Sep- tember, when he met his only grand-daughter for the first and last time, Jenny was able to conceal from him her desperate condition, her confinement being so recent as to account for her debility. The birth of the child had not relieved but, on the contrary, exacerbated her illness, and she finally wrote to Tussy in Ventnor disclosing the full horror of her situation, with strict injunctions that the news should be withheld from Marx. "This inflammation of the bladder", she wrote, "is *not a danger- ous*, but the most unbearable of all diseases. To no one in the world would I wish the tortures I have undergone now since eight months, they are indescribable and the nursing added thereto makes life a hell to me."[55] Though unable to leave her bedroom, she could not get the rest she needed, not only because of the children, but because Longuet was now also at home all day, making an effort to devote himself to the house- hold, while in fact adding to "the work and confusion". His mother, too, was behaving in a sympathetic and generous manner, though remaining firmly in Caen. Jenny worried about her Johnny, for "illness makes one so nervous"[55]; and since her father would be staying on in Ventnor alone, she feared that the plan for Harry to go there would not be feasible. It says much for Jenny that this letter of 8 November 1882, written in agony, should begin with expressions of pleasure and interest in Tussy's work and the conviction that her talents would ensure success.

A week later Paul Lafargue was summoned to appear before the Montluçon magistrate's court to show reason why he should not stand trial for subversive speeches he, Guesde and others had made. His failure to comply was followed by his arrest in Paris on the evening of 12 December. Laura immediately wrote to Engels who forwarded the letter to Marx the next day adding his own comment: "Just received this 9.20 p.m. After appearing at Montluçon Paul will of course be released at once. In the meantime I shall send Laura the needful tomorrow . . ."[64]*

The news elicited from Marx some of the kindliest comments he had ever made on Paul, whose recent articles he went out of his way to praise when he wrote to Laura, adding that her husband's "gallant fight with the powers that be make the man sympathetic, to use this, a French penny-a-liner's phrase". He hoped that, when her duties permitted, Laura would come and stay with him in Ventnor. Though suffering from tracheal catarrh he was free from pleurisy and bronchitis. "This is very encouraging", he wrote, "considering that most of my *contemporaries*, I mean fellows of the same age, just now kick the bucket in gratifying numbers. There are enough young asses to keep the old ones alive."

But Laura was not at liberty to go to Ventnor, for Jenny's circumstances roused her from what appears to have been a life of total selfishness—apart from her devotion to her husband's interests—maintained in France, as in England, entirely at Engels' expense, and on no mean scale.

On the day of Paul's arrest she managed to work into her letter to Engels the news that she had 5 francs in her pocket and later gave this as the reason for having been unable to make the journey across Paris from the boulevard Port-Royal to Argenteuil: "I hadn't got the wherewithal. . . . For out of the five francs I had in hand three had to go for coals and one for lamp oil."[65] Her letter went on to announce that they were to dine

---

* In the event Paul was tried in April 1883 for incitement to murder and loot, fined and committed to Ste. Pélagie prison for six months from 21 May.

with friends who had received a *poularde truffée* from the country and: "I want to compare notes with you on the subject of some new wines with which I have just become acquainted . . ." However, despite these graver considerations, she had eventually bestirred herself to visit Jenny whom she found "in a very precarious condition. . . . The inflammation she suffers from was rather worse than better when I saw her and she is altogether out of spirits."[65]

Engels sent the letter on to Marx with his usual words of reassurance. But Marx was not reassured and wrote to Tussy that he feared the worst if Jenny's illness were neglected. Could she not take poor Harry off her hands? If necessary she could bring the child with her to Ventnor: it was obviously impossible for anyone to give the necessary attention to their own health with all those babies. He also feared that if Johnny were to return home, as planned, he would be neglected unless another of the children made way for him. Throughout the end of December and into the New Year apprehension grew. On 6 January 1883 Paul wrote to Engels: "Jenny's condition saddened us greatly; we thought it hopeless." He and Laura had been to see her and "were astonished to find her laid up and in a very sorry state . . . she was sunk in a torpor broken by nightmares and fantastic dreams. Since her last confinement she has had constant haemorrhages whose cause . . . the doctors have not yet been able to discover; she insisted upon suckling the baby which, combined with a chronic lack of appetite, completely drained her strength." Longuet had gone away at this juncture and there was no one to look after her. She had been unable to eat and, though the haemorrhages stopped, she was plagued by diarrhoea. "We did not know of her desperate condition", Paul unashamedly confessed, "so you can imagine our shock when we found her . . . delirious." Now Laura was going daily to Argenteuil: a journey, he complained, that took four hours by omnibus and train there and back. It does not seem to have occurred to either of the Lafargues that to spare herself the expense and inconvenience of her transport, Laura might have stayed with her dying sister in a household clamorous for help. Paul's letter ended in the usual way: "Can you send me £10, for I am devilishly hard up."[66]

Marx longed to be with Jenny but knew it would be folly

to cumber her with an invalid. He had begun to suffer from spasmodic attacks, unable to get his breath on getting out of bed, which he believed to be of nervous origin brought on by his terrible fears for Jenny. Eleanor, too, wished to go to her sister, but she had Johnny on her hands. "You had *much* better let him stay on for the present", she wrote to Jenny on 9 January. She described the little boy's pleasure in being taken to a party, complete with conjurer, given by a Mrs. Bircham, the headmistress of the school in Kensington where Eleanor was teaching. His hosts had been delighted by the child who was "*wonderfully* well and in the highest spirits". In this, her last letter to Jenny, Tussy wrote: "I think of you day and night, and only wish I could *do* something. Tell Charles he is to send me a p.c. for I am too anxious to go on waiting like this."[67]

It was suggested that Lenchen should go to Argenteuil and, while the matter was debated, letters flew from Paris to London and back, day by day. On 10 January Marx forwarded to Eleanor Paul's latest news from which—though he thought it might have been written out of kindness—it seemed that the danger was passed. He had been enchanted by the reports of Wolf (Edgar) and Par (Marcel) and, momentarily cheered, he allowed himself to hope.

At five o'clock on the following afternoon, 11 January 1883, Jenny died. She was not quite 39 years of age. Her death certificate was registered at the Argenteuil Town Hall by Paul Lafargue and Gustave Louis Dourlen, her doctor. Her funeral took place on 13 January attended by many of the former Communards and by representatives of all the socialist papers in France. Engels wrote an obituary notice for the *Sozialdemokrat*[68] in which he paid a tribute to her activities on behalf of the Fenians and recalled her ordeal at the time of her arrest at Luchon. Her sorrowing father, he ended, had at least the solace of knowing that hundreds of thousands of workers in Europe and America shared his grief.

Solace it may have been, but Eleanor recalled in later years that she felt she was bringing him his death sentence when she left at once for Ventnor. "On the long anxious journey I tortured my brain thinking how to impart the news to him . . . my face betrayed it—Moor said at once 'Our Jenny is dead'. I have lived many a sad hour, but none so sad as that." No sooner had she arrived than Marx urged her to go to Argenteuil to help with the children and "would not suffer any contradiction", though she would have preferred to stay with him in his unutterable woe at the death of his "first-born, the daughter he loved most". Within half an hour she was on her way back to London and then set off for Paris. "I can only think with a shudder of that time," she wrote.[30]

Marx himself immediately returned to London, but he had come home to die. Eleanor was right in saying that Jenny's death was the last terrible blow. He now suffered a series of the spasmodic attacks which reminded him of how distressfully Jenny must always have suffered from her asthma, while laryngitis and bronchitis made his voice hoarse and he found it painful to swallow. In February he developed a tumour on the lung. When Eleanor returned from France she brought with her poor little sick Harra whom she placed under the care of the children's hospital in Shadwell,* for the child was beyond the help of this stricken household. On 14 March 1883 at two o'clock in the afternoon, having been nursed by "good old Lenchen . . . as a mother nurses a child", Marx died suddenly and peacefully at the age of 65. Eleanor, who was present, notified the death. "Mankind is shorter by a head, and by the most remarkable head of our time", wrote Engels.[69]

He was buried on 17 March in the same grave as his wife. A week later, it was reopened to receive the remains of his grandson, Harry Longuet, who had died in hospital on 21 March at the age of four-and-a-half.

Marx's funeral was attended by a relatively small company, which included Engels, Eleanor, Longuet, Lafargue, Liebknecht, Lessner, Schorlemmer and Edwin Ray Lankester. Laura did not leave Paris. Eleanor, who had received, among condolences from a multitude of her own and her father's friends, a warm letter from Richard Garnett, invited him to the ceremony though he was unable to be present.

The Congress of the illegal German Social Democratic Party was to be held in Copenhagen from 29 March to 2 April. Bebel wrote to Engels on the day of the funeral saying that he proposed to move a resolution that a monument to Marx should be erected, not as a grandiose memorial, but as a token of the

* See fn.†, p. 154.

gratitude and solidarity of the workers of the world. To this Engels replied on 30 April: "I don't know what should be done about a memorial to Marx. The family is against it. The simple gravestone designed for his wife and now bearing his own and his little grandson's name, would be desecrated in their eyes if it were replaced by a monument." Eleanor echoed these sentiments in her later writings: "Marx did not want a 'memorial'. To have desired to put up any other memorial to the creator of *The Communist Manifesto* and of *Capital* than that which he had built himself would have been an insult to the great dead. In the heads and hearts of millions of workers, who have 'united' at his call, he has not merely a memorial more lasting than bronze, but also the living soil in which what he taught and desired will become—and in part has already become—an act."[30]

Before he was laid in earth many people were allowed to see him in his coffin: days of lying-in-state, as it were. Mrs. Comyn wrote: "The last time I saw Dr. Marx he lay in his coffin, his hands folded over his breast—a warrior who had fought valliantly until weapons were taken from him by a force greater than his own. The serenity of his face was wonderful, wrinkles were smoothed out, old age had retreated, all traces of suffering were swept away. A tranquil . . . power remained." She was alone with Eleanor in the room and wished to express her sympathy, but "she stopped me imperiously. . . . 'I want no condolences. If he had lingered during a long illness, and I had seen his mind and body decaying before my eyes, I should have stood in need of consolation. But it was not so. He died in harness, his intellect untouched . . . He has earned his rest. Let us be grateful for so much'."[*1]

Another of those who claimed to have paid his last respects

---

* It is, of course, quite possible that Mrs. Comyn recorded at the time and accurately quoted Eleanor *verbatim* some 39 years later. However, in Engels' letter to Sorge of 15 March the following passage occurs: "All events occurring of natural necessity bring their own consolation with them, however dreadful they may be. Medical skill might have been able to vouch him a few more years of vegetative existence, the life of a helpless being, dying—to the triumph of the physician's art—not suddenly, but inch by inch. Our Marx, however, would never have borne that . . . To see this mighty genius lingering on as a physical wreck for the greater glory of medicine and the mockery of the Philistines whom he had so often reduced to dust in the prime of his strength—no, it is a thousand times better as it is, a thousand times better that we bear him, the day after tomorrow, to the grave where his wife lies at rest."

to the dead man in his coffin was Edward Aveling, who had met Marx but once, briefly, many years before. "I stood by the side of his corpse, hand in hand with my wife", he wrote.[70] It is quite on the cards that Edward Aveling never stood by the coffin at all, hand in hand with anybody; but if he did it was not with his wife. His readers were being given to understand that it was he who stood lovingly at Eleanor Marx's side in the solemnity of her father's death chamber. Though she lived openly with Aveling for the last fifteen years of her life, the conjuring up of this intimate scene of March 1883 is more in keeping with Aveling's propensity to falsify facts than with Eleanor's sense of fitness.

REFERENCE NOTES

Abbreviations

BIML	Institute of Marxism-Leninism, Berlin.
Bottigelli Archives	Letters in the custody of Dr. Emile Bottigelli, Paris.
Bottigelli L & D	*Lettres et Documents de Karl Marx 1856–1883.* Previously unpublished texts edited by Dr. Emile Bottigelli. Annali dell' Istituto Giangiacomo Feltrinelli, Anno Primo. Milan, 1958.
ELC	*Frederick Engels Paul and Laura Lafargue: Correspondence,* Volumes I–III. Lawrence & Wishart, 1959–1963.
IISH	International Institute of Social History, Amsterdam.
Liebknecht	*Wilhelm Liebknecht Briefwechsel mit Karl Marx und Friedrich Engels.* Edited by Georg Eckert. Mouton & Co., The Hague, 1963.
MEW	*Marx Engels Werke.* Dietz Verlag, Berlin. 1956–1968. Unless otherwise stated Volumes 27–39.
MIML	Institute of Marxism-Leninism, Moscow.

(1) Marian Comyn. "My Recollections of Karl Marx". *The Nineteenth Century and After.* Vol. 91, No. 539. January 1922.

(2) *Aus Meinem Leben.* Stuttgart 1911.

(3) An obituary article published in *Die Neue Zeit* No. 30 1897–98. BIML.

(4) Eleanor to Jenny, 18 June 1881. Bottigelli Archives.

(5) *My Years in Exile*. Trans. by B. Miall. Parsons, 1921.

(6) 17 June 1879. MEW.

(7) H. M. Hyndman. "Something Better than Emigration: A Reply to Lord Brabazon". *The Nineteenth Century*. Vol. XVI. December 1884.

(8) *Record of an Adventurous Life*. Macmillan 1911.

(9) *Tom Mann's Memoirs*. The Labour Publishing Co. Ltd., 1923. New edition MacGibbon and Kee, 1967.

(10) *La Rupture Marx-Hyndman*. Annali dell'Istituto Giangiacomo Feltrinelli. Anno Terzo. Feltrinelli. Milan 1960. (MEW Vol. 35).

(11) Engels to Laura, 16 February 1884. ELC, Vol. I.

(12) Mrs. Marx to Laura, n.d. (but obviously first week in July 1881) from 43 Terminus Road, Eastbourne. MIML.

(13) James G. Hutchinson. "Progress and Wages. A Workman's View". *The Nineteenth Century*. Vol. XVI. October 1884.

(14) Eleanor to Hirsch, 16 September 1880. IISH.

(15) November 1880. Liebknecht.

(16) 7 October 1881. IISH.

(17) Eleanor to Liebknecht, 12 February 1881. Liebknecht.

(18) 12 February 1881. Liebknecht.

(19) 4 March 1879. BIML.

(20) 1 January 1880. BIML.

(21) 1 October 1880. Original English MIML. (German MEW).

(22) *Justice*. 9 April 1898.

(23) Jenny to Marx, 3 December 1881. BIML.

(24) Havelock Ellis. *Adelphi*. New Series. Vol. 6. September 1935.

(25) To Jenny, 7 April 1881. Bottigelli Archives.

(26) Pre-26 July 1881. IISH.

(27) 7 October 1881. Bottigelli Archives.

(28) 18 October 1881. Bottigelli Archives.

(29) Eleanor to Jenny, 31 October 1881. Bottigelli Archives.

(30) Reminiscences of Liebknecht. *Karl Marx Selected Works*. Vol. I. Lawrence & Wishart, 1942.

(31) Eleanor to Jenny, 4 December 1881. Bottigelli Archives.

(32) Published in the *Sozialdemokrat* on 8 December and in *l'Egalité* on 11 December 1881. Though delivered in English, the original text of the speech has not been traced.

(33) Letter to Olive Schreiner, 16 June 1884. Quoted in (24).

(34) Eleanor to Marx, 7 August 1881. Bottigelli Archives.

(35) Information kindly provided by Dr. Felix Brown, M.A., F.R.C.P., F.R.C.M., Member Royal Medico Psychological Association.

(36) In the Radford family collection.
(37) Engels' articles have been reprinted in pamphlet form as *The British Labour Movement*. Martin Lawrence 1934.
(38) Eleanor to Jenny, 8 January 1882. Bottigelli Archives.
(39) Eleanor to Jenny, 15 January 1882. Bottigelli Archives.
(40) Jenny to Laura, 10 January 1882. BIML.
(41) Jenny to Marx, 24 February 1882. MIML.
(42) Jenny to Eleanor, 7 March 1882. IISH.
(43) Marx to Engels, 11 November 1882. MEW.
(44) Eleanor to Jenny, 21 February 1882. IISH.
(45) Jenny to Eleanor, 10 April 1882. IISH.
(46) Jenny to Eleanor, 17 May 1882. IISH.
(47) Eleanor to Carl Hirsch, 24 February 1882. IISH.
(48) To Eleanor, 10 April 1882. IISH.
(49) Jenny to Eleanor, 12–13 April 1882. IISH.
(50) Marx to Bracke, 18 August 1877. MEW.
(51) English edition trans. Edward Fitzgerald. John Lane 1936.
(52) Bottigelli Archives.
(53) 3 April 1882. Bottigelli Archives.
(54) Eleanor to Jenny, 25 March 1882. Bottigelli Archives.
(55) Jenny to Eleanor, 8 November 1882. IISH.
(56) Eleanor to Jenny, July (n.d.) 1882. Bottigelli Archives.
(57) "Letter from England" in *Russkoye Bogatstvo* (Russian Wealth), No. 5 1895. MIML. (Retranslated from the Russian by Mr. John Gibbons.)
(58) 2 August 1882. ELC. Vol. I.
(59) 2 October 1882. Bottigelli Archives.
(60) Jenny to Eleanor, 15 January 1882. IISH.
(61) 3 May 1882. IISH.
(62) 22 June 1882. BIML.
(63) Jenny to Laura, early September (n.d.) 1882. IISH.
(64) ELC, Vol. I.
(65) 21 December 1882. ELC, Vol. I.
(66) ELC, Vol. III.
(67) Eleanor to Jenny, 9 January 1883. Bottigelli Archives.
(68) No. 4 1883, published 18 January. Vol. 19, MEW.
(69) To Sorge, 15 March 1883. MEW.
(70) Edward Aveling. "Charles Darwin and Karl Marx". *New Century Review*. April 1897.

THE GRAVE IN HIGHGATE CEMETERY

PART IV

THE NONCONFORMIST

1

Edward Bibbins Aveling, born on 29 November 1849 at 6
Nelson Terrace, Stoke Newington in the borough of Hackney,
was the fifth of the eight children—six sons and two daughters
—of the Rev. Thomas William Baxter Aveling and his wife,
Mary Ann.

Nelson Terrace, from which Aveling derived the pseudonym
he later adopted legitimately as playwright and critic, fraudu-
lently in contracting his second marriage, was in the heart of
Kingsland of whose Independent (Congregational) Chapel in
Robinson's Row, High Street, his father was the incumbent
for close on half a century.

Compared to the raffish environment of Eleanor's birthplace,
with its shifting and foreign population, Aveling's was one of
solid respectability. While at the lower end of the short terrace
the residents followed such occupations as stonemason, laund-
ress, gardener and dressmaker, the social scale rose with the
house numbers to the firm gentility of a retired major on full
pay. Even when allowance is made for some slight overcrowding
among the manual workers, the number of persons to the house
in Nelson Terrace was roughly six, an average that included
a plethora of domestic servants—cooks, footmen, housemaids,
nurses—in some cases heavily outnumbering their employers.

Such a household was No. 14 where an elderly gentlewoman
lived with her three servants. She was called Elizabeth Bibbins
and it is inconceivable that the Rev. Aveling should have saddled
his fourth son with her surname simply because it caught his
fancy. "All the family were called after people with money",
one of his surviving granddaughters remarked.[1]

As a small boy Edward was occasionally sent to dine with
Miss Bibbins. In later life he recalled that she would ask him
"Will you take peas or potatoes?" to which he would reply,
characteristically, "Both, please".[2]

The next and fifth son, Frederic (or Frederick) Wilkins

Aveling was named after the Treasurer of Kingsland Chapel, Frederick Robert Wilkins, a bullion merchant who conducted his business from Winchester Street in the City. The Rev. Aveling, with his large brood, can hardly be censured for these baptismal ploys. Though he supplemented his income by journalistic work, including the editorship of *The Jewish Herald* from 1848 until 1853, the Kingsland living was worth no more than between £400 and £500 a year.* Nor were the pious man's hopes disappointed. Under Miss Bibbins' Will, drawn up on 22 January 1859, he was appointed one of her two executors and when she died six weeks later at the age of 85, he and his family received a goodly portion of her estate valued at some £15,000.†

While Miss Bibbins remained in Nelson Terrace until her death, the Avelings had moved some years before to 13 Amhurst Road, Shacklewell, in Hackney, where the last child, a boy, was born when Edward was six years of age. This was a larger house, as, indeed, was required. The 1861 census shows that theirs was the most populous dwelling in the street, with twelve members, though by then the eldest son, aged 20, had already left home. Their neighbours, boasting more servants and fewer children, showed an average of no more than eight persons to a household.

Here Edward lived until 1863 when he was sent with his brother Frederick, 18 months his junior, to the West of England Dissenters' Proprietary School in Taunton.‡ Rough notes jotted down for his memoirs by the Rev. Frederick Aveling shortly

---

* If this should be thought adequate for the times, there is the abiding witness of Trollope's Mr. Quiverful, the Rector of Puddingdale, whose income at the same period was also £400.

† After various bequests to distant relatives, faithful servants and the religious and charitable Institutions recommended by her pastor, the Rev. Aveling, Miss Bibbins left him £500, the same amount to Mrs. Aveling and £500 on trust in 3% Consolidated Bank Annuities Stock for each of his eldest children: Thomas Goodall, then 18, and Mary Elizabeth who was 17. The two next sons, Charles Taylor and William Arthur, and the three younger children received nothing, but Edward Bibbins was left £300 of Stock on trust. The trust funds were to be disbursed for the education of the minors who would be paid the money on attaining the age of 21. Provision was made that in the case of any legatee dying before that age, the money should revert to the father, who also received £100 as executor, all the old lady's books and book-cases and an equal share with his co-executor of the residue of her personal estate and effects.

‡ Founded in 1847. In 1868 the name of the school was changed to the Independent College, to which the Rev. Frederick Wilkins Aveling, M.A., B.Sc., returned as Headmaster at the early age of 29, to remain for 14 years (1880–1894). It is now known as Taunton School.[3]

THE SCHOOLBOYS: EDWARD (SEATED) AND FREDERICK AVELING

EDWARD AVELING: A PROMISING YOUNG MAN

before his death in 1937* contain the following passage: "Edward, at school with me at Taunton. Bad egg. Had fever, recovered. So father made us both join the Church. We were far too young. I was only 12, Edward 13½."[4]

Whether too young or not, these two, in being sent to a boarding school, differed from their elder brothers whose education ended roughly at an age when theirs began, Thomas having set out to earn his living as a youth (despite Miss Bibbins' Will), Charles† and William,‡ though still living at home, being employed as clerks while in their early 'teens: one in a grocery shop, or "Italian warehouse", the other by a shipping agent.

In the same year—1863—as the two boys entered Taunton, their elder sister, Mary, then 21, married Francis Robert Wilkins, the son of the bullion merchant whose glittering trade he followed. From that time forth the Rev. Aveling was relieved of his responsibility for this daughter whom he specifically referred to in his Will as being "through her marriage well provided for". There can be little doubt that this circumstance also accounted for her younger brothers' superior education.

Frederick stayed at Taunton for four years, but Edward left after two, whereafter he was privately educated, for some part of the time in Jersey—by a tutor he hated[6]—until he entered University College, London, as a medical student in 1867. When he was 20 he transferred from the Medical to the Science Faculty, obtaining a £40 Exhibition to study botany and zoology. He took his B.Sc. Honours degree in zoology in 1870, doing so brilliantly that he qualified for an annual £50 scholarship for a further three years. Thus by the time he had reached his majority he had proved himself a young man of outstanding ability.§ In passing it may be said that his brother

* He and his wife lie buried, like the Marxes, in Highgate cemetery.
† 1844–1902. Later in life Charles qualified in medicine and became a highly successful general practitioner.
‡ b. 1846. Emigrated to Canada where he died in his thirties. He was the father of Dr. Francis Arthur Powell Aveling, M.C., Ph.D., D.Sc., sometime Professor of Psychology at King's College, London, after leaving the Roman Catholic priesthood.[1,5]
§ One anecdote illustrating his gifts, attested to by both his surviving nieces in almost identical terms, was obviously handed down in family lore by the brother concerned. "Edward was so brilliant", writes Mrs. Gwendoline Redhead, "that when he wanted to take Logic for some exam. and had never touched the subject, he came to my father two days before the exam. My father said 'you can't cram up for it in two days'. Edward said he could and the two of them went ahead and

Frederick was such another. Though he won a scholarship to Oxford he refused to put his father to the expense it would entail[1] and entered New College, the School of Divinity in the University of London, then at Swiss Cottage (now at 527 Finchley Road) in 1870, was awarded two scholarships and an Essay Prize, to leave in 1874 with the degrees of M.A. and B.Sc.[7]

For a short period Edward worked as assistant to the eminent physiologist Sir Michael Foster in Cambridge,* returning to London in 1872 when he became a teacher of elementary physics and botany on the staff of Miss Buss's North London Collegiate School for Ladies in Camden Road. This was one of the many establishments which enjoyed his father's patronage and his influence may well have helped Edward to an appointment which, on a part-time basis, he kept until his resignation at the end of 1876.† Another institution in which the Rev. Aveling took a special interest was the Orphan Working School in Maitland Park, at whose 110th Anniversary dinner he was the guest of honour.[10] Again this could be the reason why it came about that, back in London and lodging near to both Miss Buss's school and the Orphanage, at 30 Bartholomew Road in Kentish Town, Edward examined the orphan boys in physiology during June 1872[11] and in the October of either that or the following year‡ was invited to give one of the lectures in his repertoire—"Insects and Flowers"—at the annual prize-giving fête before an audience of patrons and local notabilities. It was on this occasion that he was introduced to Dr. Karl Marx, his wife and their young daughter, Eleanor.[12] He never met either of the parents again.

By this time Edward was a married man. On 30 July 1872 his wedding to Isabel Campbell Frank was solemnised at the Union Chapel, Compton Terrace, Islington,§ the ceremony

---

worked till 2 a.m. and then slept for four hours, and grandfather called them at 6 a.m. and they carried on all day. The next day Edward took the exam. and passed it. He said to my father 'That's all right. I'll forget it all in a couple of days.' "[1]
* At that period there was no Physiology Department at Cambridge. Sir Michael Foster, who had been called to that University in 1870, had previously taught at University College, London, and the likelihood is that he employed this most promising of his former students privately since there is no record of Aveling's admission in any capacity to Cambridge University.[8]
† Reported to the Governors in January 1877.[9]
‡ Whether 1872 or 1873 is uncertain.
§ Founded in 1799, it was rebuilt in 1876 and is still extant.

THE REV. THOMAS WILLIAM BAXTER AVELING IN 1872

BELL AT ABOUT THE TIME OF HER MARRIAGE

being conducted by the Rev. Thomas Aveling according to the rites of the Congregationalists.

Isabel Frank, known as Bell, was one of the five children of a Leadenhall poulterer, John Frank who, dying in August 1868 at the age of 54, left an estate of £25,000. For many years the Franks had lived, though more opulently, in the same street as the Avelings, and it is probable that Edward and Bell, members of the same congregation and much of an age—she was but a few months younger than he—had known each other in Amhurst Road since childhood. At the time of her marriage Bell lived with her widowed mother at 178 Highbury Park Road in Islington. The Aveling family thought Bell a thoroughly nice young woman and her photograph, taken at about the time of the marriage, when she was 22, shows her to have been a plump and decorative one.

Edward's own account has it that he and Bell parted two years later "by mutual agreement". Engels, on the other hand, was given to understand that she had run off with a clergyman. Either way it will be seen that Edward was blameless in the matter. In later years he put it about that the whole Bell episode was foredoomed to failure: that in his green youth he had been caught by a spoilt and bigoted Miss who refused him a divorce even though she would not live with a man of his atheist and socialist beliefs, neither of which had, in fact, manifested themselves as early as he claimed to have separated from Bell. Small discrepancies of this kind did not trouble Aveling and his story passed muster in various circles where it was also believed, several years after Bell's death, that his wife was still living and that he was not free to remarry. His brother Frederick, who knew better, told Eleanor Marx "long before Bell died, that at Bell's death Edward would not marry her".[4] He noted: "He married Bell Frank for her money (300 a year). She could only get half. He soon made her do that. When not able to get any more out of her, he left her."[4] And the Rev. Frederick Aveling's daughter writes: "Eleanor Marx said to father when Bell died 'Now Edward will marry me'. But father said 'Oh no he won't. I know Edward.' "[1] It was also said that he clung to the marriage tie in the hope of laying hands eventually on the remainder of her fortune and, further, that when he left her she was stripped of everything she

I

possessed and without the means to sue for the divorce she wanted.[13]

The truth is slightly different. By the terms of her father's Will, Bell inherited a half-share with her sister Emeline Elizabeth of an annual income of £210 5s. od. derived from freehold properties in Upper Holloway. Insurance and repairs had to be paid for out of this income which came to the daughters on trust without power of anticipation. If Bell died childless—as she did—the property reverted to her sister, her sister's children or, failing these, to the trustees. All this Edward must have known. In the event, Emeline Frank, who had been one of the witnesses at Bell's wedding, never married and outlived her sister. But John Frank also left his daughters £1,000 each on attaining the age of 21 or upon marriage. It was this dowry that Edward could have run through when he married Bell four years after her father had died. He could not have touched the capital of her small income at any time and the derisory sum she left at her death she must have saved from that income or earned by her own efforts.

There was so little to poor Bell's life that the meagre facts are soon told. She lived for 20 years after the marriage and at some stage during her solitary existence joined an Anglican Sisterhood, working as a nurse.* On 12 September 1892, at the age of 43, she died intestate at 36 Brooke Street,† Holborn, in a diabetic coma, with no member of her family present and none but paid attendance. This was a stone's throw from the chambers then occupied by Edward in Chancery Lane. Within three weeks the "lawful husband", having been granted Letters of Administration, pocketed her estate whose gross value was £126 15s. 4d.

Yet when he married Edward was launched on a successful career that would seem to have made it quite unnecessary for him either to seek a rich wife or to pluck her. In 1874, while regularly employed on Miss Buss's staff, he was giving a series of evening classes on botany and zoology at the Polytechnic College in Regent Street‡ and published his first work *Botanical*

---

* One of the many Mission Houses of the "Sisters of the Poor", as they were called, was in Baldwin's Gardens, two streets away from where Bell lived. These Sisterhoods, founded by Pusey in 1845, provided the entire nursing staff at one time of, among others, University College Hospital.[14]

† The rather sordid little house still stands.

‡ On its present site it was then the Educational Department of the Royal

Tables. In the following year, having been appointed as a Lecturer in comparative anatomy and biology at the Medical School of the London Hospital, he gave his Polytechnic lessons in the mornings and, although it is not known for how long he was connected with this institute, he gave it as his permanent address up to the end of May 1881.[16] His lectureship at the London Hospital lasted until 1882, according to official records,[17] though he was in fact dismissed at the end of the 1881 academic year. In 1876 he obtained his D.Sc. at University College, London, was elected a Fellow of the Linnean Society, his sponsors being two botanists and two zoologists of note,* and in 1877 published his *Physiological Tables.* In 1878, when still under 30 years of age, he was made a Fellow of University College, and in June 1879 he applied for the vacant Chair of Comparative Anatomy at King's College, London, but on finding that the list of rules made adherence to the Church of England obligatory, he did not pursue his application and, with a fine gesture, "consigned them to the flames".[19]

The facts about Aveling's life have had to be culled from sources unpolluted by his own coloured versions and other people's opinions. Thus his claim to be an Irishman—jocularly accepted by Bernard Shaw as a counterweight to the overwhelmingly Scottish influence in literary London[20] and wholly believed by Eleanor Marx—was founded upon no more than his mother's and paternal grandmother's emigrant ancestry. It was widely and erroneously held that he had been to Harrow.[21] A biographical sketch in the 1895 *Labour Annual* published not only that he had been Professor of Chemistry and Physiology at New College, London, on whose teaching staff he never was at any time, but also that he had held the Chair of Comparative Anatomy at the London Hospital where, on his own showing, he was a lecturer who, for a salary of £25 a year, gave two lectures a week.[22]

Polytechnic Institute in association with the Society of Arts, the Science and Art Department in South Kensington and the City of London College. In 1880 this Regent Street Department suffered from lack of support and ceased to function. The building was put up for sale and bought in 1881 by Quintin Hogg, whose statue stands nearby. After extension and alteration, the premises were re-opened in September 1882 and known as the Youth's Christian Institute and subsequently as, quite simply, the Regent Street Polytechnic. It is now called the Polytechnic of Central London.[15]

* George Henshaw, Maxwell T. Masters, James Hurie and St. George Mivart. In November 1881 his name was removed from the list of Fellows for non-payment of subscriptions.[18]

2

The thundercloud of obloquy and abhorrence which, long gathering about his head, descended on Edward Aveling after the death of Eleanor Marx, never to be dispersed in the brief time that remained to him, has largely hidden from posterity both his early achievements and his solid background. Thus he was said to have come from the gutter, to have fawned upon Marx—whom he never knew—and Engels, worming his way into Eleanor's affections only to exploit and discard her to "marry money", whereafter he vanished again into the shadows from which he had emerged.

The distinction of his scientific career as a young man is beyond question; his origins were no less reputable. Though his father, unlike Eleanor's, did nothing world-shaking, he was the spiritual descendant of Milton's "faithful and freeborn Englishmen" who, hunted, hated and harried since the 17th century, became, as convinced Republicans, the backbone of the Commonwealth, identifying the struggle of conscience with that for liberty, thus earning for themselves on the Restoration the most savagely discriminative legislation ever to reach the Statute Book.[23] Under these crippling measures the Dissenters were driven out of the Church. Ordained ministers who refused to take the Oath adopting the revised Book of Prayer and repudiating the Solemn League and Covenant were forbidden to preach or teach in corporate towns. It was illegal for five or more persons to gather together for Nonconformist religious purposes, a third offence of this nature carrying the penalty of transportation. Constables could break into any house where they suspected that Dissenters met. It is estimated that one-fifth of the parochial clergy resigned their livings.

Although the Declaration of Indulgence, granting religious freedom under James II, followed by the Act of Toleration, written into the Revolution Settlement and the Bill of Rights to which William III gave his assent in 1689, lightened the penal code and again allowed Dissenters to build their own places of worship, it was possible for Lord Mansfield to protest, almost a century later and after the passing of the Dissenting Ministers Act, that "the City of London, in paltry thieving spirit, nominated Nonconformists to offices they could not fill, so that they might fine them for the non-fulfilment". The repeal of the Test and Corporation Acts did not come into force until 1830, while Dissenters were disqualified from holding office under the Crown and were excluded from the ancient Universities—Oxford, Cambridge and Durham—until 1871.

In Cromwell's time the idea of a "glorious University" in London had been conceived by the Independents, but it was not until 1828 that the University of London, "open to all creeds", came into being. The "Godless College", as it was called, became University College, founded on its present site in Gower Street in 1831. It gained its Charter as a Constituent College of the newly created University of London in 1836.

Edward Aveling's father thus grew up at a time when his denomination saw new opportunities opening. Throughout his adult life he was a minister of the Congregational Church— the most ancient of the 20 Protestant dissenting bodies in England and Wales—which, as "the Independents", had renounced the authority of "pope, prelate, presbytery, priest and parliament". In the 19th century the Nonconformist minister was looked upon as the only friend to Cobbett's "mass of unregarded humanity in the factories and mines".*

Thomas William Baxter Aveling was born on 11 May 1815 in Castletown, the ancient capital of the Isle of Man, where his father, William, a non-commissioned officer, was stationed. His mother was an Irish girl from Ennistimon, Co. Clare, but the Avelings came of an old Cambridgeshire family centred in Wisbech where, on buying his discharge from the army, William Aveling retired, only to die in 1818. The young widow was left in great poverty but the child, Thomas, was taken into the guardianship of a local burgess who sent him to the best school that Wisbech offered.† The boy showed such aptitude

---

* Greville recorded that on the 1833 petition in the House of Commons to admit Dissenters to Cambridge "Old Cobbett made as mischievous a speech as he could to blow the coals between the parties".[24]
† The Wisbech Free Grammar School was founded by a Guild in 1592. The premises are now the Youth Centre of the Unionist and Conservative Club.

that he not only became an usher at the school but, having voluntarily joined the Independent Church at 16 years of age, he was preaching in the surrounding villages before he was 18. A certain Mr. Byrnes of Wisbech left an account of the youthful lay-preacher: "He looked so young, had such command of language, was so poetical in his conceptions, and possessed such a charming voice, that wherever he went he was followed by crowds anxious to hear . . . his marvellous oratory."[25]

Thomas had also published a small volume of devotional poems which met with so singular a success that when, on the recommendation of a minister visiting Wisbech, he was entered at Highbury College in 1834 he was able to pay for his four years' residence at the theological seminary from the proceeds.

On 11 October 1838, at 23 years of age, he was ordained and immediately offered no fewer than four ministries. An elderly friend, the Rev. William Clayton, persuaded him to accept that of co-pastor to Kingsland Independent Chapel in Stoke Newington.

"My own mind", he wrote, "was strongly disinclined to accept it; my heart was fixed on another people in a different suburb. . . . But Mr. Clayton's judgment was entirely opposed to my own; and he most vigorously combatted all my objections. When I observed that there were, among the 150 people assembling in Kingsland chapel, not a dozen young persons with whom a minister was likely to grow up, and from whom he might look for co-operation—that it was literally an 'assembly of elders'—for there were, out of 68 members of the church twelve about 80 years of age—he only replied, 'Go, and call such young people in'. When I said that the place was very small, his answer was, 'Go, and enlarge it'. When I remarked that there was a sparse population among which to work— Kingsland then was a mere hamlet—cornfields and pasture lands lying between it and London—he said. 'Though the beginnings be small, its latter end will greatly increase'."[26]

The young minister's reluctance was understandable. The "mere hamlet" of Kingsland had barely cast off its rude and rustic 18th century character. It was a place of Sunday resort for the nearby City population to indulge in bull- and badger-baiting, cock-fighting and wrestling. Its inhabitants were for the most part unschooled—and godless—brickmakers. The church, such as it was, had been consecrated in 1790 in a disused workshop, originally a leper hospital known as La Loque. The Rev. John Campbell,* a man of high principle and benevolent disposition, whose pastorship Aveling was to share, had held the living since 1804, when nightingales sang in Dalston Fields. He was now 72 and infirm.

Before Campbell died and Aveling, then 25 years old, succeeded to the full pastoral office, he married Mary Ann Goodall. She was of the same age and, though born in Co. Carlow, her father had migrated and become both a farmer and innkeeper in Wisbech where the marriage, according to the rites of the Independents, took place on 3 October 1839 in Castle Square Chapel. Only one member of either family was present at the ceremony: the bride's maternal uncle, Joseph Bishop. More surprisingly, though the bridegroom was a fully ordained minister of the Church, he signed the register as "Gentleman", without profession. The eight children of this marriage were born in the course of the next 17 years, all but the youngest at 6 Nelson Terrace.

When Aveling took over his Kingsland ministry the church seated 400 people. Seven years later it was enlarged to hold 900 and in 1852 the foundation stone was laid for a bran-new Gothic edifice seating 1,350 with a gallery for 800 children. It was so vast a place, furnished with a pulpit of surpassing ugliness bought by the parishioners at the Great Exhibition of 1851, that its flourishing congregation named it with pride the "Cathedral of North London". Ever again enlarged and improved, it remained to ornament, though not embellish, that most depressing area of the metropolis until its demolition in the 1940s.

Another feature of Aveling's ministry was the building and inauguration of schools for the Kingsland children of both sexes, and, indeed, as his patronage of Miss Buss's establishment proved, he was a great believer in the education of females. His own family life, though he presided over a strict Christian

* An Edinburgh man (1766–1840), he had been accustomed to "free prayers" on moors and mountains and, on accepting the Kingsland incumbency, had stipulated that the liturgy and Church prayers should be discontinued, whereupon many of the founder-trustees resigned and the Independent character of the Chapel was established. John Campbell Road, off Kingsland High Street, still commemorates him.

household with no fun on Sundays nor frivolity at any time, was not a gloomy one, as it hardly could be with so many youngsters whose father had at heart the welfare—not only spiritual—of all children.

He was a prolific writer of both verse and prose throughout his life, during which he held innumerable honorary positions, including a Doctorate of Divinity at Howard University in the United States, the Chairmanship of the Congregational Board of London in 1873, that of the London Congregational Union in 1874* and, for the year 1876, he was elected to the highest office in his denomination as Chairman of the Congregational Union of England and Wales.[25]

In addition to a talent little short of genius for raising funds—£50,000 was subscribed by an overwhelmingly working-class congregation in less than 20 years for the benefit of his Church and the charities he supported—the Rev. Aveling was distinguished by his splendid gifts of voice and delivery as an orator: traits which his son Edward inherited in good measure, though directed to different ends. But the pastor was a comely man, as may be seen both in the engraving opposite and the family photograph taken in 1850 (p. 253). Edward, the "unprincipled windbag" as his brother called him,[4] is seated on his mother's lap here in the centre of the group. It is not easy to identify the infant Aveling, his curls cascading from under an inappropriate hat—everyone else seems to be indoors—with the ill-favoured schoolboy of 1863 shown seated by his handsome younger brother Frederick (p. 255).

At about the age of 21 Edward went through a phase of vaguely romantic good looks—the curls now trained to cluster at his neck in a poetic sweep—but in maturity there was a disturbing lack of harmony in his features. It is also true that he carried himself in a hunched manner and was not well-grown, but whether his unprepossessing person was a misfortune or a fault, it excited animadversions not usually committed to paper or publicly printed. His "basilisk eye" was more than once referred to as the sign of his awful character. William Morris's daughter called him "a little lizard of a man",[27]

* It is of interest to note that the Rev. Andrew Mearns was Secretary of the London Congregational Union when he wrote his famous pamphlet *The Bitter Cry of Outcast London: An Inquiry into the Conditions of the Abject Poor*, the first edition of which was published anonymously in October 1883.

and was not the first to do so, Bernard Shaw having used the simile and also said that "he had no physical charm except a voice like a euphonium".[28] Olive Schreiner, in whom Aveling aroused feelings of dread and horror, compared him to an illicit diamond buyer: "the real criminal type",[29] while Hyndman, who found his "forbidding face . . . ugly and even repulsive", said that "nobody can be as bad as Aveling looks".[30] One wonders whether, had he been an Adonis, outraged virtue would have been more tolerant of Aveling's conduct. Certainly, in Hyndman's *obiter dictum* that with women "he needed but half an hour's start of the handsomest man in London", it is possible to detect behind some of these strictures on his appearance the unspoken cry: It isn't fair.

When all but their two youngest had left home, the Aveling parents moved to 208 Amhurst Road where on 5 August 1877 Edward's mother died of apoplexy.* Her children were said to have been devoted to her and took it ill that, within a twelve-month of her death, the widower, then 63 years of age, married a much younger lady: Miss Agnes Sarah Joscelyne, the sister of a Congregationalist minister who officiated at the wedding. The first Mrs. Aveling was thought to have known and heartily disliked this member of her husband's flock who was forever sewing exquisite clerical bands and only too plainly "making a set at him". Her offerings were returned and she was sent about her business. Certainly she was not welcomed by her stepchildren, most of whom she outlived, surviving her husband by over 30 years. Edward is not known ever to have communicated with her, while his brother Frederick detested her and would not allow his family to meet her.[1]

The Rev. Thomas Aveling himself died of an attack of gastritis on 3 July 1884 while on a visit to the Reedham Asylum for Fatherless Children, near Croydon, of which he had been the honorary secretary for close on 40 years.

By that time Edward was not only an avowed atheist but also an active socialist who had lost much of his standing in and more or less abandoned the academic world, yet he received, without discrimination, his due share of the £8,400 left by his

---

* Family lore has it that, though a lovable woman, Mrs. Aveling was much given to the bottle, suffered from cirrhosis of the liver and expired after falling downstairs when drunk.[1] Her death certificate, signed by her doctor son, Charles, does not bear this out.

father. It is not known how much he inherited but, with provision for a large family, a youthful widow and his grandchildren by the two sons who had predeceased him,† the Rev. Aveling is unlikely to have endowed Edward with a competence.

† Ernest Henry, the youngest son (1856–1884) had died but a few weeks before his father, leaving a widow and daughter. His death on 26 May 1884, notified by Edward who was present, occurred at 12 Fitzroy Street, at which same address Frederick Lessner is known to have lived from 1873 to 1893.

3

The path leading from Nonconformism to Freethinking and from there to Socialism was neither long nor untrodden. It was more like a public highway along which marched many of the founders of the British working-class movement from the Welsh valleys, the Scottish hills, the rural parishes and industrial centres of England and the London slums.

Edward Aveling's first steps to secularism coincided with a period when high-minded men in Holy Orders wrestled with spiritual doubt, discarded the faith of their fathers and resigned from their comfortable sinecures at the older Universities. Aveling's progress to disbelief was marked by no particular anguish. It was, indeed, almost inevitable that this highly intelligent and scientifically trained young man of Nonconformist background should be drawn towards the dissenting movements of his time.

Nevertheless, viewing his character and career in perspective, it is not immediately obvious why he took this road. Like his father, he had the gift of eloquence and he wanted to preach. In the secularist movement he swiftly rose to prominence and was given a platform for the exercise of his talents. So much is clear. It is also axiomatic that the field of the natural sciences offers few opportunities for self-display. Though he could have continued to make a fair showing had he pursued his scientific career, he was a teacher and populariser rather than an original thinker.

It is unfortunate that, though a Doctor of Science, he considered himself to be a master of all the arts, in particular the art of drama, which offered him the limelight and the plaudits that he craved. He was a playwright of sterling insignificance whom nothing could discourage. Elizabeth Robins* recalls

* Born in America, Elizabeth Robins (1865–1952) came to London in her twenties making her first stage début in England in 1887. She was chiefly renowned as not only among the first but one of the finest exponents of Ibsen, the English rights of whose plays she owned. She played Martha Bernick in *Pillars of Society* in

"dingy Dr. Edward Aveling . . . appearing at my door with a *suit case* full of plays".[31] She does not remember inviting him in, not to speak of opening his suitcase. He was an amateur performer of below average stability, bursting into tears at the beauty of his renderings of poetry, and, of course, a poet in his own right. He was also a many-sided critic while, in a little over a twelvemonth,* in addition to a long series of articles on Darwin and other matters on which he was qualified to expound, he wrote and spoke on such diverse subjects as Purity, Etymology, Mahomet, the Celts, Shakespeare, Pitt, the Armada, Tennyson, Loyalty, Luther, the Meaning of Life and Death, the National Anthem, Publicans, the Sense of Colour, the Stuarts, Swinburne's literary defects, Courage, Burke and Old Mother Hubbard and all.

In the summer of 1879 he claimed to have held secularist views for two or three years, deterred from making them public because he doubted not the cause but his own worthiness and strength to serve it,[32] but he had not in fact played any active part in the National Secular Society until the beginning of that year, when he began to contribute regularly to its 2d. weekly organ, *The National Reformer*, edited by Charles Bradlaugh† and Annie Besant.‡

At first Aveling hid his identity by signing his articles "E.D." but used his own initials after his public declaration of faith,

1889, Hedda Gabler in 1891 and, one of her finest parts, Hilda Wangel, in *The Master Builder* in 1893.
* 1880–1881.
† 1833–1891. Born in Hoxton, Bradlaugh was in turn errand-boy, coal merchant, enlisted trooper, builder's timekeeper and lawyer's clerk before he became a Freethought lecturer. He was a considerable force for progress and enlightenment in the 'seventies when he enjoyed a large following. A vigorous opponent of socialism, he lost much of his influence with its later revival. With Mrs. Besant he stood trial in 1876 for circulating an American pamphlet that advocated birth control and was sentenced to six months' imprisonment and a fine of £200: a verdict quashed on appeal. He stood successfully as parliamentary candidate for Northampton in the interests of religious Radicalism in 1880, but refused to take the Oath—the indulgence of affirmation being then allowed only to Quakers, Moravians and Separatists, not to atheists—and was re-elected twice more before, following scenes of violence in the House, the setting up of two Select Committees and his own four speeches at the bar, he finally took his seat in 1886, introducing the amendment to the Parliamentary Oaths Bill which received the royal assent on 24 December 1888.
‡ Née Annie Wood (1847–1933). In 1867 she married Frank Besant, a clergyman by whom she had two children, separating from him in 1873. The many causes she espoused veered with her enthusiasm for the men who led them and she ran the whole gamut from established religion, through High Church Anglicanism, the Oxford Movement, Theism, Atheism, Malthusianism, Radicalism, Science, Philanthropy, Fabianism, Feminism and Socialism to Theosophy. She showed not

by which time he had formed an attachment to Mrs. Besant, whom he shared with Bradlaugh. She hailed the "New Soldier" in the most fulsome terms: "His language is exquisitely chosen and is polished to the highest extent, so that the mere music of speech is pleasant to the ear. Since to this artistic charm are added scholarship and wide knowledge, with a brilliancy of brain I have not seen surpassed . . . our friends will not wonder that we . . . rejoice that our mistress Liberty has won this new Knight."[33]

From that time forth and for the next few years he wrote for the secularist press—taking on the editorship of the new monthly magazine, *Progress*, in 1883 when its founder, the militant atheist G. W. Foote, was imprisoned* for the blasphemies published in his *Freethinker* of which Aveling also became interim editor—was elected Vice-President of the National Secularist Society in 1881, showed zeal in Bradlaugh's electoral campaigns and the fight for the amendment to the Parliamentary Oath, lectured throughout the country, inaugurating science classes and giving regular lectures on English history and literature at the Hall of Science in Old Street. In addition he published pamphlets, stood for and obtained a seat on the London School Board in 1882, took on the private cramming of medical and science students,† wrote plays, adapted plays, and engaged in amateur theatricals and poetry recitals whenever time permitted.

These activities were not all undertaken in the order given, nor simultaneously. While his public—and some hint of his private—life was excellently advertised, so that it would be possible to render a week-by-week account of where he went and on what he spoke and wrote, there is an ineluctable dreariness about it all. Had he amounted to something in the end, had he become a figure of significance and worth, it might be of interest to record his multifarious doings—for he did so much, buzzing like a fly—but no sooner had he ceased to be a promising young man than he became, so far as posterity

only the courage of her lovers' convictions, but was a bold and energetic campaigner who, like Bradlaugh, did much to broaden men's minds and, unlike him, played an active part in the working class-movement.
* From May 1883 to February 1884.
† H. G. Wells, when he in his turn took to tutoring, said that he and his friends "put all sorts of competing coaches out of business. One of those for whom we made life harder was Dr. Aveling".[34]

is concerned, a thundering bore. Though he was able to move vast audiences—Will Thorne acclaimed him as "one of the greatest orators this country ever heard"[35]—in cold print his speeches, punctuated at the time by prolonged applause and even cheers, appear sorry stuff: pompous, florid, empty and so much hot air. Aveling, in fact, was a gasbag whom time has rudely deflated. The same cruel fate has overtaken his articles which lie today in the files of old newspapers whose pages testify that his contributions to the secularist and socialist press, save in his own field of the natural sciences, are less convincing, less original and far more embarrassing than most of the matter published in these proselytizing journals.

Yet the question remains: why should this self-indulgent, exhibitionistic character have become a socialist at all. Though of an age to do so, Aveling had never heard of the International during its existence, had not read the writings of either Marx or Engels* nor evinced the smallest interest in the Commune or its victims.† Not until the late '70s did he turn his attention to social—and then not socialist—questions.

His motives, like those of most people, were exceedingly mixed, and it would be crass to claim that principle played no part in them. "No man is scrupulous all round. He has, according to his faculties and interests, certain points of honour, while in matters that do not interest him he is careless and un-scrupulous. One of the several models who sat unconsciously for Dubedat",‡ wrote Shaw, referring to Aveling, "was morbidly scrupulous as to his religious and political convictions and would have gone to the gallows sooner than recant a syllable of them. But he had absolutely no conscience about money and women. In contrast with men who were scrupulously correct in their family and business life he seemed a blackguard, and was a blackguard; but there were occasions on which they would cut a poor figure beside him: occasions when loyalty to their convictions called for some risk and sacrifice. . . . He had his faith and upheld it."§[36]

---

* Though the first English translation of the *Communist Manifesto* appeared in 1850.
† In July 1879, at the time of the amnesty agitation, *The National Reformer* published one letter on the French Communard proscripts exiled in London signed by, among others, Charles Longuet.
‡ In *The Doctor's Dilemma* (1911).
§ Shaw was 91 when he wrote this passage: 38 years after he had created the character of Dubedat and 51 since Aveling's death.

Shaw repeated the same view when he wrote to a friend in 1946 that Aveling had been "quite a pleasant fellow who would have gone to the stake for Socialism or atheism, but with absolutely no conscience in his private life".* [28] Shaw further told his biographer, Hesketh Pearson, that Aveling's case was not unique and that he, Shaw, had been "on pleasant terms with three others, two clergymen and a retired colonel . . . with a total lack of conscience in money and sexual relations".[38]

Yet there is in Shaw's characterisations of Aveling something which does not altogether meet the case. One factor omitted is that the Nonconformist tradition never dies; another is that the man—in both his scrupulous and unscrupulous aspects—was cold-hearted.

Like his forbears, Aveling set his face against the order of things that stifled men's freedom of conscience and creed—however differently he interpreted these—and, given his epoch, how better could he express the refusal to conform than by denouncing, first, all organised religion and then the entrenched State—capitalism—itself? Having once made these decisions, he stuck to them, nor can they be regarded as the choice of a vulgar careerist. If, by reason of personal weaknesses, he fell into disrepute, thereby injuring the causes he embraced, it may be conjectured that he would have been something of a liability in whatever walk of life he had chosen.

The socialist movement, even in its infancy, was bound to attract men of his type, as it has done ever since. They are not so much moved by human misery and injustice as they are rebellious against society, contemptuous of the gullibility, blindness or hypocrisy of those who uphold the *status quo*. This is not Marxism, it is not socialism of any kind, but there was no place, certainly not in Aveling's day, for such nonconformists other than in the only movement pledged to the overthrow of the existing social system.

His anarchic individualism and egotism, never entirely held in check, were to some extent counteracted by his desire to play a prominent part, to which end he sometimes had to subordinate one greed to another, as a child will refrain from

---

* Shaw's reference to Aveling going to the gallows or the stake for his beliefs is quoted in a slightly different but distinctly Shavian version in Stephen Winsten's *Salt and His Circle*[37]: "If it came to giving one's life for a cause one could rely on Aveling even if he carried all our purses with him to the scaffold."

taking the largest piece of cake for the greater satisfaction of winning approval. This conflict within Aveling was unequal at best: again and again he forfeited approval, but he snatched a lot of cake on the way.

In background, upbringing, training and experience he was as far removed from Eleanor Marx as he well could be. Their differences of temperament emerge most clearly in their writings. Every line that Eleanor penned, whether in happy or unhappy private letters or for the public—as every recorded word she spoke—is eager, warm, alive, and rings true as a bell. Although his excessive facility enabled Aveling to pour forth lectures, journalism, pamphlets, plays, reviews, reports and a multitude of ephemera that have come down to us, his voice is not merely without character: it is muted, dead. Nothing rings through the words. Nothing at all. There is no means of knowing how he spoke or wrote to his family, friends and lovers, but his perfunctory little postscripts to Eleanor's letters and the occasional notes to colleagues that have been preserved make precisely the same muffled impact. Veiled in facetiousness or dry didacticism, his voice is as inexpressive as Eleanor's is revealing of personality.

This was the man with whom she threw in her lot.

REFERENCE NOTES

Abbreviations

Bottigelli Archives   Letters in the custody of Dr. Emile Bottigelli, Paris.

Liebknecht   *Wilhelm Liebknecht Briefwechsel mit Karl Marx und Friedrich Engels*. Edited by Georg Eckert. Mouton & Co., The Hague, 1963.

(1) Privately communicated.
(2) Eleanor to Liebknecht, 2 June 1897. Liebknecht.
(3) Information kindly provided by Dr. John M. Rae, Ph.D., Headmaster of Taunton School and Mr. Bernard Honess, Manager and Librarian of the Memorial Hall.
(4) Aveling family papers.
(5) Information kindly provided by Mr. B. M. Baker, Provost's Secretary, University College, London.

(6) Aveling to Laura Lafargue, 30 August 1887. Bottigelli Archives.

(7) Information kindly provided by the Rev. G. F. Nuttall, M.A., D.D., Librarian at New College, London.

(8) Information kindly supplied by Professor Sir Bryan Matthews, C.B.E., F.R.S., of the Physiology Laboratory, Cambridge.

(9) Information kindly provided by Miss Madeline McLaughlan, Head Mistress of North London Collegiate School, Edgware.

(10) Annual Report of Orphan Working School, 1868.

(11) *Hampstead and Highgate Express* and *Camden & Kentish Towns Gazette*, both of 22 June 1872.

(12) Edward Aveling. "Charles Darwin and Karl Marx: A Comparison". Part II. *The New Century Review*, April 1897.

(13) Flysheet issued by Ferdinand Gilles from 6 Everleigh Street, Tollington Park. "Is he the Son-in-Law of Marx?" 10 November 1891. (See Ref. 4).

(14) Maria Trench in *The Nineteenth Century*, Volume XVI. August 1884.

(15) Information kindly provided by Mr. Wilfred Ashworth, Chief Librarian of the Polytechnic of Central London.

(16) *The National Reformer*. 1881.

(17) Information kindly provided by Dr. H. B. May, M.D., F.R.C.P., Dean of the London Hospital Medical School.

(18) Information kindly provided by Miss Sandra Raphael, Librarian to the Linnean Society of London, Burlington House.

(19) *The National Reformer*. 6 July 1879.

(20) Letter to David O'Donoghue, 9 May 1889. *Bernard Shaw: Collected Letters* 1874–1897. Edited by Dan H. Laurence. Max Reinhardt, 1965.

(21) Thanks to the Headmaster of Harrow School, Dr. R. L. James, C.B.E. (retired July 1971), the School Registers were examined for the period 1800 to 1895 during which time no Aveling was a pupil.

(22) In an indignant article on his dismissal in *The National Reformer*, 18 December 1881.

(23) The Corporation Act 1661, the Act of Uniformity 1662, the Conventicle Acts of 1663 and 1670, the Five-Mile Act 1665 and the Test Act 1673, collectively known as the Clarendon Code.

(24) *The Greville Diary*. Edited by Philip Whitwell Wilson. Heinemann 1927.

(25) This quotation and many other details concerning the life of the Rev. Thomas Aveling are from *Memories of Kingsland*

by "A.S.A." (Agnes Sarah Aveling, his second wife) published in aid of the Church Restoration in 1887, and from records kindly provided by Mr. Bernard Honess of the Memorial Hall.

(26) Thomas William Baxter Aveling. *Memorials of the Clayton Family*. Jackson, Walford & Hodder, 1867.

(27) May Morris. *William Morris, Artist, Writer, Socialist*. Vol. II. Basil Blackwell, 1936.

(28) Letter to L. Preger, 22 February 1946. Quoted by Warren Sylvester Smith in *The London Heretics 1870–1914* from material in the Berg Collection, N.Y. Constable, 1967.

(29) *Olive Schreiner: Letters 1876–1920*. Edited by S. Cronwright-Schreiner. T. Fisher Unwin 1924.

(30) H. M. Hyndman. *Further Reminiscences*. Macmillan, 1912.

(31) Elizabeth Robins. *Both Sides of the Curtain*. Heinemann, 1940.

(32) "Credo Ergo Laborabo". *The National Reformer*. 27 July 1879.

(33) *The National Reformer*. 17 August 1879.

(34) H. G. Wells. *An Experiment in Autobiography*. Macmillan, New York, 1934.

(35) *My Life's Battles*. George Newnes n.d. *c.* 1925.

(36) "Biographers' Blunders Corrected" in *Sixteen Self-Sketches*. Constable 1949.

(37) Hutchinson 1951.

(38) Hesketh Pearson. *Bernard Shaw. His Life and Personality*. First complete edition, Methuen, 1961.

PART V

TRANSITION

Early in April 1883 Dr. Aveling, editing *Progress* during Foote's trial for blasphemy, asked to buy the block of Marx's portrait which had appeared in *The Republican*,* with a biography, in November 1882. The block was not available, having been sent to the *Sozialdemokrat*, but Aveling had wanted it to accompany Eleanor's two articles on her father which appeared in the May and June issues of *Progress*.

"There is no time perhaps", she wrote, "so little fitted for writing the biography of a great man as that immediately after his death, and the task is doubly difficult when it falls to one who knew and loved him."[1] Her first essay was confined to "strictly historical and biographical details", her second to a clear concise exposition of the theory of surplus value.[2] The two articles taken together reflect Eleanor's grasp of the essentials of Marxism and her power to convey them in the simplest and most telling manner. Without any pretensions to great intellect, she demonstrated here that, by temperament and ability, she was peculiarly fitted to wield in practice with style and vitality the weapons Marx had forged, combining to a rare degree an understanding of theory with deep human feeling, uncommon in the world of politics.

In general, the obituary notices that appeared in English and German were, as Engels wrote to Laura, "inexact and badly informed, but upon the whole decent".†[3]

The lease of 41 Maitland Park Road had still a year to run and there was talk of finding a tenant; but in the meantime it became clear that there would be at least six months' work to do in the house: the reams of manuscript Marx had left, the multitude of letters that came to light—dating back to correspondence with his father in 1837—and the "garret full

---

* A monthly Radical paper issued from 1880 to 1886. It published an obituary of Marx in April 1883.
† Many of the national newspapers (including *The Times*) received the news of Marx's death from their Paris correspondents; some published that he had died in France. But, as the *Pall Mall Gazette* commented on 16 March, the extraordinary thing was that Karl Marx's death should have been allowed to pass almost unnoticed.

of boxes, parcels and books"[4] had to be sorted and examined. The massive material for what had been planned as the second volume of *Capital*—of which only two chapters had been put into order—consisted of endless drafts, with quotations collected from every possible source without any indication of their intended use, all in Marx's impossible handwriting "which the author himself was sometimes unable to decipher"[5]. It was to occupy Engels for the remainder of his life. "If I had known, I should have left him no peace day or night until it was finished and printed," he wrote to Bebel.[5]

In his preface to the 1893 edition of Volume II of *Capital*,* by which time Volume III, never foreseen by Marx, was in preparation for the press, Engels described the problems he had confronted: "It was no easy task to put the second book of *Capital* in shape. . . . The great number of available, mostly fragmentary, texts worked on added to the difficulties of this task. . . . The bulk of the material was not finally polished in point of language. . . . Thoughts were jotted down as they developed in the brain of the author. Some parts of the argument would be fully treated, others of equal importance only indicated. . . . At conclusions of chapters, in the author's anxiety to get to the next, there would often be only a few disjointed sentences. . . . This is the material for Book II, out of which I was supposed 'to make something', as Marx remarked to his daughter Eleanor shortly before his death. . . ."

At first, as the house was gradually cleared, the papers assembled and dusted by Nim, more and more letters appeared. These, where they touched on incidents in the '40s known to Nim, were read aloud to be greeted by her shouts of appreciative laughter but, as Eleanor later wrote, once the letters had been transferred to his house, Engels, as Nim had told her, "burnt lots of letters referring to himself",[6] while, when after Engels' death she herself tried to order the correspondence for a projected biography of her father, it proved "rather difficult work . . . because I find all the letters are higgledy piggledy. I mean that the parcels the dear old General made up are *quite* unsorted, not merely as to date, but that the letters of various writers are all mixed up, and different portions of a letter are occasionally in different parcels."[7]

---

* The first German edition appeared in 1885.

Naturally Eleanor did not reproach Engels for the confusion in which she found these letters: she had been unable to cope with the task herself at the time. "This sorting of the papers will be terrible work", she wrote to Laura. "I hardly know how it is to be got through." This was more particularly the case since she had her own work to do and "I am more anxious than ever now to earn my own living". There were "at *least* 500 pages of the second volume", but, while she knew that Engels would take these over, she did go through many of the letters and: "I need not tell you that I have taken the *utmost* care to prevent our good General from seeing anything that is likely to give him pain. Indeed *all* the private letters I shall put aside. They are of interest only to us. . . . Would you like me to send you all your and Lafargue's letters? If so as I find them I will put them together. . . ."[8] Eleanor begged Laura to come to London. Engels added his entreaties, putting his house at her disposal and emphasising that Tussy wanted and needed her there.[4]

Marx had died intestate, but while Laura had been too unwell to attend his funeral or to help now in the disposition of his effects, she was well enough to make an angry fuss at being, as she felt, slighted.

On reading Engels' articles in the *Sozialdemokrat* "On the Death of Marx",[9] the first of which ended: "By word of mouth he appointed his youngest daughter Eleanor and myself as his literary executors", her resentment knew no bounds. "Will you oblige me", she wrote to Engels on 2 June, "by telling me whether Papa told you that he desired Tussy to be, with you, his literary executrix? Not having been with my dear father at the end you will, I know, understand that I am desirous to learn what were his ultimate directions. What his wishes and intentions were at Vevey *I know*."[10] A few weeks later she returned to the attack, repudiating any notion that she was concerned "about the fate of his chairs and tables", but insisting that when she had been with Marx in Switzerland he had "said he would give me all the documents and papers required for a history of the International and with his usual goodness he asked me to undertake a translation of *Kapital*. . . . He invited me to stay at Ventnor, to work with him, and under his direction, there. I accepted his invitation very gladly and but for

Jenny's illness and other tribulations should have joined him there."[11] She harked back to old grievances: Tussy's letter asking her to come to London had not reached her until the day after her father's death,* entirely ignoring the letter Engels—who was not nursing Marx—had written to her on 10 March, four days before her father died, to say: "I conclude that in this frosty and snowy weather with east winds you will not be in too great a hurry to come to London. Anyhow, should you make up your mind to come, everything is prepared for you", and then, as reassuringly and tactfully as was his wont, to describe Marx's failing strength.[12] Laura made no move, though it was a letter that should have sped her to her father's side. "When after Jenny's death I expressed a wish to see Papa I was told that my coming would alarm him", she huffed. "I requested you the other day", Laura continued to Engels, "to inform me. . . . whether Mohr had told *you* that he wished Tussy to be his literary executrix. You have not answered me. Had you answered in the affirmative I should have simply concluded that long illness had changed my dear father. . . . Papa, in health, would not have made *his eldest and favourite daughter* his sole executrix, to the exclusion of his other daughters —he had too great a love of equality for that—let alone the last of his daughters. Thus much I know. . . ."[11]

Thereupon Engels replied: "When you spoke of your knowledge of what poor Moor's views and wishes had been at Vevey, it was in connection of a more or less testamentary nature. . . . After poor Mohr's death, on my inquiry, Tussy informed me that he had told her she and I were to take possession of his papers. . . . If you wish to have Mohr's exact words, Tussy will no doubt give them to you if you ask her to do so. . . . As to the expression *literary executors*, I am alone responsible for it. I could not find another at the time, and if by it I have in any way offended you, I humbly ask your pardon. How the disposition *itself* can wound you, I cannot see. The work must be done *here on the spot*. The real work, that you know as well as Tussy does, will mostly have to be done by me. But as Mohr had one daughter living in London, I find it but natural that he should associate her to me in such work as she could do. Had you been

---

* But Engels' telegram, sent on 15 March, had brought Paul to London post-haste.

living here instead of in Paris, all the three of us would have been jointly appointed, no doubt about that.

"But there is another view of the case. According to English law . . . the only person living who is the legal representative of Mohr in England is Tussy. Or rather, the only person who can become his legal representative by taking out *letters of administration*. This must be done by the *next of kin living* in England— Tussy. . . . Of the projects Mohr discussed with you at Vevey I was of course utterly ignorant and only regret you did not come over since 14th March, when we should have known and complied with them as much as possible. . . ."[13]

How bad the relations between the two sisters were at the time of Marx's death is illustrated by the fact that one of the letters of condolence addressed to Laura,* inadvertently opened by Tussy, had to be passed to Lenchen for Engels to forward.

To be sure, Laura's life was not bathed in sunshine: all her children had died, she was 38 years of age and had none of the satisfactions of work to fill her time and mind or to relieve her of the permanent want of money to live in that station of life to which Engels was accustomed. Moreover, her husband—also of no settled occupation—was now, from 21 May, in gaol, where she visited him daily bringing a basketful of the choicest food and wine to take luncheon with him. Certainly she had reason for cheerless reflections. Notwithstanding Paul's valuable contribution to the French socialist movement,† when all is said and done the Lafargues were a trivial pair. Leaving aside the dedication and majesty of her father's labours, the sacrifices of her mother and the yoke Engels had borne uncomplainingly for the best years of his life, Laura's circumstances have only to be matched against the sufferings of her sister Jenny, so lately dead, and Eleanor's stalwart efforts to become self-supporting, to see her pettiness at this juncture as both indelicate and undignified.

Engels, however, had no wish to interfere between the two sisters and strongly advised Laura to write direct to Eleanor or, better still, to come to London. Nothing could throw greater obstacles in the way of the important work to be done, he

---

* From Rudolph Meyer.
† He is perhaps best known to English readers for his splendid pamphlet *The Right to be Lazy* [14], on which subject he was an expert.

wrote, and the help she could give "than fresh unpleasantness" between herself and Tussy. "What we are, all of us, desirous of seeing carried out, is a befitting monument to the memory of Mohr, the first portion of which must be the publication of his posthumous works. Let us then contribute what we can towards that end."[13] He had said nothing to Eleanor of Laura's plaints: the only person he had told was Nim.

It was therefore natural for Eleanor to correspond quite freely with her sister, reporting on her efforts to sort the letters and also her concern about her nephew Johnny, whom she felt she could no longer keep with her, though quite unable to elicit any reply from Longuet about arrangements for the boy's homecoming. She also worried about Nim, who "after all the terrible work and trouble of these last awful months"[8] sadly needed a little holiday away from "this dreary abode".[15] Thus, killing two birds with one stone, for Eleanor did not know how else to arrange either matter, Lenchen took Johnny back to Paris and, though it had not occurred to Laura to invite her in the first place, she put Nim up at the end of April, Eleanor pleading that she should keep her as long as possible: "Let her have at least two clear weeks", she asked, modestly enough.[15]

Though the major work, as Engels recognised, must fall to his lot, Eleanor played her part and, in June, went to see the publisher Kegan Paul with a view to an English translation of *Capital*, to be undertaken by Sam Moore. "He is by far the best man", said Engels, "slightly heavy, but that can be mended."[16] James Knowles, the editor of *The Nineteenth Century*, had already approached Engels on this question in April and had been told that Moore alone was fitted for the task.*

Although Laura had said no word to Nim of any intention of coming to London, where Engels invited her to make his house her headquarters during Paul's incarceration and share in his holiday plans for a couple of months at least, she did eventually show her "bright face in this dull climate" when it was at its least dull, that is, in July, to stay for some ten days.

A week after her departure, on 18 August 1883, Letters of Administration were granted to Eleanor for Marx's estate valued at £250.

---

* He had also been told: "Allow me to point out that I am no 'Dr.' but a retired cotton manufacturer."

By this time Eleanor had put a few sticks of furniture into rooms she had taken at 32 Great Coram Street* to be nearer the British Museum and also to her friends, Dollie and Ernest Radford, who had married in July and were living round the corner in Brunswick Square. Moreover it was not far from Aveling's quarters in Newman Street, on the other side of the Tottenham Court Road.

Nim had now moved into 122 Regent's Park Road where, for the rest of her life, she was Engels' most treasured housekeeper. 41 Maitland Park Road stood untenanted, according to the Ratebooks which bear final dusty witness to the end of the Marxes' family life.

Eleanor continued to write for *Progress*—her two articles reviewing Stepniak's† *Sketches and Profiles* appearing as "Underground Russia" in the August and September issues‡—to teach and, at all times, to work at the Museum. It was here that she had met Miss Potter who noted in her diary on 24 May 1883:

"In afternoon went to British Museum and met Miss Marx in refreshment room. Daughter of Karl Marx, socialist writer and refugee. Gains her livelihood by teaching 'literature' etc., and corresponding for socialist newspapers, now editing 'Progress' in the enforced absence of Mr. Foote. Very wroth about imprisonment of latter.

" 'I couldn't see much joke in those particular extracts but there was nothing wrong in them. Ridicule is quite a legitimate weapon. It is the weapon Voltaire used and did more good with it than any amount of serious argument. We think the Christian religion is an immoral illusion and we wish to use any argument to persuade the people we have to deal with. The striking difference of this century and the last is, that free thought was the privilege of the upper classes then and it is becoming the privilege of the working classes now. We want to make them disregard the mythical next world and live for this world and insist on having what will make it pleasant for them.'

---

* Renamed Coram Street on 30 January 1900. No. 32 was at that end of the street which no longer exists and is now a building site.
† Pseudonym of Sergei Mikhailovich Kravchinsky (1852–1895) who emigrated to Geneva in 1876 and to London in 1885. His own book with the title *Underground Russia* was published in an English translation in 1883.
‡ See Appendix 5, p. 303.

"It was useless to argue with her. She refused to recognise the beauty of the Christian religion. She read the gospels as the gospel of damnation. Thought Christ, if he had existed, was a weak-minded individual with a good deal of character but quite lacking in heroism. 'Did he not, in the last moment, pray that the cup might pass from him?'

"When I asked what 'socialist progress' was, she very sensibly remarked that I might as well ask her to give me in a short formula the whole theory of mechanics. Socialist progress was a deduction from socialist science which was the most complicated of all sciences. I replied that from the little I knew about political economy (the only social science we English understood) the social philosophers seemed to limit themselves to describing forces that were more or less necessarious. She did not contradict this. I do not know whether it is true or not? In person she is comely, dressed in a slovenly picturesque way with curly black hair, flying about in all directions. Fine eyes full of life and sympathy, otherwise ugly features and expression and complexion showing signs of unhealthy excited life kept up with stimulants and tempered by narcotics. Lives alone, is much connected with the Bradlaugh set, evidently peculiar views on love, etc., and should think has somewhat 'natural' relations with men! Should fear that the chances were against her remaining long within the pale of respectable society."[17]

That Eleanor Marx should fall below the standards of the railway magnate's daughter is not altogether a surprise*— it is conceivable that their papas would not always have seen eye to eye—but the opinion that Eleanor was something of a slut and a drug addict into the bargain does seem a shade bizarre considering her attitude to narcotics—"not much better than dram-drinking and . . . almost . . . as injurious"—and the innumerable testimonies to her neat if not modish attire.

When the school term restarted in September, Eleanor went back to teach at Mrs. Bircham's school in Kensington but was looking for other pupils as well. "It is *so* difficult to get work, or at least regular work", she wrote to Laura. "The kind of lessons I give are not like teaching 'all subjects'."

* One is consequently less stunned to find Emma Cons—who founded the Old Vic as a popular Shakespearean theatre on the Surrey Side in the belief that the people of that deprived neighbourhood needed entertainment as much as sanitation— nailed by Miss Potter as "not a lady by birth".[18]

She then asked whether Laura and Paul could not send articles to *Progress* which "little magazine is beginning—to the great annoyance of Bradlaugh—to have a really good circulation". Aveling, as its acting editor, was "not *quite* a free agent", but could do more or less as he pleased. She ended her letter—headed "London", without further address—"Dr. Aveling sends kind messages to you and Lafargue",[19] thus indicating that, on Paul's attendance at Marx's burial and Laura's visit in July, the parties had met, and also that Engels was mistaken in saying to Laura in a letter of the same date that he believed Eleanor to be "out of town".[20]

By October Engels, who knew that he alone could decide on the importance or unimportance of Marx's mass of papers and that Eleanor, with her many undertakings must leave these decisions to him, was far from well. He suffered from rheumatism in the legs and was forced to keep to his bed for eight weeks. While he was laid up Karl Kautsky* came to visit him on his birthday—28 November—where he met Eleanor again and Aveling for the first time. With Bernstein, Kautsky was later to become Engels' "eyes" in learning to decipher Marx's handwriting, and one of the presumptive heirs to the literary remains of both Marx and Engels on the latter's death.† On this occasion he stayed only briefly in England and, on 4 December, Eleanor dropped him a note at Wedde's Hotel in Greek Street, Soho, to say ". . . if you have the time, and could come to 13 Newman Street, Oxford Street, at about 11 o'clock, you could meet me there. I am working there with Dr. Aveling."

This relationship, not openly announced as yet, was now obvious enough to make Mrs. Besant scream aloud. In the pages of the *National Reformer*, to which Aveling was still contributing, she attacked an article in *Progress* saying "I do not know who Mr. 'Paul Lafargue' may be"[21] and, on 23 December, vigorously protested at some "gross and scandalous libel on Dr. Edward Aveling" invented by "a Miss Eleanor Marx". The whole

---

* 1854–1938. Writer and journalist, Kautsky was the editor of *Die Neue Zeit*, the theoretical organ of the German Social Democratic Party, from 1883 to 1917. Until 1890 it was a monthly paper and thereafter, until 1923, a weekly. He had been in London from mid-March until early July 1881, when he met the Marxes, including Eleanor, the Lafargues and Engels, of whose household Pumps was then in charge. In 1882 he became engaged to Louise Strasser but, though married at the time, came alone for his brief visit to London at the end of 1883.
† He lost the heritage to Bebel.

matter, except for her uncontrollable rage, is wrapped in mystery. Mrs. Besant, who did not choose to enter into any details, accused this Miss Marx of "hoping . . . to cause a break and to hinder and impede the Freethought cause by introducing discord and quarrel among co-workers in the ranks". She warned all London Freethinkers against "any statements made in my name by Miss Eleanor Marx or by any of her friends".[22]

Thus Miss Potter is once again and this time doubly confuted: Eleanor, who is certainly not editing *Progress*, is neither "much connected with the Bradlaugh set" except by hostility, and she no longer, save to keep up appearances, "lives alone".

The facts widely known about Eleanor Marx are that she lived with a man of evil reputation who married someone else and that she killed herself. Of this the stuff of theatre is made: a neurotic woman, a villain, an unhallowed union, betrayal, suicide and, hey presto, the Marx-Aveling melodrama is produced: the Emma Bovary of Sydenham (minus the style). The sub-plot concerns the awful fate and actuarial risks attendant upon being one of Karl Marx's daughters. Laura's death by her own hand has been telescoped in time—even made to precede that of Eleanor—in many a vivid account, while there are those who will have it that Jenny participated in this riot of self-destruction.

Eleanor's union with Aveling may have been, was, disastrous in the long run; his character may have been, was, deplorable. Nonetheless, from the time her life was joined with his, it became purposeful. She does not doubt where she is going, she goes. Her manner, unassuming and frank as always, now takes on authority. She has lost none of her humour or humanity— on the contrary, these qualities deepen—but she is a woman complete: responsible, fearless and supremely capable of using her gifts to the full in the service of her fellowmen.

REFERENCE NOTES

Abbreviations

Bottigelli Archives   Letters in the custody of Dr. Emile Bottigelli, Paris.

ELC   *Frederick Engels Paul and Laura Lafargue: Correspondence*, Volumes I–III. Lawrence & Wishart, 1959–1963.

EDWARD AVELING: THE SECULARIST

ELEANOR MARX. THE END OF FAMILY LIFE

IISH   International Institute of Social History, Amsterdam.

MEW   *Marx Engels Werke*. Dietz Verlag, Berlin. 1956–1968. Unless otherwise stated Volumes 27–39.

MIML   Institute of Marxism-Leninism, Moscow.

(1) *Progress*. May 1883.

(2) *Ibid*. June 1883.

(3) 25 March 1883. ELC, Vol. I.

(4) 22 May 1883. *Ibid*.

(5) Engels to Bebel, 30 August 1883. MEW.

(6) Eleanor to Kautsky, 15 March 1898. IISH.

(7) Eleanor to Laura, 12 November 1896. IISH.

(8) Eleanor to Laura, 26 March 1883. Bottigelli Archives.

(9) In Nos. 19 and 20 published on 3 and 21 May 1883.

(10) 2 June 1883. ELC, Vol. I.

(11) 20 June 1883. *Ibid*.

(12) 10 March 1883. *Ibid*.

(13) 24 June 1883. Original in English, MIML. (German MEW.)

(14) *Le Droit à la Paresse* appeared first in *L'Egalité* in 1880 and was reprinted as a pamphlet, with an introduction written in Sainte-Pélagie prison, in 1883. The first English edition was translated and published by Charles H. Kerr in Chicago (n.d.)

(15) Eleanor to Laura, 27 April 1883. Bottigelli Archives.

(16) Engels to Laura, 2 June 1883. ELC, Vol. I.

(17) MS. Diary. By courtesy of the British Library of Political and Economic Science. I have to thank Mr. Malcolm Muggeridge for drawing my attention to this passage in the manuscript diaries.

(18) Beatrice Webb. Quoted from her diary of 12 August 1885 in *My Apprenticeship*. Vol. II. Pelican Books 1938.

(19) 19 September 1883. Bottigelli Archives.

(20) 19 September 1883. ELC, Vol. I.

(21) *The National Reformer*. 2 December 1883.

(22) *Ibid*. 23 December 1883.

AUTHOR'S POSTSCRIPT

Those who have read thus far will have noted that in the course of this book I have frequently taken refuge in such phrases as "nothing has been traced" and "the reason is obscure".

They do not mean that the matter is untraceable or need remain forever in the dark. They should be regarded not only as admissions of pure ignorance but also as so much bait laid to catch younger and more diligent researchers.

Some of these points may not be worth bothering about—though it has galled me not to bring them to light—but the seeds of this book were curiosity, aroused by tantalising glimpses of Eleanor Marx as she flitted in and out of other people's reminiscences and letters. Should it also bear the fruit of curiosity, it will have served a useful purpose.

Y.K.

FREDERICK DEMUTH

Helene Demuth's son, Henry Frederick Demuth, was born on 23 June 1851 at 28 Dean Street in the parish of St. Anne, Soho. There can be no reasonable doubt that he was Marx's son. Engels, however, did not contradict the assumption that he was the father until he lay dying, when he charged his friends to make the truth known if—but not unless—he were to be posthumously defamed for behaving badly to a natural son.

Nothing certain is known of Frederick's childhood and youth, though from his manner of writing—its phrasing and spelling no less than its simple directness, suggesting that it was much as he must have spoken—it is a fair inference that he was brought up in a London working-class environment and received a limited education.

That he was given into foster care shortly after birth is not surprising. Mrs. Marx's own child, born three months before Freddy, was also put out to nurse for a few months because "the poor little thing" could not be reared at home under the prevailing conditions. Two vivid descriptions of that overcrowded interior at 28 Dean Street have come down to us.

The first relates to Easter 1852, when the year-old Franziska had severe bronchitis. Mrs. Marx records in her reminiscences: "For three days the poor child wrestled with death. She suffered terribly. When she died we left her little body lying in the small back room; all of us went into the front room together and when night came we lay down on the floor, the three living children beside us. . . .". Eleanor, who drew on this passage of her mother's notes for the preface to *Revolution and Counter-Revolution* adds: "In that 'front room' in Dean Street, the children playing about him, Marx worked. I have heard tell how the children would pile up chairs behind him to represent a coach, to which he was harnessed as horse and would 'whip him up' even as he sat at his desk writing."

The second description was written by a Prussian police spy reporting to his masters in 1853: ". . . He (Marx) lives in one of the worst and therefore one of the cheapest quarters in London. He occupies two rooms; the one looking out on the street is the living room and the bedroom is at the back. There is not a single clean or solid piece of furniture to be seen in the whole place . . . in the centre of the living room there is a large old-fashioned table covered with oilcloth on which lie manuscripts, books and newspapers along with children's toys, bits of his wife's sewing things, a few teacups with chipped rims, dirty spoons, knives, forks, candlesticks, an inkpot, tumblers, clay pipes, tobacco ash—in short, everything jumbled together on the same table; a second-hand dealer would shudder at this hotch-potch. . . . Sitting down is quite a dangerous affair: here is a chair with but three legs; there another, which by chance is still intact where the children are playing at being cooks. Courteously this is offered to the guest, but the children's cooking is not removed and you sit down at the risk of ruining your trousers. None of this occasions Marx or his wife the slightest embarrassment. You are received in the most friendly manner, cordially offered pipes, tobacco or whatever else is available. In any case the clever, agreeable talk compensates to some extent for the domestic short-comings and makes the discomfort endurable. . . ." * The police report mentions the three "really handsome children",† one of whom, the only boy, was to die two years later.

It may well be asked why Marx, longing for a son, did not claim Freddy, who survived to grow up as a total stranger. Since economic considerations did not hinder further legitimate additions to the family it must be conjectured that Mrs. Marx never knew that Freddy was her husband's child.

Existing records show that, as an adult, he was known as Frederick Lewis Demuth, having dropped the name Henry, which is on his birth certificate, and probably incorporated that of his foster-parents. He served an engineering apprenticeship and joined the King's Cross Branch of the Amalgamated Society of Engineers as a skilled fitter in February 1888. He was by then a married man of nearly 37, but both in the Union Report of his Branch and in all subsequent documents he appears as almost two years younger than his true age, which suggests that he was under a misapprehension about his year of birth. Possibly a mild deception had been practised upon him to fit in with the ages of his foster-siblings.

Freddy's life was not a happy one. He was devoted to his son, Harry, but he was a lonely man, dogged by misfortune.

It is not known when Eleanor formed her close friendship with him nor when the other members of the family came to know him. As Helene Demuth's son, whatever his paternity, he would have been a person to cherish as soon as that identity was known. In May 1882

---

* *Akten des kgl. Polizeipräsidiums zu Berlin, betreffend die neuerdings bemerkbar werdenden Bestrebungen der Kommunisten 1853.* (Pr. Br. Rep 30, Berlin C. Pol. Präs. Tit. 94, Geheime Präsidial-Registratur Lit. C. Nr. 286.) Cited by Gustav Mayer in *Neue Beitrage zur Biographie von Karl Marx* in *Archiv für die Geschichte des Sozialismus und der Arbeiterbewegung* 10 Jg., Hirschfeld, Leipzig, 1922.
† Jenny, Laura and Edgar.

Jenny wrote to Laura: "You cannot imagine what it is to me to think that I still owe poor Freddy his money, and that it is probably my insolvency which prevents our dear Nim* from carrying out her projects of going to Germany."† It is unlikely, however, that much was seen of Freddy in Marx's lifetime, but he is said to have visited his mother regularly after 1883 when she became Engels' housekeeper until she died in 1890, by which time Eleanor evidently knew and liked Freddy well. Clearly under the impression that she was speaking of Engels' son, she wrote to Laura a few weeks after Helene Demuth's death: "Freddy has behaved admirably in all respects and Engels' irritation against him is as unfair as it is comprehensible. We should none of us like to meet our pasts, I guess, in flesh and blood. I know I always meet Freddy with a sense of guilt and wrong done. The life of that man! To hear him tell of it all is a misery and shame to me."‡

Engels, Eleanor and Aveling had witnessed the Will drawn up on the day Helene Demuth died by which she left everything she had to "Frederick Lewis Demuth of 25 Gransden Avenue, London Lane, Hackney". Ten days after she had made her mark upon this Will—"being too weak bodily to sign my name"—her "monies, effects and other property" were granted to him. The amount in all was £95.

Some eighteen months later it emerged that not only Eleanor but Laura and their brother-in-law Charles Longuet had accepted some financial responsibility for Freddy, though naturally it was Eleanor, as the only one in England, who was in direct touch with him and knew what was going on. "The facts are these," she wrote in July 1892 to Laura who had sent 50 francs, which she could ill afford but had been unable to get from Longuet since he never answered letters, "Freddy's wife some time ago ran away taking with her not only most of Freddy's own things and money, but worst of all, £29 placed in his keeping by his fellow-workmen. This money belongs to a small benefit fund of theirs—and on Saturday he has to account for the money. You will understand now why this is such a bad business. . . . It may be that I am very 'sentimental' —but I can't help feeling that Freddy has had great injustice all through his life. Is it not wonderful when you come to look things squarely in the face, how rarely we seem to practise all the fine things we preach—to others? . . ."§

* The Marx grandchildren called Helene Demuth Nim, Nym or Nimmy, nicknames adopted by the whole family.
† 17 May 1882. IISH.
‡ Eleanor to Laura, 19 December 1890. Bottigelli Archives.
§ Eleanor to Laura, 26 July 1892. Bottigelli Archives.

In writing these censorious passages Eleanor plainly did not know to whom they should have been applied. When she did, the shock was dolorous. Not until a few days before Engels' death in August 1895 was she confronted with the truth of Freddy's paternity. According to Louise Freyberger* she refused to accept the statement when Sam Moore,† in whose presence it had been made, immediately went to see her. She is reported to have said it was a lie and insisted upon hearing it from Engels himself. She visited him the day before he died when, with cancer of the oesophagus, he was no longer able to speak and he wrote down the words for her on a slate.

At the time of this disclosure Eleanor had been living for some eleven years with a man to whom she was not married and it is unlikely that her prudery was outraged. But for most of those years— and possibly even longer—Freddy's sad life had induced in her feelings of misery, guilt and shame whenever she met him. If she broke down and wept, as she is said to have done, it was not because Marx had begotten an illegitimate son but because he had been unkind. That Freddy's wrongs must be laid at her father's door lacerated her heart.

Engels made no provision for Freddy, but the Marx heirs— Eleanor, Laura and Jenny's widower as the trustee for her children —arranged to give him regular support, though the lawyer‡ was under the impression that these remittances were a loan to Charles Longuet.

How long this arrangement lasted is not known, but though Eleanor left nothing to Freddy in her own Will, her affection for and trust in him grew with the years until he became the only person in whom she confided during the last months of her life. To no one else, neither to her oldest friend, Wilhelm Liebknecht, nor to Karl Kautsky, who had become very close to her, and to both of whom she wrote only a few days before her end, did she reveal anything of her agonies of personal unhappiness.

After her death, Freddy remained in touch with her friends and relatives; his own situation, and something of his character, may be discerned from two letters which he wrote many years later. The first of these, to Laura, written on 7 October 1910 from 54 Reighton Road, Upper Clapton, Stoke Newington, says that he is fortunately in work and now more pleasantly lodged than formerly, being with a congenial workmate and his wife. His main concern is his son

* 1860–1950, *née* Strasser, married Karl Kautsky 1883, divorced 1889, married Dr. Ludwig Freyberger 1894. Was Engels' housekeeper from December 1890 until his death in August 1895.
† See fn. p. 113.   ‡ Arthur Willson Crosse.

Harry, then working night shifts at a French taxicab company, which Freddy calls "Namier Renaud". The hours were 8 p.m. till 6 a.m., six nights a week, for which he earned 22s., but, a married man with a family, Harry was glad of the work. "His wife and little ones," Freddy writes, "are well although I am sorry to say there has been another little girl born. To me it seems very sad, seeing they have had so much trouble in their young lives, to bring more children into the world appears to one only short of a crime. But I suppose it will go on till the time comes when the birth of children will be hailed with joy instead of sadness. . . ." In the same letter he asks whether Laura knows if his mother had any relatives in the engineering trade as he has come across the name Demuth, a Union member "of Austria". His reason for making the enquiry is that, if this were some connection, "they might have a place in England and through them I might be able to get my son a better and more remunerative employment. . . . You will realize he and his are the only Beings I have in the world who I can call mine and although I do not see them very often it gives me great Pleasure to help in any way I can do." He ends his letter: "Dear Laura, affectionately your, F. Demuth".*

The following year Laura committed suicide and another friend was lost. But in 1912 Freddy wrote to Bernstein, whom he thanks for great kindness to his son, then recently emigrated to Australia, leaving behind his wife and, by this time, four small children. On arriving in Adelaide Harry was not met by the people who had written to say there was plenty of work to be had and he proceeded to Custon where they lived, only to find there were no openings at all. He then went further up country, prepared to take on anything. Freddy had promised to send out his wife and the children as soon as Harry was settled. "The one great consolation I have", he wrote to Bernstein, "is in knowing that they will not be materially worse off than when he was at home. I am very thankful that I am able to see after them . . . at any rate I feel I have done the right thing in sending him to the place he had set his mind on going to, and if things do not turn out as well for him and his family that we all hope for I do not think he can blame me as I have done everything for him that laid in my power."† Harry did not succeed in Australia and came back to England.

In the meantime Freddy himself had become a toolmaker, but no direct documentary evidence of his life during the next 14 years has come to light. He was over 63 when the First World War broke out and he remained at work for another decade when, as a member

* 10 October 1910. IISH.   † 29 August 1912. IISH.

of the Hackney Branch of the AEU,* he drew superannuation for the remainder of his life. In his late years he lived at 7 Reighton Road, Upper Clapton, with a Miss Laura Payne who moved with him to his last home at 13 Stoke Newington Common in North Hackney. She was present when he died of cardiac failure on 28 January 1929 at nearly 78 years of age,† drew the £12 funeral benefit from the Union and inherited a quarter of his estate.

This gentle, unassuming man has left two puzzles behind: his loving concern for his son and devotion to "the only Beings I have in the world who I can call mine" are strangely disavowed in his last Will and testament, drawn up on 26 July 1926, where the remainder of his personal estate and effects are bequeathed to "Mr. Harry Demuth my nephew known as my son." The second mystery is how an engineering worker drawing superannuation pay of 9s. a week‡ could leave, in 1929, the sum of £1,971 12s. 4d. There may be a connection between the two facts. If so, it signifies that these descendants of Karl Marx wished to be left in decent peace and obscurity.

*   *   *   *

That such a wish should be disregarded was inevitable and in recent times there have been many efforts to bring the full Freddy Demuth story to light, some in the interests of truth, others for different reasons. The toilers in this field owe their thanks first and foremost to Louise Freyberger.

In a letter to August Bebel written on 2 and 4 September 1898 she recounted Engels' death-bed statement to herself, her husband and Sam Moore concerning Frederick Demuth's parentage. It is a most extraordinary letter,§ which, throwing all caution to the winds, forfeits credence on many points. In a vein of high fantasy, Louise Freyberger elaborated the theme of the relationship between Marx and his wife at the time and as a consequence of the Demuth

---

* By the amalgamation of nine smaller unions with the ASE it became the Amalgamated Engineering Union (AEU) in July 1920. In 1970 with further amalgamations the name was changed to the Amalgamated Union of Engineering Workers (AUEW).

† The death certificate gives his age as 76, as do the AEU records.

‡ Superannuation pay at that date was 8s. a week after 30 years membership, 9s. after 35 years, 10s. after 40 years. Photostats of Branch Records kindly supplied by Mr. George Aitken, formerly Research Officer of the AEU, other information by the present Research Department of the AUEW.

§ Published, though not in full, in Karl Marx by Werner Blumenberg. (Rowohlt, Hamburg, 1962). Grateful acknowledgment is made to Mr. Bert Andréas for providing the passages omitted from that text and to the IISH Amsterdam for permission to see a transcript of the complete letter in the original German.

episode. Eleanor, she claimed, was fully apprised of this situation: she "knew very well" that for many years her parents did not sleep together "but it did not suit her to recognise the true reason for it; she idolised her father and concocted the most beautiful myths". Now one thing that Eleanor cannot have known very well, or at all, was the nature of her parents' sexual life—unless, of course, they recounted it to her—in the years before her own birth in 1855: itself an event never ascribed to immaculate conception. By the time she had reached an age to make her own observations, they will not have shed much light upon the circumstances surrounding Frederick Demuth's advent in 1851. Further, while Louise Freyberger at the time of writing may not have been conversant with conditions in the Dean Street lodgings of 45 years earlier, where the Marxes lived for seven months before and five-and-half years after Freddy's birth, they were not such as to afford the luxury of separate bedrooms for the parents and, indeed, the painful lack of privacy was the worst feature of family life there. Another matter that Eleanor was said to know perfectly well was that her mother had once deserted her father in London and gone to Germany and that, for Marx, "the fear of a divorce from his wife, who was dreadfully jealous, was ever present".

To be sure, at the end of 1850 Mrs. Marx was distraught owing to the death of her little son Guido. It is equally true that in March 1851, following the birth of the next, her fifth, child she was depressed and not made happier, one may suppose, by her husband's openly expressed disappointment that she had been delivered of a girl.

Marx reported all this to Engels in detail as, in later years, he confessed his lack of patience with his wife's tears and reproaches which he found bothering, though he could not find it in his heart to blame her   as the money worries piled up. But there is no evidence whatsoever, either before or after Freddy's birth, that the threat of separation, desertion or divorce was in the air. Had it been "ever present" it could not but have received some mention in the letters that passed between Marx and Engels which, however winnowed in after years to eliminate private disclosures, are not without exceedingly frank accounts of Marx's domestic situation and troubles with his wife at all times.

Apart from a brief visit to Marx's uncle in Holland in August 1850, when she herself was pregnant but Frederick Demuth not yet conceived, Mrs. Marx never left her husband in London nor went abroad at all until, in July and August 1854, with Eleanor on the way, she stayed at her old home in Trier on her doctor's orders. That her mother again went to Germany in 1856 Eleanor naturally knew, since she herself, aged 18 months, was of the travelling party; but as, shortly after her return to England, Mrs. Marx became pregnant with the child who was born and died in July 1857, the most precocious knowledge on Eleanor's part could have suggested only that her parents' marital relations were fairly normal. It is true that no further children were born, but Mrs. Marx was now 43 years of age and it would be a cause of wonderment if, eight years and two pregnancies after the event, Frederick Demuth's birth should have been the explanation for any abstinence. How, then, was Eleanor to know the "true reason" for all this sleeping apart and wanton desertion had she chosen to do so but for blind idolatry of her father?

The most dubious of all Louise Freyberger's claims is that she had seen the letter Marx had written to Engels in Manchester "at the time". She added, unwisely, that she believed Engels had since destroyed this letter. In the first place, there was no earthly reason why Marx should have written at all: Engels was living in London throughout the whole of 1850 until mid-November. He was there for Christmas, when Helene Demuth was four months pregnant and the fact could hardly be hidden or ignored. At the beginning of March 1851 Marx wrote to Engels to say that he must see him, that letters "confuse, delay and get one nowhere" and Engels accordingly came to London early that month when, in view of Mrs. Marx's approaching confinement, two extra rooms had been temporarily rented in the house where Engels was invited to stay. Marx visited him in Manchester in April for a few days and Engels was in London again from 8 to 14 June that year, when Frederick's birth was imminent, if not overdue. Thus there were no fewer than five occasions during the relevant period with ample opportunity for the two men to discuss the matter and decide upon what was to be done and what was to be said without either of them writing a line to each other about it. In the second place, if Engels ever received a letter on the subject it would have been most irrational of him to keep it for some forty odd years (including seven after Marx's death) on the off-chance of a Louise Freyberger turning up to read it, and then—concerned as he was at the last to repudiate the fiction of his paternity—inconsequently to destroy the unassailable proof.

Finally, Louise Freyberger states as a fact that Frederick did not use the name Demuth until after his mother's death in November 1890, regardless of documentary evidence to the contrary of which perhaps she was unaware.

These details would be of small consequence but that they give a distorted picture of the Marx family relationships and, in particular, show Eleanor in a false light, while stamping Louise Freyberger as an unreliable and destructive person of coarse mind who waited four years—when Eleanor had been safely dead for six months—to betray Engels' trust. This is not to say that the whole should be dismissed as a fabrication. There is no reason to doubt her contention either that Marx was Frederick Demuth's father or that Engels informed her of the fact, if only because she could not have had the hardihood to invoke Sam Moore's name, which was above suspicion, and run the risk of claiming him as a witness to the scene described when he was alive for another thirteen years to deny it. And if there is any part of her account which emerges credibly it is her twice-repeated assertion that when that scene took place Engels laid it upon the three people present to use the information only if he were accused of treating Frederick Demuth shabbily: he did not, he told them, want to have his name reviled, particularly when it no longer served any purpose. That had not happened. There had been no ugly gossip bringing him—or Marx—into disrepute. So Louise Freyberger, flouting Engels' dying wish, puts pen to paper and kindly provides material for the scavengers of the future.

For those who have gone mad with glee on discovering that Marx had an illegitimate son, as for those who turn pale at the very thought and take to their beds, it is small comfort to reflect that the evidence reposes in so flawed a vessel as Louise Freyberger.* Yet a fact remains a fact even when embedded in vulgar twaddle, and Marx's importance to the history of mankind is not lessened by one jot because he fathered Frederick Demuth. Frederick Demuth, humble and rejected, has made for himself a small place in history, too, as the closest and most loyal friend of Eleanor Marx when her need was greatest.

". . . Dear Freddy", she wrote, "you are the only friend with whom I can be quite free . . . I tell you what I would tell to no other person. I would have told it to my dear old Nymmy but I have lost her and have only you . . ."†

---

* Naturally there has been much hearsay evidence from other sources. Thus it was privately communicated to the present writer that, in the early years of this century, Laura Lafargue introduced Frederick Demuth to Clara Zetkin in Paris as "my half-brother".
† 3 February 1898. *Labour Leader*, 30 July 1898.

APPENDIX 2 (see p. 72)

LETTER FROM KARL MARX TO PAUL LAFARGUE

London 13 August 1866

My dear Lafargue,

Allow me to make the following observations:

1. If you wish to continue your relations with my daughter, you will have to discard your manner of "paying court" to her. You are well aware that no engagement has been entered into, that as yet everything is provisional. And even if she were formally your betrothed, you should not forget that this concerns a long-term affair. An all too intimate deportment is the more unbecoming in so far as the two lovers will be living in the same place for a necessarily prolonged period of purgatory and of severe tests. I have observed with dismay your change of conduct from day to day over the geologic epoch of a single week. To my mind, true love expresses itself in the lover's restraint, modest bearing, even diffidence regarding the adored one, and certainly not in unconstrained passion and manifestations of premature familiarity. Should you plead in defence your Creole temperament, it becomes my duty to interpose my sound sense between your temperament and my daughter. If in her presence you are unable to love her in a manner that conforms with the latitude of London, you will have to resign yourself to loving her from a distance. I am sure you take my meaning.

2. Before definitely settling your relations with Laura I require a clear explanation of your economic position. My daughter believes that I am conversant with your affairs. She is mistaken. I have not raised this matter because, in my view, it was for you to take the initiative. You know that I have sacrificed my whole fortune to the revolutionary struggle. I do not regret it. On the contrary. Had I my career to start again, I should do the same. But I would not marry. As far as lies in my power I intend to save my daughter from the reefs on which her mother's life has been wrecked. Since this matter would never have reached its present stage without my direct intervention (a failing on my part!) and without the influence of my friendship for you on my daughter's attitude, a heavy personal responsibility rests upon me. As regards your present circumstances, the information, which I did not seek out but which has reached me nevertheless, is by no means reassuring. But to proceed. Concerning your position in general, I know that you are still a student, that your career in France has been more or less ruined by the Liège incident, that you still lack the language, the indispensable implement

for your acclimatisation in England, and that your prospects are at best entirely problematic. Observation has convinced me that you are not by nature diligent, despite bouts of feverish activity and good intentions. In these circumstances you will need help from others to set out in life with my daughter. As regards your family I know nothing. Assuming that they enjoy a certain competence, that does not necessarily give proof that they are willing to make sacrifices for you. I do not even know how they view your plans for marriage. I repeat, I must have definite elucidation on all these matters. Moreover, you, as an avowed realist, will hardly expect that I should treat my daughter's future as an idealist. You, a man so practical that you would abolish poetry altogether, cannot wish to wax poetical at the expense of my child.

3. To forestall any misinterpretation of this letter, I can assure you that were you in a position to contract marriage as from today, it would not happen. My daughter would refuse. I myself should object. You must be a real man before thinking of marriage, and it will mean a long testing time for you and for her.

4. I should like the privacy of this letter to remain between our two selves. I await your answer.

Yours ever,
Karl Marx*

* MIML. A German version of the French original appears in MEW.

ENGELS' "CONFESSION"*

Your favourite virtue	jollity
,, ,, quality in man	to mind his own business
,, ,, ,, ,, woman	not to mislay things
Your chief characteristic	knowing everything by halves
Your idea of happiness	Château Margaux 1848
,, ,, ,, misery	to go to a dentist
The vice you excuse	excess of any sort
,, ,, ,, detest	cant
Your aversion	affected stuckup women
The character you most dislike	Spurgeon
Your favourite occupation	chaffing and being chaffed
,, ,, hero	none
,, ,, heroine	too many to name one
,, ,, poet	Reineke de Vos, Shakespeare, Ariosto, etc.
,, ,, prose writer	Goethe, Lessing, Dr. Samelson
,, ,, flower	Blue Bell
,, ,, colour	any one not Aniline
,, ,, dish	cold: salad, hot: Irish Stew
,, ,, maxim	not to have any
,, ,, motto	take it aisy.

F. Engels*

* For Jenny's album. August 1868. MEW.

LETTERS SENT BY ELEANOR TO 38 LONDON AND PROVINCIAL PAPERS

To the Editor of the ...

Sir,

A Reuter's telegram some days ago announced that a state of siege had been proclaimed in Hamburg, Altona, etc., and some 175 persons expelled from these towns. But the circumstances under which these proceedings have been instituted, the inhumanity with which the expulsions are carried out—these are unknown in England, or assuredly some protest would have been raised. Englishmen have sympathized with Bulgarians and Turks, with Russians and Greeks, will they not give some measure of justice at least if not of sympathy to the Social Democrats of Germany?—

The "Socialisten Gesetz" (*sic*) requires that some act or acts "endangering public safety" shall have been committed before the "minor state of siege" can be proclaimed. But in Hamburg and in all the places concerned, positively no excuse of any kind exists for exceptional legislation. There have been no "excesses", no unauthorized meetings, no "seditious" or "incendiary" publications, no conspiracies. Despite the efforts of the police to discover any plot wherewith to justify their own illegalities, they have been unable to find a trace of one; their continual domiciliary visits to the houses of the "suspected" have been absolutely fruitless. The Socialists have abided strictly by the law—even by the exceptional laws which Prince Bismarck framed, and which he—incapable of governing even with these (a state of siege has been declared in his own rural possessions in Lauenburg!)—is the first to break.

Without rhyme or reason, without the shadow of an excuse 175 persons—many of whom had already been driven from Berlin—have been expelled from Hamburg etc; the houses of poor working men have been broken up, their families turned adrift, to find work and a new home elsewhere—or starve, as the case may be. One poor woman, the wife of a printer, seeing her home destroyed and starvation staring her in the face has lost her reason and is now in a madhouse! As to the manner in which the orders of expulsion are executed, let the following case serve as an example. A Social Democrat, confined to his bed for the last six months and in the final stage of consumption, was removed in this cold November weather by railway from Pinneberg in Holstein to Neustadt, where he arrived in a dying condition.

Such eloquent facts need no comment. At a moment when the German press is gagged, and all expression of public opinion impossible, when Prince Bismarck meditates fresh illegalities by proclaiming a state of siege in Leipzig, and uses his utmost efforts to coerce the Swiss government into expelling the Socialists who have taken refuge in Zurich and Geneva, at such a moment it is the duty of the free press of England—the only free press in Europe—to denounce acts as harsh as they are unjust, as merciless as they are illegal.

I am, Sir,

Yours obediently

E.M.

London, November 1880.

41, Maitland Park Road. N.W.

To the Editor of the ...

Sir,

The illegal persecution to which the Socialists of Germany are now being subjected is so opposed to all sense of justice and legality, that I trust I shall not appeal in vain in asking you to give the publicity of your journal to making known the inhumanity with which a section of the German people are being treated. It is no question of sympathy for Social Democracy—but simply one of common justice and fair play.

I am, Sir,

Yours obediently

ELEANOR MARX*

London, Nov. 1880.

* Liebknecht.

"UNDERGROUND RUSSIA"

Extracts from two articles by Eleanor Marx published
in the August and September 1883 issues of *Progress*.

That a book on the Russian revolutionary movement, written by
Stepniak, with a preface from the pen of Lawroff, would be of the
utmost interest was to be expected. The little volume which Stepniak
modestly calls a series of "Sketches and Profiles", is in reality a work
of the utmost historical value, for though written by an active Nihilist
it is full of just appreciation and critical insight. It is to be hoped
that all the romancing historians and would-be historical romancers;
all the emotional and tender-hearted old statesmen, and tract-
distributing prison-visiting divines will read it before again expressing
their views on Russia and the condition of the Russian people.

In his excellent "Introduction" Stepniak has, in masterly fashion,
traced the history of the Socialist—or, as it is improperly called—
Nihilist movement from its beginning in 1861 to its latest phase,
the "terrorist" phase of to-day. . . .

The so-called emancipation of the Russian peasants was begun
by the Czar Nicolas. The Czar has always been, and still is, the
greatest landed proprietor of Russia. In 1845 the surveyed State
domains in the European part of the Empire amounted to 261,824,541
desjatines, that is rather more than 50,000 square miles—one
desjatine being a little over a hectare—and the State peasants numbered more than half the rural population. The latter were actually
serfs, though legally free men, and though the commune had been
preserved more intact amongst them than the rest of the peasantry.
The ruler was not the landlord but the gendarme, the tax-gatherer,
and the privileged distiller. In this domain, where his sway was
unchecked, Nicolas opened the campaign of autocracy against the
landed nobility. . . .

The emancipation of the serfs had become a moral necessity
after the Crimean failure. Occidentals looked upon the battlefield
only; but Russians saw with their own eyes the incomparably
greater masses of troops dragged from all corners of the immense
Empire, who, never reaching the theatre of war, perished miserably
by the way, inglorious victims of administrative incompetency and
corruption. The iron-fisted system of Nicolas had thus broken down
before the first serious emergency it had to cope with. Commotions
amongst the peasants, and intellectual revolt in the higher ranks of

society, simultaneously signalised serfdom as the corner-stone of the old system, and the true reason of the collapse. The strange condition of the popular mind may be gathered from the rumor widely spread amongst the serfs that their emancipation was one of the clauses of the Treaty of Peace dictated at Paris by Napoleon III, whom they, more or less, confounded with Napoleon I! No Czar, however strong-willed, could have resisted this tide. He would have been only too glad to make his nobles the scapegoats for the accumulated sins of autocracy. . . .

I have spoken of the *moral necessity* of the abolition of serfdom; but if Nicolas already felt that the interest of the crown lay that way, any further doubt on this subject was impossible after the Crimean war. The war left behind it an exhausted exchequer, depreciated paper-money, and rapidly-increasing arrears of the direct taxes, falling only upon the peasants and workmen generally. What was wanted was the power of applying the tax-screw freely, *and making the government the tax-gatherer*. This was impossible with a state of serfdom, where the landowners were liable for the taxes of their serfs. . . .

Still more heavily did military considerations weigh in the eyes of the autocrat. The Crimean war had given the finishing stroke to the clumsy old army organisation, which consisted of a standing army levied from the peasantry—the guards serving twenty-two, all other troops twenty-five years. With such a time of service it was quite out of question to increase its numbers. This was fully under-stood by the government, which therefore extended more and more, and as an irregular supplement of the standing army, independent of it, Cossack colonies over the whole of the empire. . . . But general compulsory service was not only impossible as long as the peasant remained the property of his landlord; it could not be extended to the other classes while military service—equivalent, in fact, to penal servitude for life—was the stigma of serfdom. The peasant had to become a nominally "free" man before the other nominally "free" Russians could be enrolled at his side. Thus, if Peter the Great, in order to create a standing army had to consolidate serfdom, Alexan-der II, under quite altered conditions, had to abolish it—in order to introduce general compulsory service.

. . . the Russian people owe no more gratitude to Alexander for his "emancipating" the serf, than English people do to John for signing Magna Charta. Nay, less, for while John's extorted signature conferred some boons upon the English people, Alexander only added to the already terrible misery of the Russian people—only made their chains heavier, their burdens more unbearable.

. . . the immense debt of gratitude owed by Russia to the Czar Alexander II exists only in the fervid imaginations of certain "West-Europeans". This once admitted, we can not only more thoroughly sympathise with Russian revolutionists, but we can better understand their course of action, and the reason why the first manifestation of the Nihilist movement began in 1860—i.e. immediately after that huge sham, the Emancipation.

The word "Nihilism" is the invention of the novelist Tourgenieff, "accepted", Stepniak tells us, "from party pride by those against whom it was employed," and now used to designate an entirely different movement from that first denoted by the word. The original Nihilist agitation had no political objects. It was "a philosophical and literary movement . . . now absolutely extinct, and only a few traces left of it". Still, it was the germ from which the other and greater movement sprang. . . .

The first battle was for religious freedom, and it was easily won. Every cultivated Russian is an atheist, and "when once this band of young writers, armed with the natural sciences and positive philosophy, . . . was impelled to the assault, Christianity fell like an old, decaying hovel which remains standing because no one touches it". . . .

Religious freedom was not all, however, for which the Nihilists fought. Nihilism recognised the equal rights of women and men. Here the struggle was long and bitter, for the "barbarous and medieval family life" of Russia stood in the way. But again it achieved a victory. In no other country are the women of the "educated classes" so entirely on the same footing as the men.

These victories gained, the Nihilists began to ask themselves what, after all, they had achieved? . . . The movement had reached the stage when, to the despairing question, "What are we to do?" the International Working Men's Association gave an answer, and the heroic Commune of Paris showed the way.

. . . Thus arose the Socialist propagandist movement of '72–'74, a movement that presented an entire contrast to that of '60–'70; and yet, by a strange though not uncommon irony, the later movement came to be known by the name of the earlier one.

. . . Among the causes that drove the youth of Russia to accept these revolutionary principles, none was more potent than the years of ferocious reaction that had followed the Polish insurrection in '66, a reaction which "swept away everything that still maintained a semblance of Liberalism," and which prepared the way for the Socialist propaganda begun in '72. The young men and women who had been studying at Zurich, and who were recalled by the ukase, equally stupid and brutal, of '73, came to swell the ranks of the revolutionary party. . . .

Yet even this was no political movement. The "propagandists" had not yet learnt that political emancipation is a necessary step towards social emancipation, and that a social revolution could no more come about by their preaching than it could have been established by Imperial ukase. . . . For two years it lasted. Thirty-seven provinces were, according to government circulars, "infected". The number of arrests is unknown. In one trial there were 193 prisoners. In 1875 the movement somewhat changed its aspect. . . . The years '77–'78 mark the end of the first revolutionary period. In '77 the trial of the Moscow "Fifty" was, by order of the government, a public trial. . . . But the ability of the prisoners who spoke, their noble heroism and simple, unaffected self-sacrifice, produced the very opposite effect to that expected by the government. . . . these "saints" were of too ideal a type to be fit for the coming struggle, and there appeared in their place a type as noble, but more strong—that of the Terrorist.

In spite of all heroic self-sacrifice and devotion, the Russian Socialists were bound to admit that they had failed, and they began to understand that to grapple with their barbarous enemy, deeds, not words, were needed. . . . "But a revolution, like a popular movement, is of spontaneous growth, and cannot be forced," and the revolutionists soon abandoned the series of "demonstrations" that had been planned, and which, in a country where towns of 10,000 or 15,000 inhabitants form only four or five per cent of the population, were impossible. But if the "demonstrations" ceased the government persecutions increased. Not only were the prisoners subjected to every sort of torture—of the "193", seventy-five "died" or went mad in prison *during the investigations*—but "that which is freely done in every country in Europe was punished among us like murder. Ten, twelve, or fifteen years of hard labor were inflicted for two or three speeches . . . or for a single book read or lent. From time to time, by ways which only prisoners know how to find out, there came from these men buried alive some letters, written on a scrap of paper in which tobacco or a candle had been wrapped up, describing the vile and useless cruelty which their gaolers had inflicted upon them . . . arousing in the most gentle and tender minds thoughts of blood, of hatred, and of vengeance."

The Terrorist movement began on January 24th, 1878, when Vera Sassulitsch shot the governor Trépoff. Vera herself was no Terrorist—she acted to avenge the man whom Trépoff had insulted and tortured, and "to call the attention of Russia and the world" to the condition of the political prisoners. . . . With cynical disregard of public feeling, Alexander ostentatiously visited Trépoff, so that even the "Liberals"—or those among them who were sincere—threw in their lot with the revolutionists. Far from attempting to conciliate, the government, with reckless insolence, sought only to aggravate the people. It forced the Socialist party to transform into a system what had been only an accident; to make an end of what had been a means to an end. Five months after Vera's acquittal and escape into Switzerland, "Terrorism, by putting to death General Mesentzeff,* the head of the police, . . . boldly threw down its glove in the face of autocracy." Since then the avenging arm of the Terrorist has struck often—and its greatest blow on March 13th, 1881.† What the end will be who can tell? But assuredly the coward despot, hiding amid his soldiers and his spies, and trembling every moment for his miserable life, is living a life more terrible than that of his unhappy peasants or of his tortured victims. . . .

This able and valuable book concludes with an interesting "Summary" of the whole movement, in which a most lucid account of the *theories* and *doctrines* of the Socialist Revolutionary Party is given. To this is added a translation of the admirable address to Czar Alexander III by the Executive Committee after March 13th. All those who believe the Russian Terrorists to be either blood-thirsty monsters or mad dreamers and fanatics, would do well to study this document. It is at once a justification of their policy, and an exposition of their moderate demands. In it the Executive offered terms of peace to Alexander. . . . Let the Czar but grant a small measure of reform, let him but give his people "freedom of the press, of public speech, of public meeting, and electoral addresses," and the Terrorists are ready to lay down arms. "And now," they said, "your Majesty, decide. The choice rests with you. We, on our side, can only express the hope that your judgment and your conscience will suggest to you the only decision which can accord with the welfare of Russia, with your own dignity, and with your duties towards the country." The Czar did choose. He replied by hanging Sophie Peroffsky and her fellow prisoners, by exiling and imprisoning thousands. But the end is not yet.

ELEANOR MARX

* He was in fact stabbed by Stepniak.   † The assassination of Alexander II.

SELECT BIBLIOGRAPHY

Adler, Victor. *Briefwechsel mit August Bebel und Karl Kautsky.* (edited Friedrich Adler). Verlag der Wiener Volksbuchhandlung, Vienna, 1954.

Allingham, William. *A Diary* (edited H. Allingham and D. Radford). Macmillan, 1907.

Anderson, Louisa. *Elizabeth Garrett Anderson.* Faber & Faber, 1939.

Andréas, Bert. *Briefe und Dokumente der Familie Marx aus den Jahren 1862–1873. Archiv für Sozialgeschichte*, II. Band. Verlag für Literatur und Zeitgeschehen. Hanover, 1962.

Ashley, Maurice. *Oliver Cromwell and the Puritan Revolution.* English Universities Press, 1958.

Aveling, Agnes Sarah ("A.S.A."). *Memories of Kingsland.* Published in Aid of Church Renovation Fund, 1887.

Aveling, Thomas William Baxter. *Memories of the Clayton Family.* Jackson, Walford & Hodder, 1867.

Bartel, Horst and others. *August Bebel. Eine Biographie.* Dietz Verlag, Berlin, 1963.

Bax, Ernest Belfort. *Reminiscences and Reflections of a Mid and Late Victorian.* Allen & Unwin, 1918.

Bebel, August. *My Life.* T. Fisher Unwin, 1912.

Briefwechsel mit Friedrich Engels. (edited Werner Blumenberg). Mouton & Co., The Hague, 1965.

Beer, Max. *A History of British Socialism*, Volume II. G. Bell & Sons, 1920.

Bernal, J. D. *Science in History.* Watts & Co., 1954.

Bernstein, Eduard. *My Years of Exile* (trans. B. Miall). L. Parsons, 1921.

Bertall. *The Communists of Paris 1871.* Popular English edition Buckingham & Co., Paris and London. J. M. O'Toole & Son, Dublin, 1873. (From the French edition published by Edouard Blot et fils ainé).

Besant, Annie. *An Autobiography.* T. Fisher Unwin, 1893.

Blumenberg, Werner. *Karl Marx in Selbstzeugnissen und Bilddokumenten.* Rowohlt, Hamburg, 1966.

Booth, Charles and others. *Labour and Life of the People.* Volumes 1 and 2, Williams & Norgate, 1889 and 1891.

Life and Labour of the People in London. Volume 9. Macmillan, 1897.

Bottigelli, Emile. *Lettres et Documents de Karl Marx 1856–1883.* Annali dell'Istituto Giangiacomo Feltrinelli, Anno Primo, Milan, 1958.

La Rupture Marx-Hyndman. Annali dell'Istituto Giangiacomo Feltrinelli, Anno Terzo, Milan, 1960.

Bowley, Arthur L. *Wages in the United Kingdom in the 19th Century.* C.U.P., 1900.

Bradlaugh, Charles. *Speeches.* Freethought Publishing Co., 1890.

Briggs, Asa and Saville, John (editors). *Essays in Labour History.* 2nd edition. Macmillan, 1967.

Brown, E. H. Phelps with Browne, Margaret H. *A Century of Pay.* Macmillan, 1968.

Bruhat, Jean, Dautry, Jean and Tersen, Emile (editors). *La Commune de 1871.* 2nd edition. Editions Sociales, Paris, 1970.

Buchanan-Gould, Vera. *Not Without Honour.* Hutchinson, 1953.

Bunel, Victor (editor and publisher). *Réimpression du Journal Officiel de la République Française sous la Commune du 18 mars au 24 mai 1871.* Paris, 1872.

Burton, Hester. *Barbara Bodichon.* John Murray, 1949.

Cole, G. D. H. and M. I. *The Condition of Britain.* Gollancz, 1937.

Cole, G. D. H. *A Short History of the British Working-Class Movement 1789–1947.* Allen & Unwin, 1948.

Collison, William. *The Apostle of Free Labour.* Hurst & Blackett, 1913.

Craig, E. G. *Index to the Story of My Days 1872–1907.* Hulton, 1957.

Cronwright-Schreiner, S. C. *Olive Schreiner.* T. Fisher Unwin, 1924.

Darwin, Charles. *Autobiography.* (edited Nora Barlow). Collins, 1958.

Documents of the First International. Volumes I–V. (edited Lydia Belyakova). Lawrence & Wishart, 1963–1968.

Dornemann, Luise. *Jenny Marx.* Dietz Verlag, Berlin, 1968.

Durkheim, Emile. *Le Suicide.* Félix Alcan, Paris, 1897.

Dutt, R. P. *The Internationale.* Lawrence & Wishart, 1964.

Ellis, Havelock. *My Life.* Heinemann, 1940.

Engels, Frederick (see also under Marx).

Anti-Dühring. Lawrence & Wishart, 1934.

Friedrich Engels' Briefwechsel mit Karl Kautsky. (edited Benedikt Kautsky). IISH. Danubia-Verlag, Wilhelm Braumüller und Sohn, Vienna, 1955.

The British Labour Movement. (*Labour Standard* articles May–August 1881). Martin Lawrence, 1934.

The Condition of the Working-Class in England in 1844. With 1892 Preface. (trans. Florence Kelley Wischnewetzky). Allen & Unwin, 1936.

Friedrich Engels Paul et Laura Lafargue; Correspondance. Textes recueillis, annotés et présentés par Emile Bottigelli. 3 Tomes. Editions sociales, Paris, 1956–1959.

Frederick Engels Paul and Laura Lafargue: Correspondence. Vol. I–III. (trans. Y. Kapp). Lawrence & Wishart, 1959–1963.

Introduction to "Class Struggles in France 1858–1850". (1895), *Karl Marx: Selected Works,* Volume II. Lawrence & Wishart, 1942.

History of Ireland (to 1014). (trans. Angela Clifford). Irish Communist Organisation, London. 2nd edition. 1970.

Foner, Philip S. *History of the Labor Movement of the United States* Volume 2. International Publishers, New York, 1955.

Fremantle, Anne. *This Little Band of Prophets.* Allen & Unwin, 1960.

Froude, Henry and others. *Frederick James Furnivall.* O.U.P., 1911.

Frow, Edmund and Katanka, Michael. *1868 Year of the Unions.* Michael Katanka (Books) Ltd., 1968.

Gemkow, Heinrich, and others. *Karl Marx. Eine Biographie.* Dietz Verlag, Berlin, 1967.

Gillespie, Frances Elma. *Labor and Politics in England 1850–1867.* Duke University Press, North Carolina, 1927.

Glynn, Anthony. *High upon the Gallows Tree.* Anvil Books Ltd., Tralee, Co. Kerry, 1967.

Gollin, R. M. *Beerbohm, Wilde, Shaw and Edward Rose.* N.Y. Public Library, 1964.

Harrison, Royden. *Before the Socialists. Studies in Labour and Politics 1861–1881.* Routledge & Kegan Paul, 1965.

Herzen, Alexander. *My Past and Thoughts.* Volumes I–VI. (trans. Constance Garnett). Chatto & Windus, 1924–7.

Hill, C. and Dell, E. *The Good Old Cause.* Lawrence & Wishart, 1949.

The History of the TUC 1868–1968. (edited Lionel Birch). General Council TUC, 1968.

Hobsbawm, Eric. *Labouring Men.* Weidenfeld & Nicolson, 1964.

Horne, Alistair. *The Fall of Paris.* St. Martin's Press, New York, 1966.

Hutt, G. A. *British Trade Unionism.* (Revised edition). Lawrence & Wishart, 1962.

Hyndman, H. M. *The Record of an Adventurous Life.* Macmillan, 1911. *Further Reminiscences.* Macmillan, 1912.

Jackson, T. A. *Ireland Her Own.* Cobbett Press, 1946.

Jellinek, Frank. *The Paris Commune of 1871.* Gollancz, 1937.

Jenkins, Mick. *Frederick Engels in Manchester.* Lancashire and Cheshire Communist Party, 1951.

Kamm, Josephine. *Hope Deferred: Girls' Education in English History.* Methuen, 1965.

Kisch, Egon Erwin. *Karl Marx in Karlsbad.* Aufbau Verlag, Berlin, 1953.

Kuczynski, Jürgen. *A Short History of Labour Conditions under Industrial Capitalism. Volume I Part I. Great Britain 1750 to the Present Day.* Frederick Muller, 1947.

Lawrence, D. H. *The Collected Letters*. Volume I (edited H. T. Moore). Heinemann, 1962.

Lewis, R. A. *Edwin Chadwick and the Public Health Movement 1832–1854*. Longman, Green & Co., 1952.

Liebknecht, Wilhelm. *Briefwechsel mit Karl Marx und Friedrich Engels*. (edited Georg Eckert). Mouton & Co., The Hague, 1963.

Karl Marx: Biographical Memoirs. (trans. E. Untermann). H. Kerr & Co. 1901 and *Karl Marx: Selected Works* Volume I (edited C. P. Dutt). Lawrence & Wishart, 1942.

Karl Marx zum Gedächtnis. Nuremberg, 1896.

Lilley, S. *Men, Machines and History*. Cobbett Press, 1948.

Lissagaray. *Histoire de la Commune*. (précédée par Amédée Dunois). Libraire du Travail, Paris 1929.

History of the Commune of 1871. (trans. Eleanor Marx Aveling). Reeves & Turner, 1886.

Lozovsky, A. *Marx and the Trade Unions*. Martin Lawrence, 1935.

Mackenzie, Compton. *My Life and Times. Octave 7 1931–1938*. Chatto & Windus, 1968.

Mann, Tom. *Tom Mann's Memoirs*. (First published 1923 by The Labour Publishing Co. Ltd.). MacGibbon & Kee Ltd., 1967.

Marek, K. *Philosophy of World Revolution*. (trans. D. Simon). Lawrence & Wishart, 1969.

Marshall, A. Calder. *Havelock Ellis*. Rupert Hart-Davis, 1959.

Marx, Karl. *The Civil War in France*. (1891 preface by Frederick Engels). Martin Lawrence, 1933.

The Eastern Question. (edited Eleanor Marx Aveling and Edward Aveling). Swan Sonnenschein & Co., 1897.

The 18th Brumaire of Louis Bonaparte. (trans. Eden and Cedar Paul). Allen & Unwin, 1926.

On the Jewish Question in *Early Writings* (trans. T. B. Bottomore). Watts & Co., 1963.

Marx, Karl and Engels, Friedrich. *Werke*. Dietz Verlag, Berlin, 1956–68.

Correspondence of Marx and Engels. (trans. and edited Dona Torr). Martin Lawrence, 1934.

Selected Correspondence (trans. I. Lasker, edited S. Ryazanskaya). Lawrence & Wishart, 1965.

Mayer, Gustav. *Friedrich Engels*. Chapman & Hall, 1936.

Mayer, Paul. *Die Geschichte des sozialdemokratischen Parteiarchivs und das Schicksal des Marx-Engels-Nachlasses. Archiv für Sozialgeschichte*. VI./VII. Band 1966–1967. Verlag für Literatur und Zeitgeschehen, Hanover.

Mayhew, Henry. *London Labour and the London Poor*. Volumes I–III. Charles Griffin & Co. (n.d. probably 1861).

London Labour and the London Poor. Volume IV. Griffin, Bohn & Co., 1862.

Mearns, Andrew. *The Bitter Cry of Outcast London: An Inquiry into the Condition of the Abject Poor*. (edited Anthony S. Wohl). Leicester University Press, 1970. (First edition James Clarke, October 1883).

Mehring, Franz. *Karl Marx*. (trans. Edward Fitzgerald). John Lane, 1936.

Mohr und General. Dietz Verlag, Berlin, 1964.

Moody, T. W. and Martin, F. X. *The Course of Irish History*. The Mercier Press, Cork, 1967.

Morton, A. L. *A People's History of England*. Gollancz, 1938.

Nethercot, Arthur H. *The First Five Lives of Annie Besant*. Rupert Hart-Davis, 1961.

Nicolaievsky, Boris and Maenchen-Helfen, Otto. *Karl Marx Man and Fighter*. (trans. G. David and E. Mosbacher). Methuen, 1936.

"Orme, Michael". *J. T. Grein*. John Murray, 1936.

Payne, Ernest E. *The Free Churches: their History and Witness* (in *Who's Who in the Free Churches*, edited L. G. Pine). Shaw Publishing Co., 1951.

Pearson, Hesketh. *Bernard Shaw, His Life and Personality*. (first complete edition). Methuen, 1961.

Ramelson, Marian. *The Petticoat Rebellion*. Lawrence & Wishart, 1967.

Registrar General's Statistical Review of England and Wales for the Year 1937. O.H.M.S., 1940.

Reminiscences of Marx and Engels. Foreign Languages Publishing House, Moscow (n.d., probably 1956).

Robins, Elizabeth. *Both Sides of the Curtain*. Heinemann, 1940.

Rose, Paul. *The Manchester Martyrs*. Lawrence & Wishart, 1970.

Rossa, Jeremiah O'Donovan. *My Years in English Jails*. (edited Sean Ua Caernaigh). Anvil Books, 1967. (First published 1874 in USA).

Rothstein, Andrew. *A House on Clerkenwell Green*. Lawrence & Wishart, 1966.

Rothstein, Theodore. *From Chartism to Labour*. Martin Lawrence, 1929.

Royal Commission on Population Report. Cmd. 7695, 1949.

Salt, Henry S. *Seventy Years Among Savages*. Allen & Unwin, 1921.

Schreiner, Olive. *Letters 1876–1920*. (edited S. C. Cronwright-Schreiner). T. Fisher Unwin, 1924.

Shaw, G. B. *Collected Letters 1874–1897*. (edited Dan H. Laurence). Max Reinhardt, 1965.

The Perfect Wagnerite. Constable, 1898.

The Quintessence of Ibsenism. Constable, 1913.

Sixteen Self Sketches. Constable, 1949.

Simon, Brian. *Studies in the History of Education 1780–1870*. Lawrence & Wishart, 1960.

Education and the Labour Movement 1870–1918. Lawrence & Wishart, 1965.

Smith, Warren Sylvester. *The London Heretics 1870–1914*. Constable, 1967.

Summerson, John. *Georgian London*. Pleiades Books, 1945.

Survey of London: Volumes 33 and 34. *The Parish of St. Anne, Soho*. (edited F. H. W. Sheppard). The Athlone Press, University of London. Published for the Greater London Council, 1966.

Thompson, E. P. *William Morris*. Lawrence & Wishart, 1955.

The Making of the English Working Class. Penguin Books 1968.

Thorn, George Ernest. *The Story of Kingsland Congregational Church 1789–1936*. Independent Press Ltd., 1936.

Thorne, Will. *My Life's Battles*. George Newnes Ltd. (n.d., probably 1925).

Tillett, Ben. *Memories and Reflections*. John Long Ltd., 1931.

Torr, Dona. *Tom Mann and His Times*. Lawrence & Wishart, 1956.

Tsuzuki, Chushichi. *H. M. Hyndman and British Socialism*. (edited Henry Pelling). O.U.P., 1961.

The Life of Eleanor Marx 1855–1898. Clarendon Press, 1967.

Webb, Beatrice. *My Apprenticeship*. Longman, Green & Co., 1950.

Webb, Sidney and Beatrice. *The History of Trade Unionism 1666–1920*. Printed by the Authors for the Trade Unionists of the United Kingdom, Christmas 1919.

Williams, Gertrude M. *The Passionate Pilgrim*. John Hamilton, 1931.

Winsten, Stephen. *Salt and His Circle*. Hutchinson, 1951.

Woodham-Smith, Cecil. *The Great Hunger*. Hamish Hamilton, 1962.

Worobjowa, O. and Sinelnikova, I. *Die Töchter von Marx*. (trans. Waldemar Dölle). Dietz Verlag, Berlin, 1963.

NAME INDEX

Listing those involved in Eleanor Marx's—and also Edward Aveling's—family life and personal experience, including references to their public activities, but omitting purely public, literary or historical figures as well as some friends and correspondents of the antecedent generations.

About the Author

A writer and translator, Yvonne Kapp was born and has lived most of her life in London. In the late twenties she was literary editor of *Vogue*, working in Paris. In the thirties she worked full-time for anti-fascist refugee committees in London. Subsequently she became, and remained throughout the war, chief research officer for the Amalgamated Engineering Union; she was then employed in the field of industrial research by the British Medical Research Council. Her translations include *Tales from the Calendar* by Bertolt Brecht, and *The Correspondence of Frederick Engels and Paul and Laura Lafargue*.